ARISTOPHANES: POET AND DRAMATIST

Aristophanes
POET & DRAMATIST

Rosemary M. Harriott

THE JOHNS HOPKINS UNIVERSITY PRESS
Baltimore, Maryland 212118

Published in 1986 by The Johns Hopkins University Press
701 West 40th Street, Baltimore, Maryland 21211

Library of Congress Cataloging in Publication Data

Harriott, Rosemary M.
  Aristophanes, poet and dramatist.

  Bibliography: p.
  Includes index.
  1. Aristophanes—Criticism and interpretation.
I. Title.
PA3879.H35   1986   882'. 01   85-17187
ISBN 0-8018-3279-9

Printed and bound in Great Britain

CONTENTS

PREFACE

My indebtedness to scholars, above all to the editors of Aristophanes' comedies, is not the less because they do not receive the detailed acknowledgment appropriate in a more specialised work than this. Those who are familiar with the literature on Aristophanes will appreciate the extent to which I depend on the scholarship, observations and ideas of others. I am conscious, too, of what I owe to writers on other genres as diverse as Greek tragedy and the Victorian novel; I must have borrowed much also from sources which I cannot now recollect. In accordance with the aims of the book, the Select Bibliography has been kept short and as a result fails to offer the full acknowledgement due to scholars and critics.

At a time when this book seemed to be making very slow progress I benefited greatly from a period spent working in the Library of the Fondation Hardt at Geneva, with generous assistance from the funds of the British Academy.

My grateful thanks are due to those who have provided help, advice, comment and encouragement at various stages in the preparation of this book: chief among them are Norma Miller, Fred Robertson, Jill Walford and Margaret Williamson. Sybil Lowery has been patient, swift and expert in dealing with the manuscript.

Finally I should like to record once more my gratitude to two scholars who long ago fostered my enthusiasm for Aristophanes, Professor Hugh Tredennick and Professor A.M. Webster (Miss A.M. Dale); the former patiently introduced a novice to *Clouds*, imparting with his inimitable courtesy and humour much more than the necessary elucidation of language and background. Some time later, when for five years I was Mrs Webster's pupil at Birkbeck College, I gained immeasurably from her personal kindness and interest as well as from her meticulous and committed teaching which so effectively communicated her love of Greek drama.

INTRODUCTION

In the mansion owned and run by the literary institution, Aristophanes occupies a fine room, but for those visitors who frequent it, for their various reasons, there is a separate, private entrance. In this book the conventional isolation of Aristophanes is abandoned in favour of the acknowledgement that he moved as freely as he wished to the quarters occupied by rhetoric or lyric, above all to the *piano nobile* where tragedy resides, and that he went as colleague and friend, not as an intruder to scorn and mock. My chief interest is in Aristophanes the craftsman, the poet in the literal sense of 'maker', whether he is making whole plays or individual lines of verse: I want to discover why *this* scene, *this* speech is included, why *here* and not elsewhere. It goes without saying that the craftsman, even the producer of comedy, is serious and that his work deserves respect and will repay scrutiny: Aristophanes would have smiled at the illogicality of those who believe that only straight-faced poets exercise skills worthy of critics' attention.

The method adopted in this study is descriptive rather than argumentative, depends heavily on comparing material from different plays and moves from small to large, from the consideration of individual passages to that of the composition of the play as a whole. My intention in following this method, admittedly rather 'bitty' in the early chapters, was to avoid revisiting familiar territory along a well-trodden route. In an attempt to study Aristophanic comedy from fresh viewpoints, I have followed the example of the Initiates in *Frogs* when they list persons banned from taking part in the Mysteries. The material and plan of this book also involve a series of exclusions; I have instructed all of these manifestations of the poet to stand aside: the careless improviser, the creator of lovable rogues, the inventor of ingenious obscenities, the writer fettered by outdated forms, the worshipper of the jest for its own sake, the satirist, the parodist. For the time being let them be replaced by the poet who makes (and makes over) the material of comic drama written in verse of marvellous versatility, 'amusing, yes, but also heartfelt'.

1 THE POET AS STORY-TELLER

It is the timber of poetry that wears most surely, and there is no timber that has not strong roots among the clay and worms.

(J.M. Synge, Preface to *First Edition of Poems*)

In the earlier chapters of this book I am concerned less with whole plays than with individual speeches or songs or passages of dialogue, with the materials and architectural detail of the plays rather than the completed edifice. Gradually the viewpoint becomes more distant so that the putting together and combining of the elements may be studied. If Aristophanes had produced even moderately homogeneous verse, I could claim in these early chapters to be analysing his style; as it is, I can only hope to describe some of the ways of writing employed by this master of many styles. Broadly speaking, in the first three chapters the unit for discussion is the individual speech or song, while repartee and rapid conversational exchange are reserved for Chapter 4: this arrangement necessitates shifting from one play to another within chapters in order to facilitate comparisons. In this chapter the material is drawn from five plays, *Acharnians*, *Knights*, *Clouds*, *Wasps* and *Frogs*, and can be classified as broadly narrative and descriptive. Narrative technique in the prologues of three plays will be considered first, then descriptive passages, mainly relating to, or sung by, the chorus and finally I shall touch on a mode unique to Old Comedy, autobiography in the parabasis.

Dramatic Narrative

In *Tellers and Listeners* Barbara Hardy writes: 'We have of course looked hard at total narrative forms like epics, novels and stories, but much less closely at the narratives within those forms.'[1] In drama, unlike most novels, there is no narrator's voice to be heard, and narrative becomes only a manner of speaking employed by characters, along with prayer, argument, abuse or conversation. All narrative in drama is dramatic narrative: it serves the needs of the play. As narrative, however, it can also be detached and studied in its own right and Aristophanic narrative in particular requires attention because the energy and impetus of comedy are conducive to over-hasty and unreflective reading with the consequence that the careful suggestiveness of the writing goes unobserved. Take, for example, the few lines from the famous contest between Euripides and Aeschylus in *Frogs* where Euripides, while accusing his rival, gives an account of his own treatment of tragedy, an account, we must remember, put into his mouth by the comic dramatist. The reader of my last sentence will not have supposed me to be using the word 'treatment' as a live metaphor: now read on.

> When I took over the Art from you she was puffed out with bombastics and ponderous rhetorics. That very minute I put her on a diet and reduced her weight with medicinal verselets, training circuits and vegetable laxatives and dosed her with oralistics extracted from boiled books. Next I used monodies to put muscle on her . . . (939-44)

The metaphor is not only live but lively: the poet has assumed the voice of the trainer accustomed to 'selling' his own programme and determined that his athlete should win. He emphasises his own actions and the sorry state in which his pupil came to him. That the pupil is not a real young man but the female personification Tragedy, a regular 'competitor' in the 'Games' held to honour Dionysus, is indicated by comparatively few words, all of them referring to verbal expression. Thus in one image, the sickly ponderousness of Aeschylean tragedy, Euripides' deliberate innovations and the continuity of tragedy are all conveyed. The message is clear: Euripidean tragedy will win.

Ask what use classical tragedy made of the narrative mode and the answer will be given 'in messenger speech and prologue', the former used to convey information to people who are on stage about a calamity which has occurred off-stage and the latter by way of exposition and preparation before the entry of the chorus. In comedy messenger speeches are rarely essential, chiefly because much more of the action can suitably be played before our eyes, so that when they occur they draw attention to themselves as intruders from the sister art.[2] Exposition, on the other hand, is essential to both forms and quite often comedy, like tragedy, begins with a speech delivered by one of the principals which lasts several minutes. Narrative is not, however, restricted to these two occasions; as well as having an important function in debate and argument, it may constitute all or part of the material of a song.

I introduce this section, not with an actual Aristophanic prologue, nor even with an early play, but with a miniature narrative from *Frogs*, the latest play considered in this book. The contest between Aeschylus and Euripides draws attention to their respective prologues (1119-247); after the younger poet has found fault with his rival's obscurity, inaccuracy and tautology, it is Aeschylus' turn: hearing only the opening line of Euripides' *Antigone*, 'A fortunate man was Oedipus at first', he opens his attack by denying that a man destined to kill his father could ever have been 'fortunate' (1182-6). Undeterred, Euripides continues: 'then he became by contrast the wretchedest of mortals.' At this Aeschylus launches into his new, concise version of the well-known myth:

> No, absolutely not; he never stopped being it, it's obvious. As soon as he came into existence they threw him out, in winter, in a broken pot to prevent him growing up to be his father's murderer. Next he limped off to Polybus, both feet swollen; and then he married an old woman, while he was still young. What's more, she was his own mother. Next he blinded himself. (1187-95)

This is not story-telling for its own sake: its tendentious purpose is to demonstrate, in the niggling manner of the fifth-century New Criticism, the incorrectness of the word 'fortunate' in Euripides' opening line. Therefore Oedipus' wealth, power, prestige and wisdom are ignored. Moreover, the only descriptive additions to the bare tale are pathetic. The story is purely a story, not the synopsis of any actual or imaginable tragedy, and so does not criticise Euripides' dramaturgy, only his diction. Yet there is a sense in which this apparently simple and naïve account is critical, in that it reduces myth and consequently tragedy's use of myth. Aeschylus drops into an everyday style, telling a tale as familiar to his hearers as to himself, and by so doing turns the tragic into the grotesque and destroys the fall from greatness to calamity on which Euripides' initial antithesis had relied.

Prologues

In this section three expository monologues will be considered and compared, two of them spoken by the principal at the play's commencement, the third by a subordinate character after a few moments of conversation. I include all of them under the heading of story-telling used in its broad sense to include passages of description or reflection. It is easy to assess the important but purely informative function of such expository material, which includes the kind of detail about settings and participants that the modern programme would make known; what is more taxing, more interesting and more controversial is to attempt to estimate the exposition's persuasive and prognostic aspects. A prologue sets up expectations and reveals attitudes as well as outlining the situation from which the action of the play will evolve.

The earliest surviving play, *Acharnians*, begins with 42 lines of monologue spoken by an as yet unnamed man alone on the stage.[3] At first he musingly recalls his sorrows (many) and his joys (a mere handful). This process turns out to be a focusing priamel which emphasises its final element, the present bitter pangs he suffers because everyone else is late for the assembly meeting (19-26); reflections on their unpunctuality lead in turn to the real crux: 'About peace and peacemaking no-one cares; oh Athens, Athens' (26-7). The speaker now reverts to his own feelings of boredom and impatience as he waits, fidgeting, and above all to his longing to get back to the country home from which the war has separated him: 'I look over at the fields experiencing desire for peace, hatred of the city and absolute yearning for my own place' (31-3: my translation fails to convey the ordering and assonance of the original). Finally the speaker declares his determination to insist that peace be discussed and announces the late arrival of the presiding officials.

Of the speaker himself we have learned only that he is a farmer forced to live in the city; about his likes and dislikes, political and cultural, we learn rather more. Only the immediate future is revealed: today there is to be a regular meeting of the assembly; for the time being the Theatre of Dionysus has become the Pnyx.[4] What will be done about peace?

This speech finds its nearest parallel in extant tragedy in the opening of Sophocles' *Women of Trachis*, where Deianeira, feeling as isolated as Dicaeopolis, enlarges on her many fears and anxieties and few joys; her musings have a clearer chronological structure than Dicaeopolis' recollections, but like his culminate in the expression of her present fear, greater than all that have gone before. However, whereas the Sophoclean prologue needs to be held in the mind and reassessed as the tragedy progresses, the hero of *Acharnians* is free to move on unfettered by his past.

The opening of *Clouds*, the next play to employ expository monologue, has similarities with that of *Acharnians*, although the principal is not alone on the stage but accompanied by his sleeping son; he also is anxious, impatient, fearful, as he reflects upon his woes, grumbling and yawning, in the way of insomniacs. As the night drags on he reveals his chief cause for concern, his son's extravagance which will shortly bring several creditors down upon him. These reflections, uttered in the tones of a man speaking half to himself, half to a crony, just as the thoughts occur to him, are followed by a chronologically ordered section of a kind found in Euripidean prologues; in this he traces the events which have led up to his present sorry state.

So far I have written as if the prologue of *Clouds* consisted of an unbroken sequence as far as the end of the narrative (1-80). In fact, other voices are briefly heard and these interruptions help to suggest atmosphere and to define the setting as well as providing breaks in the long speech. Thus, for instance, the speaker does not merely refer to debts, but sends a slave for his accounts; he does not merely lament his son's expensive obsession with chariot-racing, but allows us to hear that the lad even 'dreams horses': 'Philo, you're cheating: keep to your own lane' (25).

It is a brief period of actual wakefulness (135 f) which divides the initial description of Strepsiades' anxieties from his account of their cause. Like the Nurse in Euripides' *Medea* (1 f) who had deplored the building of the ship which enabled Jason to reach Medea's native land, he begins, or seems to begin, with a wish: 'Would that the matchmaker – go to perdition for encouraging me to marry your mother' (41-2). This wish, or rather curse, is followed by three lines in which he describes his former rustic happiness as a bachelor; in three more he sets out his wife's family, status and milieu ('city-bred, classy, indulgent, multi-millionairessy') and in the next four he shows in what ways they were an ill-matched pair.[5]

At this moment the lamp runs out of oil. Resuming, Strepsiades comes to his son's birth, dwelling on the ensuing squabbles; the first of them, over choice of name, illustrates their fundamental disagreement over money (68-73). As a result of maternal influence the son's horse fever has destroyed the father's fortunes and he is awake, as he now lies before our eyes in the theatre, in anxious deliberation. At last he reveals that his cogitations have produced a plan and 'If I can persuade this lad here, I'll be saved' (77).

On the basic level the *Clouds'* prologue speech introduces the participants, their relationship and current problems, from the point of view of the head of the *oikos*. At its end one would probably expect further developments in the dispute within the family (perhaps including report of intensification of the discord between husband and wife) and also encounters between debtor and creditors. These expectations are in fact largely fulfilled eventually. But *Clouds* therefore differs from *Acharnians* in the unexpectedness of what happens immediately after the intro-ductory monologue: *Acharnians* has its predicted assembly scene but in *Clouds* there is an abrupt change caused by the nature of the principal's 'solution'.

Turning from action to attitudes it may be said that the speech which is primarily concerned with money and the family exposes two conflicting sets of values, those of the wife's family, adopted with pleasure by the son, as against the rustic, hardworking frugality of the father.[6] It is here suggested, I think, that the father's values are 'right' and admirable (and if so the spectators will feel approval as well as sympathy for him). Any view of the morality underlying the speech will depend in part on one's estimate of its tone or tones. Obviously it lacks the extraneous jokes of many Aristophanic opening scenes and its material could even be described as 'relevant' or 'realistic'. Moreover, there are features reminiscent of tragedy in the presentation of a hero sleepless during the long hours of night, particularly one who searches for understanding of the causes of his suffering. Nevertheless, such hints can be sharply contradicted: 'Now therefore pondering the whole night long', he tragically resumes after his autobiographical excursus (75) only to continue 'I've discovered one simple, absolutely splendid way out'. This unexpected conclusion, typical of comedy, goes along with the puns, lists and coined words which could not occur in a more 'serious' genre and yet in the whole speech the comic elements seem to be subordinate rather than foregrounded.

Taking this example of narrative in a historical context, its novelty and difference from other passages is noteworthy (although we must allow for the fact that our material for comparison is small). For autobiographical narrative in early Greek literature our chief source is the *Odyssey*, but nothing there, certainly not Odysseus' occasional anxious reflections (*Od.* 9. 316-8, for example), provides a model for this passage. The modern novel reader may find here the now familiar expository combination of present and past in the self-revelation and self-awareness of the hero; the fifth-century spectator had no such experience.

Let me end this account of *Clouds* by quoting and commenting on seven lines about the husband and wife (46-52). 'Then it was the niece of Megacles (son of Megacles) I married; she the city-bred and I the rustic.' (In these lines only the name Megacles does not begin with a vowel.) The wife is now described by three adjectives in tricolon crescendo as 'classy, spoilt, Coesyra-like'. After the marriage 'I used to lie down beside her smelling of newly-made wine, of the rack for drying figs, of wool – of super-abundance; she for her part of perfume, of saffron, of passionate kisses, of extravagance, of gluttony, of Aphrodite, of her natal goddess'. This description of the husband takes one single line and moves from actual farm produce to the idea of plenty associated with harvesting fruit and shearing flocks, and from two-syllabled to three- and finally a five-syllabled word. Two lines are needed for the wife; in the former the simple 'perfume' and 'saffron' followed by the compound 'tongue-kisses' associated with and maybe consequent upon the use of scent. So far the description of the wife parallels that of the husband, the two of them in bed together, characterised by contrasting odours but sharing enjoyment. In the second the wife is removed, as it were, from the marital bed and bluntly condemned as uneconomical and self-indulgent in the first two words: the last two, the first proper nouns since 'Megacles', are not blunt but allusive: she has the air of one who frequents a particular shrine of Aphrodite and of those divinely favoured by birth. (The associations are aided by assonance as well as by climaxing.) In these lines there is a kind of punning which goes further than word-play: people may smell accidentally of what they have worked with or deliberately of costly scent; their own preferences and the impression they make on others are formed by scents. The wife employs scent and has the air of a sexy, self-indulgent woman of a familiar aristocratic kind. The mere listing of seven 'scents', apparently a stylistic extravagance, is in fact economically suggestive of character, class and background.

As in *Clouds*, the exposition of *Wasps* falls into descriptive and narrative parts. Like *Clouds*, *Wasps* also sets out a conflict between father and son: here the father is pursuing an obsession and the son trying to restrain him. The initial statement (by a household slave) of the master's passion for the jury courts and its exemplification takes 26 lines, while the account of past and present attempts to cure and manage the old man occupies 18 (87-132). The two plays however differ in the speaker's point of view. Here we cannot be persuaded to share the old man's feelings by hearing his own account; instead we see how he appears to a not unsympathetic observer, Xanthias, a subordinate who shares in the chore of restraining him. If one reads the old juror's later justification of his life (548-630) by the side of Xanthias' prologue, the importance of viewpoint becomes even clearer.

To begin with a brief summary: we learn of the extent to which the passion of the 'compulsive juror' (Sommerstein's phrase) affects his daily life and behaviour, his eagerness for his day's employment keeping him awake at night or sending him very early to doze at the court entrance, for example. In the second section Xanthias recounts how the young master had first tried to reason with his father, next resorting to religious cures; now that these too have failed they 'keep guard all round the house' to prevent his egress.

This picture the slave gives of his master is partly that of a lover, partly that of an invalid. Sometimes lover and invalid are indistinguishable. Thus longing to be elsewhere, inability to sleep, dreaming of the beloved, inscribing the dear name on walls, characterise the *erastes*, while the initial diagnosis of his love as a sickness (87), 'litigious mania', is followed by reference to symptoms like groans, insomnia and obsessional behaviour shown in an account of the way the sick man spends his day. The remedial measures taken are recounted in the narrative section. Here for the most part the son takes action as the subject of the verbs and the father, as befits a patient, becomes merely the object of curative endeavours. The son, distressed by his father's illness, attempts counselling, medication, various 'cures', including a visit to a healing centre on the island of Aegina and at last a kind of house arrest. Now the wily inventiveness of the old man is revealed in an account of the actions he undertakes, such as making holes and scaling walls, only to be foiled each time by the busy vigilance of the household.

The efforts described near the end of this long speech are at once illustrated before our eyes as son and slaves push their prisoner back down the chimney (147), barricade the door (155) or detect him clinging under a donkey like another Odysseus evading the Cyclops. For the play's major concern it is the earlier part of the exposition that matters, together with the last three lines. In these Xanthias identifies the old man as 'lover' of Cleon (Philocleon) as well as of courts, and his son as 'loathe-Cleon' (Bdelycleon).[7]

I return now to Xanthias' picture of the old man as mad lover to suggest the precise detail of his behaviour which differentiates him as an individual and also introduces the play's public dimension in which father and son are seen as politically divided over issues which concern the *polis* and the family. Eventually Philocleon himself will explain why he values jury service. For the present we are shown how his behaviour appears to an observer: he keeps his fingers curled as if grasping his voting-pebble; where another man would write 'I love Benedict' on a wall, he prefers 'I love verdict'; he complains that the cockerel whose cry usually rouses him has been bribed to silence so that he will sleep late; he cultivates a private pebble beach, in case of a shortage of voting-pebbles. The devoted juror is not only a maniac but an elderly idiot whose bizarre activities bring the juror's role into disrepute even as their eccentricity arouses laughter.[8]

Description

I turn now to examples of Aristophanic description, drawing them first from passages concerning the choruses of *Acharnians*, *Wasps* and *Frogs*. We have looked at passages in which description of a person's tastes and behaviour form an essential part of the exposition: in the case of Philocleon the impression given by the slave may be altered or confirmed when the man himself is before us, but for Strepsiades' wife his word must suffice; she is part of his explanation and never appears, except in so far as she is reflected in her son. Because preliminary sketching of people and places has become a matter of routine in many kinds of writing at all levels, it is worth pointing out the rarity with which it occurs in Greek drama. By and large setting is ignored, unless, like Philoctetes' cave, Prometheus' isolated crag or the Birds' new city, it is altogether exceptional: comedy is interested in an ordinary house only when a Philoclean is trying unconventional exits. The physical appearance of characters often goes unremarked, except for features which are grotesque or significant in the way that General Lamachus' military splendour is significant, or Dicaeopolis' rags. And so, when information of a descriptive kind is presented, it should not be neglected.

In *Acharnians* the hostility of the chorus to the peacemaker is the motive for some four hundred lines, or roughly a third, of the play. Before the audience sees the chorus, Amphitheus explains that, as he was hurrying to bring the wine of peace, 'some old men caught its scent, Acharnians, solidly made veterans, oak-like, tough, survivors of Marathon, maple-like. Next they all yelled "You villain, carrying wine when our vines have been cut?" ' (178 f). Judged realistically these lines are odd: the speaker might report the fact of pursuit and the words of his pursuers but how could he instantly perceive all the qualities he ascribes to the old men? A general impression of age and toughness, perhaps, but not the particulars as here stated. There is at this moment a sense of haste: the samples must be delivered before the old men arrive. Description should be brief, and it is. In two lives of verse, in only seven words, helped by assonance, Aristophanes emphasises the age and toughness of the pursuers and suggests their patriotism and 'woodiness' (and whether this last element gave the audience a hint of the Acharnians' occupation of charcoal-burning we can only guess). These lines spoken by the informing voice have a preparatory function, like characterisation in a novel. For example, when the Acharnians enter (204), they lament their age and decrepitude: the treaty-bearer wouldn't have got clear away 'in my youth when I could keep pace with a champion runner, even carrying my load of charcoal'. Amphitheus' fear of them is justified by their repeated insistence that age will not stop their pursuit. That they are formidable adversaries is shown further as they attack Dicaeopolis (280, 320); their vulnerability is therefore worth examining as it goes 'against the grain' of the previous characterisation, and may again be thought improbable by realistic standards. Dicaeopolis, denied a hearing on pain of death, uses the real Euripides in order to save himself by borrowing firstly a motif and a metaphor from his *Telephus* and secondly clothes and 'props' from a fictive Euripides (393 f). As Telephus had seized a baby as hostage in the famous tragedy, so Dicaeopolis takes and threatens to kill 'the dearest of your dears' (326), a charcoal basket. Interestingly, the hostage here is not presented as an infant but as one who shares age and deme with the chorus. The cohesiveness suggested in the lines already discussed (178 f) allows the fantastic threat to succeed: the Acharnians' mutual, ingrained loyalty is not yet to be shaken.

The particularity of the description of the Acharnians as charcoal-burners is laid aside when Dicaeopolis sees them as merely typical country dwellers or as aged men, dim-witted and vindictive (370 f), but it is resumed in the first of their songs in the parabasis in a new aspect. Charcoal-burners, who need expertise in tending fires, themselves display a fiery vigour so that they aptly call on an ardent Muse, a specifically Acharnian Muse, to bring them an energetic tune: 'just as the sparks leap up from the burning oak when the fire is fanned . . . come to me your fellow-demesman, bringing a forceful, fierce, rustic tune' (665-75).[9]

In *Wasps* it is not until the parabasis, which occurs when two-thirds of the play is over, that a full description of the eponymous chorus is to be found.[10] Apart from the 'anapaests', discussed later in this chapter, the whole of the rest of the parabasis consists of a self-portrait by the Wasps, dealing in Song A with their reflections on the passing of their youth, in Speech A and Song B with their former prowess in battle and in Speech B illustrating true 'waspishness' by contrast with the behaviour of drones (1060-1121). At this stage characterisation is unlikely to be used to further the plot. Although there is a similarity between *Acharnians* and *Wasps* in that the age of the chorus is an important theme of each parabasis, the placing and treatment of the topic is very different. The vindictiveness of elderly jurors, glanced at in *Acharnians*, is fully demonstrated in the action of the later play, chiefly in the person of Philocleon, but it is a more sympathetic aspect which appears when the Wasps introduce themselves (in the song which occupies the same position as the Acharnians' invocation to their Muse of fire) with words rather reminiscent of the Acharnians' regret for lost youth in their entry song: in their youth they had been 'valiant performers in festival choruses and in battles, exceptionally valiant in this' (that is, sexual activity); not all that is gone, their hair whiter than swan's plumage; 'but even from these relics a young man's energy must be found' and the worth of age maintained (*Wasps* 1060 ff, cf. *Ach.* 209 ff).

In the first of their paired speeches the chorus refer to their 'waspishness' and offer an explanation of their sting intelligible 'even to an ignoramus' (1073-4). What follows is a characteristic piece of eulogy praising the speakers as autochthonous, patriotic and brave fighters against the Persians (1076 f).[11] 'As a result all the barbarians still say "Nothing more manly than an Attic wasp!" ' (1089 f). At last it is clear that the wasp jurors are proudly maintaining battle honours won long before and that the preceding lines both justify their boast and amplify their general resemblance to wasps. For instance, they recall how the Persians set fire to Athens as men smoke out wasps' nests (1080) and how they eventually fled as though stung (1088).

Just as the earlier song had contrasted the morality of young and old, so the matching verse (Song B 1091 f) repeats this idea and adds a new item: when invading enemy territory these warriors, unlike others, they imply, reserved their praise for the truly deserving, the best oarsmen. The sung verse thus continues the account of military excellence begun in Speech A but turns from land fighting to sea and from defence to attack. The wasp image, here dropped, is prominent again in the second of the paired speeches. Like Speech A this begins (1103) with an assurance addressed to the audience: 'If you look at us in detail you will find we exactly resemble wasps both in our character and in our way of life.' This time the promise is carried out point by point: firstly when provoked the old men are ill-tempered; secondly, in their swarms they crowd the jury courts and finally they are well equipped for attack and for foraging. In the earlier sections the use of contrast was noted in passages where the old men criticised the young; in the final lines of the parabasis the same device is found, expressed in terms applicable only to wasps: 'However there are drones seated among us who have no sting. They don't go out on active service but eat what we produce, without exertion or hardship' (1114 f). Immediately they apply the analogy to humans: any citizen who fails to fight and suffer for Athens has no right to the juror's pay (1117 f).

This description of the speech and song pairs is intended partly to bring out links between *Acharnians* and *Wasps* but more particularly to show the intricate combination of thematic material in the Wasps' self-congratulation. The songs, about men, and the speeches, about men-wasps, are less sharply differentiated than at first appears and all four sections foreground the chorus's lasting unanimity. If the structure repays scrutiny, so do details of the language. Heavily dependent upon echoes and quotations from a variety of sources, it yet does not sound like pastiche and seems able to incorporate also phrases that would not be found in Homer, Herodotus or any 'serious' writer, as when the Wasps liken their pursuit of the barbarians to tunny-fishers throwing harpoons, the comparison being helped by a pun.

What is the point of this careful and lengthy characterisation so late in the play? Perhaps its essential features may be clarified by turning back to a description that is manifestly a preliminary, the account given before his first appearance of the single old juror round whom the play pivots. Whereas the Wasps' self-congratulation revealed their cohesiveness as a group, Philocleon is unique and eccentric and Aristophanes' presentation of his 'madness' is put, as it must be, into the mouth of a third party, a not unsympathetic observer of the old man and his son. Unlike Philocleon, for whom jury service provides a means of self-aggrandizement, the Wasps, by recalling their patriotic use of their 'stings' to terrify Athens' enemies and by presenting their 'swarming' in the jury courts partly as a civic duty and partly as a reward for retired warriors, go some way towards restoring the ordinary juror in public esteem. This is all the more desirable because it is the Wasps' acceptance of Bdelycleon's arguments in the agon or formal debate which leads to the isolation of Philocleon; moreover, their silence during the trial of Cur could have created an unwanted impression of vacillation or even disloyalty to their calling.

The majority of the passages considered so far have been spoken, not sung. For my next example of self-characterisation by a chorus I have chosen the song of the Frogswans and shall follow this with other descriptive songs drawn from the same play, but performed by the main chorus of Initiates. The opening scene of *Frogs*, discussed in Chapter 5, brings Dionysus and his servant to the lake which separates this world from Hades. Charon, the ferryman, introduces their song as an aid to rowing, in answer to a question from Dionysus, plainly no oarsman (203 ff): 'How shall I be able to row, seeing that I lack training, lack seamanship, lack service at Salamis?' 'Easily. You'll hear splendid songs, the minute you start rowing.' 'Whose songs?' 'Frogswans'. Fantastic.'

The song which follows is a rare exception to the observation made in my introduction, that Aristophanic poetry has received comparatively little detailed attention.[12] Two questions have been raised regarding the Frogs' single contribution to the play named after them: were they seen as well as heard?[13] Is their song intended as parody (that is, mockery) of existing lyric? The first of these questions has to be considered by anyone planning to direct the play, but the second has little theatrical significance. I should like to consider here the Frogs' dramatic role in so far as it clarifies the nature of their song.

When Heracles, himself a traveller to the underworld, had foretold the sights and experiences that awaited the traveller to Hades he promised: 'You will also see a brilliant light, like that of Athens; you will see myrtle-groves and happy groups of worshippers . . . the Initiates' (155-8). The alert auditor may have gathered from this that the chorus would be composed of people who had been initiated in a mystery religion and that their parodos would not take place until Dionysus had passed the lake, the monsters and the quagmire which held criminals. If experienced as well as alert, he may, however, have suspected that the dramatist was promising more than he intended to perform. In fact the monsters and criminals (in reverse order) make an appearance of sorts, but the monsters are imaginary and the 'criminals' just the audience in the Theatre of Dionysus (273-96).

The Frogs then are unexpected. What is their dramatic function? In one sense it is merely to accompany and embellish the crossing of the lake, the essential change from this world to the other, made traditionally in Charon's boat which on this occasion must be propelled by its passengers. What more appropriate than to provide musical accompaniment for their rhythmic action? Dionysus had earlier recalled being on board a ship (48 f), but certainly not as a humble oarsman. Now he has to row, a task he finds both awkward and painful. The song allows no respite and moreover its rhythms, particularly their variation, are a hindrance, not a help, as had been promised. Thus Dionysus is shown as an individual struggling against a group who are no less powerful for being invisible.

As a result, from the formal aspect, this lyric scene consists of choral song with loud interruption or comment from a soloist, a pattern used in tragedy at moments of great tension. The Frogs perceive nothing about the oarsman, save that he attempts to interfere with their singing (228).[14] Ironically, they justify their song first by claiming that they perform in honour of Dionysus himself at the Anthesteria held in their own precinct. Taking the Frogs' hymn on its own, it belongs to that category in which members of a chorus exhort one another to perform in honour of various divinities and draw attention to the excellence in music and dancing which fits them for this task. Thus here they mention their 'melodious song' (213), their leaping among the reeds and their bubbly dances in the deep waters (243 f). As well as playing a part in the worship of Dionysus, they claim that the Muses, Pan and Apollo love them in return for the services offered to them. In essence all of this is conventional enough both in subject matter and expression, the kind of thing expected from a chorus of human or divine worshippers: what makes it novel is only the identity of the singers and of their 'rival', the fact (if it is a fact) that they are unseen and the occasion on which they are presently performing. The entertaining and unparalleled detail of their song follows on naturally from the comic creation of frogs who can sing like swans. Granted that they have musical ability and the desire to worship (just as swans honoured Apollo), then this is the kind of song they would sing, when 'on days of sunshine we leaped among the galingale and reed, enjoying our deep diving songs, or to avoid the rainshower, we uttered our varied music in the watery depths with our splish splosh splashings' (242 f).

Aristophanes' narrative or descriptive material is not always so easy to follow and *Frogs* also contains songs which are confusingly impressionistic. The two songs I wish to examine now precede and introduce the literary contest between Aeschylus and Euripides and each in its own way prepares the auditor for the ferocity of the coming struggle. In form, the second and simpler of the two is an invocatory dactylic hymn to the Muses inviting them to supervise the contest.[15] It is natural and fitting to invoke Muses as expert witnesses in literary matters and natural also to preface the contest proper with a religious ceremony beginning with a hymn. Partial quotation of the hymn will demonstrate its conventional features: 'Ye nine, Zeus' daughters, chaste Muses, you who behold from above . . . come, oversee . . .' (*Frogs* 875-82). Inviting deities to be present in time of battle, contest or competition is also customary. The amount of idiosyncratic material in this little ode may be small but it is sharply incongruous. Here is the ode in full:

> Ye nine, Zeus' daughters, chaste Muses, you who behold from above the subtly-worded intelligent minds of men who forge maxims, when to battle they come with their contra-assertions, their planned, keen wrestlers' shifts and twists; come look upon the power of their two dread mouths to provide phrases and shavings of words. For now this great contest of your art approaches its enactment.

These contestants are shown to wrestle and smite their foes with the techniques and weapons not of epic battle but of the newer intellectual and verbal warfare, practised not only by Euripides the 'modernist' but also by Aeschylus.

This juxtaposition of material both physical and verbal in a frame and on an occasion conventionally religious forms a whole which is reasonably simple by comparison with an earlier song which heralds the entrance of the two tragedians. Dionysus' slave Xanthias has just asked his new crony, a slave of Pluto's, about the yelling and insults he can hear (757 f). He learns that Euripides has laid claim to the 'tragic throne' occupied by Aeschylus and that the resultant dispute is about to be settled by a contest or arbitration. At this preliminary stage it sounds as though the plays will be weighed and measured, bit by bit, so as to produce an objective, unassailable decision (797-802) but this impression is countered by the stress, a few lines later, on finding an expert adjudicator.[16] Euripides, it seems, favoured the objective method but Aeschylus was angry, 'lowered his head and glared like a bull' (804).

It is at this point that the chorus sing their four stanzas

anticipating the conflict to come (814-29). These stanzas offer an impressionistic view of contestants and contest in which there is no direct reference by name to either poet and in which a Homeric veil obscures the distinction between image and reality, between old and new, between physical and intellectual conflict. To simplify the deliberately complex, by way of preface to detailed comment, the first stanza presents on animal angrily anticipating attack by another, while in the second incidents in a battle between human adversaries are foreseen. Stanza three reverts to an attacking animal and stanza four (probably) to his adversary's counter-attack. In this song there are only slight indications, mainly in the last verse, that words not blows will be the medium of warfare and that intellectual powers, not physical skill and prowess will be tested.

> Fearful shall be the spleen now of Thundermutter withinside
> when the riptooth-sharpening he sees of his multiloquacious
> antagonist to encounter him. Then shall ensue dread
> eyewhirl of fury.
>
> Horse-encrested phrases shall shock in helmtossing combat,
> chariots collide in whelm of wreckage and splinter-flown action,
> warrior beating off brain-crafted warrior's
> cavalried speeches.
>
> Bristling the hairy mane on his neck of self-grown horsehair
> bellowing he shall blast the bolts from compacted joinery
> banging plank by plank nailed sections of verse in
> stormburst gigantic.
>
> Next, mouthforged tormenter of versification, the slim-shaped
> tongue unraveling to champ on the bit of malignance
> wickedly shall chip and chop at its tropes, much
> labor of lungwork.
>
> > (*Frogs* 814-29, trs. R. Lattimore)

The expression 'Homeric veil' which I used just now requires clarification. That the song emphasises the 'epic' quality of the coming contest is made clear by its metre, diction and content: much of the rhythm is dactylic, like the Homeric hexameter, and the frequent compound adjectives use or imitate Homeric formations. Heroic poetry too compares the warrior preparing for single combat with lion or boar but, whereas in Homer such comparisons are presented in the form of simile, in this ode human and animal have lost the distinctness of simile.[17] Even the verbal nature of the contest has its Homeric counterpart in the jeers and insults flung at each other by heroes about to engage in combat, or at its conclusion. Just as a veil both forms a surface cover and may prevent a clear view of the variety that lies beneath, so the Homeric atmosphere of these verses is their most obvious characteristic and may be thought the clearest indication of the importance, or at least the grandiose nature, of the encounter.

Clearly the Homeric and the Aeschylean overlap. As Aeschylus claims in the agon itself to be Homer's direct successor in the presentation of heroes and heroic virtues (1034-42), so too his metre and style often recall his model. Moreover the earlier comparison of Aeschylus to an angry bull aids the identification of the enraged animal of the opening lines. At the verbal level what can be labelled exclusively 'Aeschylean' by the scholar may or may not have been so distinguished by Aristophanes' contemporaries. With regard to Euripides, however, what is discernible is 'modern' usage and emphasis rather than linguistic elements exclusively Euripidean.

The failure to name names causes uncertainty here as well as elsewhere in the contest.[18] As the chorus mention 'the one' and 'the other', do they indicate by look or gesture whether they mean Aeschylus or Euripides? The nature of these stanzas rather suggests that mystification is intended. At any rate the opening description of the angry loud-roaring contestant who sees his adversary sharpening a tusk suggests a lion-man facing a boar-man. (I use these inelegant compounds because it would be misleading to speak of lion fighting boar: Aristophanes is recalling the comparison of warrior with animal in those transformations which, in Redfield's words, 'mark moments of high heroic action.')[19] The identification of Aeschylus partly depends on the mention of 'anger', as does that of Euripides on the second element of a compound epithet ('shrill-babbling'); in addition the boar is the challenger in this situation. In the second stanza, the preliminaries to Homeric duel over, fighting from chariots is about to begin: now the adversaries, having dropped their animal natures of a moment ago, are referred to as men who fight by hurling verbiage from chariots which crash and splinter. The mention of chariots, the product of men's skill, permits the introduction of terms of a kind applied to literature seen as a craft, the view implicit in the earlier reference to weighing and measuring the dramatic art: and thus the chariots bridge, as it were, the gap between the heroic past and the late fifth century.

The third stanza as a whole pictures an enraged animal with bristling hair, frowning and roaring while he hurls phrases the size of ships' timbers. The animal Aeschylus now most resembles is a boar which as it charges can root up and toss aside brushwood. The boar is resisted in the final stanza by an opponent whose nature is hard to describe (partly because of textual problems) but whose main feature is a tongue which functions both creatively and as a cutting weapon eagerly destroying the adversary's words.

Whatever he makes of the sense of this passage, the auditor will be aware of prominent stylistic features: abundant, often compound, epithets, distinctive sound and rhythm and close-packed images, all contribute to a fierce and energetic whole. At the conclusion we see emerge from Pluto's dwelling Dionysus, a petulant Euripides and an Aeschylus who, far from hurling phrases like timbers, maintains a dignified, or sulky, silence.

The Poet's Autobiography

Early in this chapter I wrote: 'in a drama all narrative is dramatic.' With regard to Aristophanic comedy this statement needs some modification to take account of passages in the opening section of those parabases, for instance *Knights*, *Clouds* and *Wasps*, in which a narrative element is present and in which the speaker's identity is debatable. When writing about Strepsiades' story of his marriage I tried to show that it was more than an artless recital, and more than a way of gaining sympathy for his difficult situation. Similarly with these passages addressed to the audience. So I wish now to look at some lines from *Knights* and *Clouds* in which the narrative mode conceals or disguises the underlying message. My approach will not be that of the scholar wishing to solve a problem in literary history but of someone interested in the various uses of narrative.[20] In Chapter 2 the rhetorical aspect of the opening section (the 'anapaests' or the 'parabasis proper') will be considered, but here emphasis will fall on the story-telling, descriptive element.

After the rival demagogues have departed to pursue their quarrel elsewhere, leaving the stage empty, the Knights who form the chorus say they have agreed to explain at the poet's bidding why he had not previously sought leave to put on a comedy in his own name; the deferral was due to his belief that comedy did not grant her favours to all suitors and to his observation that audiences were fickle in their tastes (and this observation he supports by describing their treatment of other fifth-century comic poets, Magnes, Cratinus and Crates) (512-40). In addition he believed that 'one should first be an oarsman before taking on the steering and then after that be bow-officer and keep watch for the winds and then finally do one's own steering' (*Knights* 541-4).

The intention of this address, as of all such, is to help the dramatist in his attempt to win first prize. The earlier action of the play has shown the Knights coming to the support of a man inexperienced in politics who is attacking an established leader and the later action will develop the idea that the populace (Demos) will grant favours only to the assiduous and persuasive demagogue wooer: in the 'anapaests' the Knights champion a dramatist admittedly inexperienced in the art of producing plays, and refer to Comedy as a choosy mistress and to the spectators as disloyal to their former favourites.

The Knights are here represented as conveying to a wider audience the dramatist's answers to the question reportedly put to him by 'many who approached him amazed that he had not long before' sought to direct a play himself and be publicly acknowledged as its author (512 f). It is as though we are to imagine Aristophanes and a group of Knights chatting in the street shortly before the performance with this topic emerging casually in conversation: this device facilitates the creation of a persona for the dramatist and permits description of his state of mind. The persona is that of a modest and hesitant man who attempts to exculpate himself from the charge of spiritless reluctance to engage openly in the competition by explaining his thought processes. He begins with, but does not dwell on, his belief that producing a comedy was extremely difficult. Next he refers to his realisation, long ago, that the spectators reacted differently each year and were disloyal to formerly popular poets as they grew old, and this theme he develops during the course of the next 21 lines (almost half of the 'anapaests'), by recounting the experiences of three of his rivals. (To these lines I shall shortly return.) It is his rivals' vicissitudes which have made him nervous, he says (541).

Now he reverts to his earlier point, the belief that comic production was difficult (541, cf. 515 f) but this time he offers an analogy between producer and mariner designed to show that patient study and thorough experience are prerequisites of command in each field. He picks out three stages for the mariner: beginning as one oarsman among many, he graduates to the post of look-out and bow-officer and from that to helmsman in command of his ship's course. The implications are that a novice might well endanger the safety of a ship and lack authority over the crew: similarly a comedy produced by a novice might well 'sink' at the festival; its inexpert director would certainly have problems in obtaining from his 'crew' of chorus members the results he desired.

Because I have omitted so far to do more than sketch the content of the central 20 lines of the 'anapaests', I have been able to emphasise the personal nature of the beginning and end, the attempt to portray a young man characterised by *sophrosyne*, prudent self-control and modesty, as opposed to rash impetuosity. This stance on the part of the dramatist makes an agreeable contrast with the postures of the two principals in the comedy, the unscrupulous demagogues competing for power, but creates a problem with regard to the central section of the 'anapaests'. That section, we recall, was (somewhat illogically) attached to the rest as follows: some of the poet's reluctance 'to ask for a chorus' resulted from his observation of the fickleness of audiences (517 f). In themselves the lines thus introduced convey a picture of the careers of three dramatists: Magnes, in his prime very successful, was found too mild in his old age and rejected (520-5); Cratinus, formerly victorious and popular, now feeble and in a pitiful condition through age, wanders round babbling incoherently, neglected by the people (526-36); Crates, finally, had to suffer passionate outbursts and ill-treatment from the audience in spite of the elegant fare he offered them, with only moderate success (537-40). On this passage Sommerstein neatly comments:

unlike Magnes (dead) and Crates (dead or retired), Cratinus
was still active as a dramatist and indeed was one of the
competitors at the very festival at which *Knights* was
produced; by sandwiching him between Magnes and Crates
Ar. insinuates that he belongs to the past and his retirement is
overdue.[21]

How can the nervous and modest poet manage to knock his
rivals' product without damaging the persona he has sought to
adopt? In addition to the 'sandwiching' observed by Sommerstein
we may note, what my summaries did not convey, the
metaphorical liveliness and abundance found almost throughout.
The final section, the least extended, presents Crates' comedies
as economical but pleasant lunches; in the case of Crates, his
unpopularity and lack of success begin as well as end the passage
referring to him. The lines about Magnes convey the variety of
his successes by a series of participles denoting aspects of
performance; for instance, 'uttering different sounds', 'using his
wings', 'dyeing himself frog-colour'. It is more likely that the
incongruous juxtaposition of these activities would make an
effect on first hearing than that each participle would at once
recall the title of one of his plays to all members of the audience.
The tone of the lines is one of attempted fairness: Magnes did
eventually fail, of course, 'but not in his youth' (524).

In the case of the centrepiece, Cratinus, the tone is nicely
judged; ostensibly a tribute to the poet's early achievement and a
commiseration with him in his later years such as might properly
come from a modest youthful competitor, the latter part in fact
suggests that Cratinus is a senile drunkard. Beginning with the
image of Cratinus' art as a powerful current carrying away
everything in its course, our poet changes the picture to envisage
his rival himself in wretched old age, victories long past, in terms
(probably) of a defunct musical instrument; 'in his old age he
wanders around' (like the man in the proverb) 'with garland all
withered and with thirst all undone' when he ought to be feasted
at state expense and be given a seat of honour in the theatre in
recompense for his earlier victories and not be left to wander
talking nonsense (533-6). By this kind of writing, which moves
rapidly from image to image, doubts and questions are swept
aside (honours for retired poets? Cratinus senile?): apparently

just recalling facts already familiar, like Cratinus' dipsomania and his recent failures, the poet uses the technique of persuasive (mis-)information to create a persona for Cratinus as fictitious, conceivably, as the one the composer of these 'anapaests' was endeavouring to create for himself.

Finally I turn to the parabasis of the revised version of *Clouds*, where the dramatist is adducing earlier successes as a reason for his confidence in the present play which he now introduces with a complimentary description. He starts 'from the time when on this spot my chaste boy and my dissolute boy received an excellent report' from, presumably, patrons of his, thus alluding to the earliest of his plays, *Banqueters*, in which a father had two sons of contrasted character and morals (*Clouds* 528 f); after this semi-ironical opening he continues in the role of the comedy's mother: 'And because I was single still and not yet permitted to be the baby's mother I exposed it and another girl picked it up and you kindly assisted its development and growth' (530-2). Since this first success the dramatist has, he says, reliable tokens of the audience's sound judgement. What is the point of this little tale and where does the emphasis lie? Surely the emphasis falls upon the spectators' welcome for the helpless, new-born play, proof of their generosity and discrimination. If so the preceding lines (admittedly of greater interest to the scholar) are to be regarded as building up to this point, the birth and fostering of the infant drama being subordinate to its reception in the theatre.

Having reminded his hearers of their own good qualities, he naturally hopes that they will be equally wise in appreciating the new play, likened now not to a baby but to Electra, the mythical heroine long parted from her brother: 'This comedy, like Electra in the tale, has come looking for spectators equally wise; she will recognise the lock of hair from her brother's head, if she catches sight of it' (534-6). The lines suggest an Electra who sets out again to find evidence of her brother's hoped-for return, in spite of previous disappointment; similarly this comedy sets out for a second attempt. She will take comfort from the slightest indication of approval from those present; if they laugh or applaud she may be emboldened to believe that her hopes, like Electra's, may eventually be fulfilled by the 'return' of victory.[22] In his recommendation of *Clouds*, the poet sustains the personification of comedy: 'Look how modest her character is,' he begins, and goes on to demonstrate by means of a negative list the various activities she does not perform. Once more these earlier lines serve chiefly to focus attention on the conclusion: the comedy has come on the stage, relying not on such extraneous aids as comic business and lewd dances, but on her own character and, above all, on what is said, on the text of the play (537-44). We can see that these descriptions, read together, suggest that a play, rather than competing aggressively, may be put forward as helpless, young, feminine, modest, appealing to the intellect and finer feelings of the hearers.

And so what the poet chooses to say in parabases in the highly picturesque language there regularly employed has no necessary relationship with truth as that term is understood, for example, in the modern court of law. Its aim, put bluntly, is self-advertisement and his task as a poet is to find sufficiently original ways of presenting his message to avoid boring his audience. Each time he has to say 'My play is good. The others are bad. Give me the prize.' A favourite way of embedding this bald utterance in attractive surroundings is to employ story-like and descriptive material rather than open step-by-step argument. Such material must be plausible, persuasive, not necessarily factual or literally true. The reader of parabases studies works of fiction, entertainments designed to win popularity sometimes by subtle rather than blatant means.

Notes

1. B. Hardy, *Tellers and Listeners* (London, 1975), 1. For further reading see Wayne Booth, *The Rhetoric of Fiction* (Chicago, 1961); G. Genette (trs. J.E. Lewin), *Narrative Discourse* (Oxford, 1980); S. Chatman, *Story and Discourse* (Cornell, 1978).

2. e.g. The 'messenger speech' at *Ach.* 1174-89, on which see Rau 139-42.

3. The opening is discussed in detail by K. Dover, *QUCC* 9 (1970), 7-23 (in Italian; there is a German version in Newiger 1975, 124 ff) and by L. Edmunds in *YCS* 26, 33.

4. As a result of this transformation the audience participates in the Assembly.

5. The translation is designed to show the crescendo from two-syllabled to six-syllabled word in *Ach.* 48.

6. The morality of Strepsiades' actions is discussed below, p. 174.

7. In D. Barrett's translation (Penguin Classics) the names are Procleon and Anticleon.

8. It is instructive to compare the Nurse's account of Medea (E. *Medea* 1-45, on which see P. Pucci, *The Violence of Pity in Euripides' Medea* (New York, 1980),

32-58) and contrast Deianeira's autobiographical narrative (S. *Women of Trachis*, 1-48).

9. The imagic potential of timber and fire has often been noted. Charcoal-burners are well chosen also because their work in the forests of Mt Parnes demanded strength, skill and endurance and because they travelled throughout Attica carrying charcoal to mines, smiths, bakers, etc. cf. E. fr. 283 (*Autolycus*) and see R. Meiggs, *Timber in the Ancient Mediterranean World* (Oxford, 1982), 451 f.

10. A complete parabasis consists of opening 'anapaests' plus a pair of songs and a pair of speeches, often in the order Speech A, Song A, Speech B, Song B. Details may be found in Pickard-Cambridge, 1962.

11. For choral self-praise see below, p. 62.

12. For a recent discussion of the function of the Frog chorus see D.A. Campbell, *JHS* 104 (1985), 163-5.

13. On the question of visibility of the Frogs see, most recently, R.H. Allison, *G & R* 30 (1983), 8-20.

14. For the competition between the singers and the noisy oarsman cf. Pratinas' *Hyporcheme*, on which see A.M. Dale, *Collected Papers* (Cambridge, 1969), 166.

15. For invocatory hymns in *Frogs* cf. 316-46, 675-85, 875-84.

16. See below, p. 112.

17. Lion (Hector) fights boar (Patroclus) at *Iliad* 16. 823-6. On Homeric similes see C. Moulton, *Similes in the Homeric Epic* (Hypomnemata 49) (Göttingen, 1977); on this passage see Taillardat, 207 f.

18. Cf. *Frogs* 901-3, 1101-2, 1413.

19. J.M. Redfield, *Nature and Culture in the Iliad* (Chicago, 1975), 192.

20. On the stages in Ar.'s career see most recently D. MacDowell, *CQ* 32 (1982), 21-6.

21. Sommerstein, *Knights*, 171.

22. It is usual to suggest that a recent revival of A. *Choephoroi* occasioned the allusion. It seems more to the point to think of an Electra who in spite of an earlier disappointment yet comes again to seek evidence of her brother's return.

2 ARISTOPHANES THE ORATOR: ATTACK AND DEFENCE

> tu quoque Pieridum studio, studiose, teneris,
>   ingenioque faves, ingeniose, meo.
> distat opus nostrum, sed fontibus exit ab isdem:
>   artis et ingenuae cultor uterque sumus.
>
> (Ovid, *Ex Ponto* 2.5)

In Plato distrust of poets and others who relied on the power of the word was allied with supreme mastery of language. Similarly Aristophanes, the enemy of orators, was himself a distinguished exponent of their art. It is my aim in this chapter and the next to substantiate and exemplify this statement in order to bring about a kind of recognition of a so far hidden and neglected side of our poet's art. In this chapter I shall discuss rhetorical attack and defence; in the next examples of praise and blame. Both chapters take much of their material from the agon, or formal debate, and from the parabasis.[1] Five plays are considered, *Knights*, *Peace* and *Frogs* taking second place to *Acharnians* and *Wasps*; full discussion of *Clouds*, in which the use and abuse of rhetoric is an important issue, is postponed until my concluding chapter.

In the poem which Ovid wrote to a friend who was in private a lover of poetry but by profession an orator, the gulf between poetry and rhetoric is accepted: *distat opus nostrum*.[2] In part it is a gulf between the public man speaking in court and senate and the private man composing verses for his readers' leisure and so it is as something of a paradox that Ovid writes, in the words quoted at the head of this chapter, that the orator, like the poet, is a devotee of the Muses and that the arts which they cultivate both derive ultimately from the same source. What would Aristophanes' contemporaries have made of Ovid's words? Some centuries nearer than Ovid to Homeric epic, regarded as the common source of both poetry and rhetoric, they nevertheless lived in an age when the mastery of words was enabling men who lacked the traditional qualifications of birth and wealth to acquire power and influence. This development was unlikely to be universally welcomed and the unpopularity of the new orator-politicians could reasonably extend to those who claimed to be able to teach the art of successful argument. If, therefore, the holders of such opinions were to consider the relationship of poetry and rhetoric, they would be likely to emphasise the distance between poetry, which could be viewed as traditional and conservative, and rhetoric which seemed an essential ingredient in an unwelcome contemporary movement.

What of poets themselves? We saw that for Ovid oratorical mastery of words was a, or the, qualification for involvement in public life whereas the poet rejoiced in staying aloof from such involvement. The Greek poet in the fifth century BC whose works were composed for state festivals could make no such distinction and may well have seen the orator as a kind of rival in that both were seeking power and influence in a public arena, the court and assembly on the one hand, the Theatre of Dionysus on the other. Drama, on this view, is inevitably a kind of public speaking.

However, rivalry and a sense of the distance between poet-dramatist and orator is not the whole story. The quality of Aristophanes' verse with its verbal ingenuity and novelty suggests that its maker cannot have found the work of teachers of rhetoric like Gorgias, Prodicus and Protagoras who began the study of language other than intriguing, even if he deplored their aims and envied their success.

In what sense can fifth-century drama be described as rhetorical? To begin with tragedy: most importantly it may contain speeches of a length and type that could be delivered, *mutatis mutandis*, in law court or deliberative assembly and the action may be so shaped as to facilitate the inclusion of such material. Thus the dramatist may engineer confrontations, like that between husband and wife in Euripides' *Medea*, in which accusation and counter-accusation are presented with the formality of public speech in carefully marshalled arguments, using conventional material and including touches of sarcasm, pathos or even humour in a calculated way.[3] Speeches of this kind which lend themselves to analysis and critical description are nothing like the utterances of people actually in the grip of rage and shock: the dramatist is making out a case for each of the antagonists, not recording a critical hour in their lives. Secondly the term 'rhetorical' may be applied to the tragic poet's style: under this heading one could include the presence of words, phrases and figures normally associated with public speaking (and in some cases mentioned in rhetorical handbooks). Passages of formal speechmaking often contain rhetorical 'markers', for instance structural signposts ('firstly', 'lastly', 'on the one hand . . .'), indications of context ('Gentlemen of the jury') and clichés ('Unaccustomed as I am . . .'). Clearly some of these markers can have no place in drama, while others require modification to adapt them to verse.

Nevertheless speeches in tragedy which have a rhetorical function can more easily incorporate stylistic markers than can their counterparts in Aristophanic comedy because the linguistic registers of tragic poetry and rhetoric are more akin. Rhetorical clichés stand out so conspicuously in most comic surroundings as to suggest that oratory, or an orator, is being 'sent up'. If those features of style which create a rhetorical surface are less common in Old Comedy than in Euripidean tragedy, where is Aristophanic oratory located and how is it to be recognised? The most obvious, but not the only, situation is of course the agon and later in this chapter we shall trace the arguments and examine the language used in one agon, that of *Wasps*. Comedy's unique element, the parabasis, also regularly offers examples of persuasive and argumentative speech: indeed its first section, the 'anapaests', in which the poet's art is defended, is like one half of an agon. In these locations, because the speaker is obviously trying to make a case, the presence of rhetoric has been recognised, however idiosyncratic the style. However I hope to show that there are other passages too which have affinities with oratory of one kind or another, even if these affinities have largely been ignored.

In a substantial article published more than 40 years ago, C.T. Murphy discussed both Aristophanes' attacks on rhetoric and his use of rhetorical features in his characters' forensic speeches (but not in parabases). Since then there has been no extended general treatment of the subject in English, although some editions, notably Douglas MacDowell's *Wasps*, offer assessment of the persuasive qualities of individual speeches.[4] Like Murphy I shall begin by mentioning Aristophanes' manifest hostility towards orator-politicians, taking my evidence from *Acharnians*.

Put briefly, in *Acharnians* orators are indicted on two chief counts: that they bludgeon the helpless and that they deceive their hearers by means of flattery. The first charge is made the more effective by being voiced by the old men of the chorus who have themselves experienced prosecution in the courts at the hands of ambitious and unfeeling young advocates (676-718). The poet also recounts how he himself 'nearly died in a foul flood of disaster' when attacked by the orator, Cleon (382). The second charge is levelled against ambassadors and others who take in and fool gullible auditors who enjoy being flattered (372-4, 634-40).

In order to estimate the force and accuracy of these remarks it will be as well to outline the placing and function of rhetorical material in the dramatic action of the comedy. The hero, having made peace with Spara for himself and his family, is threatened by the Acharnians who regard him as a traitor to Athens. Eventually he manages to persuade them not to attack him and thereafter is able to demonstrate that peace brings prosperity and success. In this action the hero uses his rhetorical ability as one, but only one, of his means of success. In the second half of the play, where the joys of peace are demonstrated, there is no use of argumentation, no attack on oratory. It is in the scenes which precede the parabasis that oratory matters and in these it becomes increasingly important. Paradoxically, in the Assembly scene at the beginning of *Acharnians*, when one would expect persuasive argumentation to be employed, probably by the hero, this is not the case, and the only hint of rhetorical skill is that displayed in the ambassador's attempt to persuade his hearers that his luxurious foreign posting had been hard to endure (65-86). For reasons which I discuss later, the Assembly ends without a debate on the subject of peace and Dicaeopolis' enforced silence on the topic he cares most about has to continue until the Big Speech begins (496). By 'enforced silence' I do not of course mean that he says nothing at all or that he stops trying to gain a hearing, merely that his early verbal efforts fail (294-325), and that even after seizing a hostage from the Acharnians he lacks the confidence to complete the speech on which he has embarked (326-82). It is only when he has returned from a visit to the tragic poet Euripides, disguised as a beggar and strengthened by drinking a Euripidean potion, that he can demonstrate his ability to argue a case, with enough success to win the approval of half of the chorus. If Dicaeopolis is not a natural orator, a Euripidean character, in pitiful attire, cannot altogether fail!

Before I describe the kind of orator Dicaeopolis turns out to be, I want to go back for a moment to the 'false start' speech where the little man volunteering to speak with his head on an executioner's block explains why he is afraid: his anxieties stem, he says, from his knowledge of countrymen's gullibility ('they're overjoyed if some conman eulogises them') and of elderly jurors' reluctance to acquit (370-6). The men he is now facing, the Acharnian charcoal-burners, are elderly country dwellers and so by implication both potentially vindictive and susceptible to flattery. How does Dicaeopolis overcome the problems of addressing this particular audience, filled as they are with bitter resentment against the Spartan enemy, not least because of damage to their own crops? Beginning the main section of his speech with a declaration of his hatred for the Spartans, he continues not with the expected arguments but with narrative of a special kind (519-39). In this he describes a chain of events which (supposedly) led up to, and caused, the outbreak of the war between the two states. Let me break off for a moment to give a parallel. Imagine a case in which a man is accused of causing an affray: unable to deny his own part in the disturbance he seeks to exculpate himself by involving other people; he and they have been caught up in an unstoppable series of events. His defence consists of narrative rather than reasoning: he tries to persuade by informing. In the same way Dicaeopolis shows that Spartan involvement in the war resulted from a chain of circumstances whose first link was forged at Athens, the second by the Megarian reaction, and so on. Finally and by indirect means, the Spartans were brought in. If such a narrative has plausibility and so gains credence, it is not for its historical accuracy but only because there is nothing improbable about behaviour of the kind described: this is how people act and how things happen. The first incident was 'unimportant and local' but 'after that' some Athenians stole a whore from Megara and 'after that' some Megarians stole two whores from Athens, and so on. 'And after that there was the din of weapons' (539).

There follows a quotation from Euripides: 'Someone will say, "It shouldn't be," ' 'What should they have done then?', Dicaeopolis asks. At this point it sounds as though a passage of argumentation might be introduced in which the rights and wrongs of possible courses of action could be discussed. Indeed, Dicaeopolis' next move is an orator's ploy. He first asks his hearers to imagine how they would have reacted if positions had been reversed ('You say A shouldn't have done what he did.

What would you have done in A's shoes?') and then answers his own question: 'Without any doubt, you would have prepared to fight.' The hearer of this second part of Dicaeopolis' defence is however more likely to be struck by the brilliant, impressionistic, extended description of a city preparing for battle than to ponder the message. Translation can convey the noisy bustling activity in city and shipyard up to a point. What is impossible in English is to capture the hammer-blow sound of 25 words ending in *-ōn*, seven at line end. Dicaeopolis, we feel on hearing this exciting account of war fever, is as capable as the next man of entering with fervour upon a military exploit – until he stops to think (540-56).[5]

At the end of a speech which has succeeded in convincing half of the bellicose Acharnians we must pause and ask what exactly Dicaeopolis has done. Has he spoken 'on behalf of the Spartans?' Yes, but only in the sense that he has absolved them from sole responsibility for the war. Has he defended the private peace which he has made? Apparently not. Is this omission to be explained by carelessness on the part of the dramatist or by his inability to find arguments which would be convincing (and not unacceptable to those eager to continue the war) or by the fact that the private peace is recommended in the play not by words but by its results: the celebration of the Country Dionysia, successful trading and feasting, for instance? We should remember that the dramatist does not allow Dicaeopolis' speech to win over the whole chorus. In the following scene (572-625), in addition to the remainder of the chorus whose hatred of the Spartans was inflamed by damage to their own crops (but who are too old to fight), he meets a new warmonger, Lamachus the *strategos*. As a result, Dicaeopolis is enabled to show the Acharnians what the spectators had already observed in the opening scene, namely that the rich and powerful not only escape the hardships of war but may actually benefit from it. Dicaeopolis uses mockery and a few pithy exchanges to floor Lamachus, but not rhetoric.

Dicaeopolis' complete defence, put into words might run like this: 'If I can prove to you that we are at least as much to blame as the Spartans for beginning the war perhaps you will modify your detestation of them and your determination to fight to the bitter end and perhaps you will open your eyes to the advantages of peace. I am neither a traitor to Athens nor a friend to Sparta but a man who longs for peace and who seeks to persuade others by his example: do as I have done and enjoy the fruits of peace.' The defence he actually makes in the Big Speech, partly in the guise of Euripidean beggar, partly in his own character, partly as spokesman of comedy, is only a portion of the defence offered by the totality of the play.

The defence made by Dicaeopolis cannot be completely separated from that put forward by his creator. I have already mentioned Dicaeopolis' admission that he feels nervous because of the credulity and spitefulness of his hearers and I now quote more fully from the 'false start' speech:

> I'm very frightened. I know the character of the country people, overjoyed at praise . . . I know the elderly folk too, their hearts set on voting sharp painful verdicts and I understand what I myself suffered at Cleon's hands because of last year's comedy. (370-8)

Of these three reasons for anxiety the first two might easily be voiced by Dicaeopolis when confronting the elderly countrymen from Acharnae but the third obviously cannot. Since the three clauses are tightly joined, it is worth enquiring whether they may all refer to the same incident, described more fully in the following lines. 'He hauled me up before the Council, accused me, mouthed lies about me, overwhelmed and pounded me in his foul torrent of politics so that I was nearly done for' (379-82). Should we infer that Cleon's near success resulted from his ability to flatter those councillors susceptible to flattery and to appeal to the vindictiveness of others?

The second allusion to the incident clarifies the charge. In the proem of the Big Speech the 'beggar' and 'maker of *trygodia*' asserts his right to speak what is 'terrible but true' about the city because on this occasion, the Lenaean festival, 'Cleon doesn't traduce me for abusing the city in the presence of foreigners' (5022-3).[6]

These two passages, in their context striking enough, but undeveloped, come back to mind when the parabasis proper begins (628-64).[7] The old men of the chorus state that the poet, falsely accused of 'making a comedy of our city' and 'insulting the ordinary people', desires to answer the charge, that is, to become as it were the defendant on trial for an offence against the community. Cleon's accusation will receive a reply before a 'jury' of the hasty and fickle Athenian citizens. The poet might recall Pindar's words: 'My necessity is to escape the teeth of reproach for excessive blame' (*Pythian* 2. 52-3, trs. R. Lattimore). The gist of his case is that he has in fact benefited the city since it is by means of insults that comic poets give the people their valuable advice! However, the line of argument presented in this discursive passage is not as easy to follow as my summary might suggest and I propose to preface discussion of it with a paragraph about the way the men of the chorus present the poet. They refer first to 'our didaskalos' (628) as wanting to make his defence against his enemies' slanders; thereafter they speak of him as the 'poet' (633, 644, 649, 654). Normally 'didaskalos', in the context of fifth-century drama, means 'chorus trainer', 'producer', but here it also, I suggest, keeps its general sense of 'teacher'. This is first implied when the poet asserts that he has benefited the citizens by putting a stop to their credulity; secondly he claims to have 'shown' how the allied cities are ruled (642) and lastly, in his promises for the future the didactic role is emphasised by repetition and by contrast between the teacher and the orator-politician. 'He declares that he will *teach* you much that is good, to make you happy; he doesn't flatter, nor offer inducements, nor try any tricks; he's not unprincipled, doesn't bedew you with compliments; he *teaches* what is best' (656-8).

Now for the content of the 'anapaests' in more detail. The opening claim, that the poet has shown the foreign envoys in their true light as wily flatterers, takes nine lines, clearly defined as a subsection by the use of ring composition (633-41). The next point, about the allied cities, receives one line only and seems merely to act as a link to the following section which illustrates and emphasises the fame of the poet (643-54). As well as the thread of argument which links the sections, there is a further link between them in the motif of official journeyings between states, beginning with the visit to Athens of flattering envoys from abroad, continuing with a reference to the arrival in the city of the tribute money from the subject allies and ending with the spread of the poet's reputation to Persia and the effect of this on diplomatic missions from Sparta to Persia.

In the first section the poet refers to a time when ambassadors who quoted the Pindaric epithets 'violet-crowned' or 'gleaming' in their compliments about Athens thereby gained anything they wanted. Now he has put a stop to the citizens' gullibility and deserves to be rewarded, he says. We may well agree, seeing how neatly he has repeated the compliment while deriding the flatterers. The next stage is less clear: in a single line the poet alludes to a second benefit, his 'showing the people of the allied states their democratic government' (642). This is so briefly and ambiguously expressed that one may suspect that the defendant is here attempting to veil the essential feature of his 'abuse of the city', namely that he had spoken harshly in the previous year's play about some aspect of Athens' treatment of the subject states.[8]

Mention of these allies leads to the theme of the following section, the fame which the poet has won by his outspoken words, as a result of which the allies will come with the tribute 'longing to see the best of poets' (644). The original concern with the effect foreigners had on Athenians has now given way to the spreading abroad of Athens' poetic renown and this is accompanied by a change from past time to assurance about the future. Whereas the Homeric warrior's fame *kleos* was conventionally exalted to the heavens, news of the poet's daring has reached as far as Persia, we are now told, as the poet sketches for his more credulous 'pupils' a short scene played by the Great King and ambassadors from Sparta. Here there is an interesting variation on earlier material: there the accusation that flattering ambassadors conned Athenian citizens, here the Persian monarch interrogating Spartan ambassadors about the relative naval and poetic strengths of their own city and their enemy, Athens. The ambassadors' answer need not be spelled out because everyone had to acknowledge Athenian naval supremacy: the King merely says that whichever side received the best poetic advice was sure to win. And, as if hyperbole had not gone far enough, from the supposed scene in Persia we are brought back to an Athens to which Spartan envoys will come, suing for peace, their only condition being control of the island of Aegina, 'not that they care about the island; they aim to remove this poet' (653-4).[9] This bold assertion introduces the peroration: the poet must be kept in Athens because he will enlighten and educate the citizens.

The defence rests. The poet has not denied the charge. Instead he has transformed the jibes and ridicule of which he had been accused into wise counsel and has gone so far as to claim that his reputation as a percipient critic has motivated the Spartans to seek an end to the war. In the course of his speech he has refrained from directly praising the audience (a common introductory motif in parabases), but praise of the city is subtly present. The poet-teacher, unable to flatter, has yet raised himself to a position of eminence and fame, not for his comic invention but for his services to the state as adviser. Like many a defendant the poet draws attention to the goods things he has done and the esteem he has won, but few defendants can have boasted that their courage has had such widespread publicity and effectiveness. It is not the voice of the man on trial that we hear in these lines but that of the hero whose *kleos* is inseparable from the renown he confers on his community by his achievement. Moreover his *kleos* is established not by the superlatives and heroic simile of epic but by hyperbolic fiction: it is almost as though we have a miniature comedy in these lines, one scene set in Persia and the second at Athens, with the poet-adviser as principal orator. He, 'best of poets', is *laudator* of his own city and above all of himself.

The coda (the *pnigos*) begins defiantly, and with a change from third person singular to first: 'So Cleon can contrive and construct whatever he likes against me' (659-60); next comes an expression of fervent assurance followed by a final descent to abuse of the enemy: 'I shall have as my allies Well and Right and (unlike Cleon) I shall never be convicted of public cowardice and depravity.'

The Formal Debate

So far I have examined speeches which present only one side of a case, the defence. Now it is time to look at situations where the dramatist has chosen to articulate the views of both sides, to write a scene in which two important characters argue from opposing standpoings.

Wasps

The set debate in the *Wasps* has as its participants the father and son whose relationship forms the core of the action and in this it resembles not only the *Clouds'* second agon (1345-451) but also, for example, Euripides' *Hippolytus*, acted five years earlier. But, if *Wasps* is a family play, its agon clearly also treats a *non-*

domestic situation, since it is the father's public duties and his power as a juror that he has to defend. Thus the agon, played before a chorus who are themselves jurors, becomes in itself a kind of back-to-front trial (although no criminal charge is involved), in which the father defends the way of life which is so dear to him and his son demolishes that defence.

The easiest way of understanding the debate *qua* rhetoric is to examine first the second speech which is made by the 'prosecutor' and victor Bdelycleon (Anticleon) in fulfilment of the programme outlined in the preliminaries to the agon. In this programme, having declared his wish that his father should adopt a more comfortable life-style, he had gone on to assert that the juror is a slave, not a ruler, and to question the size of his share of Athenian revenue (515-20). Now the son's case in the agon itself may be summarised: a rough calculation shows that, of the foreign and internal revenue received annually in Athens, the jurors get less than one-tenth while the demagogues enrich themselves (656-67). Moreover, the generous presents the subject allies give to these politicians show their understanding of the location of real power in the state: the jurors, who had actually fought in battles to achieve the enlargement of Athenian might, get nothing (669-79). Thus the jurors are 'slaves' because of their relative poverty and also because they are at the beck and call of men like court advocates who, to make matters worse, are actually enriching themselves by fraudulent, but unobserved, conspiracy (682-95). Finally, since Athens is so wealthy that every citizen could live comfortably, the impoverished state of the poor could be ended if it were not deliberately maintained by the politicians (who are thus enabled to offer bribes of grain when they think fit); as a result, the jurors' pay is on a par with a casual labourer's pittance gained by a day's fruit-picking (698-717).

It is clear from this summary that Bdelycleon's argument concentrates on riches and power and that the section purporting to deal with the juror's 'slavery' is still mainly concerned with the acquisition of wealth by politicians and official prosecutors. Bdelycleon succeeds in showing that political power (including that exercised by advocates) enriches, and that riches, however dishonestly acquired, bring power. Poor men, even poor men serving the state, are powerless and must remain so. The argument (its focus is rather different from the programme

originally stated) not only excellently demonstrates to Philocleon
the gulf between the haves and the have-nots, but also shatters
his illusions of power (to such an extent that he nearly faints from
shock, 713 f). Thus the victorious speaker, in persuading his
opponent of the rightness of his case, effects in him in addition a
kind of tragic Recognition; as the chorus note: 'he recognizes all
those former errors [*hamartias*] . . . and now he has transformed
himself, under your influence, and holds rational views' (744-9).[10]

A summary may be helpful in bringing out the main emphasis
of a speech, or even in demonstrating that there is a line of
argument beneath the rococo surface, but it inevitably omits the
features of style and detail which give life and individuality.
Bdelycleon here begins like an orator ('My task is difficult', 650),
but, apart from occasional rhetorical features, in general the tone
and style of the speech is not rhetorical, for all its careful
composition. Its rhetoric is not on the surface but in the deep
structure. It gains some of its force from repetition of words (for
office or rule, for the different denominations of coins, for giving,
offering, paying, bribing), but the repetition is never tediously
obtrusive because of the abundance of varied detail with which it
is surrounded. Athens' wealth, for example, several times stated,
is also illustrated by a list of sources of revenue (657-8). Another
feature is mimicry. Bdelycleon can mimic both words and
actions: asked to whom, if not to jurors, revenue is disbursed, he
replies, no doubt in demogogic tones, 'To those "I won't betray
the masses" chaps' (666), and later, describing a bossy official, he
imitates his stance and mannerisms (687-8). Bdelycleon's lively
delivery is assisted by vigorous images: I have already mentioned
his comparison of jurors to day-labourers and a similar point is
effected by another reference to everyday life when he says that
the politicians 'drip' the jurors' pay 'into you, drop by drop, just
enough to keep you alive, as one drips olive oil down a strand of
wool' (701-2).[11] In his attack on lawyers open to bribery, the
interdependence of two crooked advocates is forcefully indicated
by likening them to men using a two-handed saw, one pushing
and the other pulling, the opposing actions being essential to one
single purpose, self-enrichment (692-5).

Particularly interesting is the consistency of the son's personal
address to his father, given that much of what he says applies to
all jurors or even to all poor and powerless Athenians. He speaks
to his father, using the singular 'you' repeatedly, often in contrast

with 'they' (demagogues, allies, advocates); this practice, slightly disconcerting in such phrases as 'you [sing.] rule the cities' (678) and 'you rowed, fought, besieged, conquered' (654-5), underlines the fact that a loving son is speaking to his father, not a politician to the masses.

It is characteristic of Old Comedy to punctuate long speeches with interjections, as we have seen for instance in the prologue of *Clouds*. A forensic speech naturally falls into sections as separate arguments are advanced and these subdivisions, marked in tragedy or prose oratory by verbal means alone, are given distinctness in comedy by shifting attention momentarily away from the main speaker.[12] Sometimes the interjection is humorous, sometimes not. In this agon in *Wasps* Philocleon breaks into his son's speech five times. On the first occasion, misunderstanding Bdelycleon's opening prayer to father Zeus, he interrupts him in mid-line with 'Leave the "our father" out of it and explain to me how I'm a slave' (652). On the next occasion the father's comment (664) shows that he has grasped Bdelycleon's opening argument that jurors receive little of the state revenue and his question 'Where does the rest of the money go?' gives his son his chance to denounce the demagogues (666-71). The third and fourth times Philocleon has to admit the effect his son's words are having upon him, to such an extent that he feels weak and loses his grip (696 f, 713 f).

When we turn back to Philocleon's defence we find interruptions of a different, less naturalistic kind, which are unparalleled in Aristophanic comedy. Bdelycleon, having sent for writing materials (529), sets out to make for himself an *aide-mémoire* of his father's arguments and does in fact carry out his plan, at least so far as three of his four interjections are concerned (559, 576, 588). These brief summaries underline the essentials in a speech which is characterised by ebullient verbosity.

Although Philocleon's defence is essentially argumentative, much of it is expressed in the form of a narrative of a typical day in a juror's life and it therefore picks up, and modifies and develops the description of Philocleon's life given by the slave in the prologue.[13] This time, of course, the narrator's voice is identical with that of the man whose experiences are narrated. Philocleon counts his blessings, speaking of his 'sovereign power' and asking 'What creature is happier or more blessed or more pampered or awe-inspiring than a dicast, tho' he's elderly?' (548-50). He goes on to describe the way even important people become his suppliants, from the moment he reaches the entrance of the court; once inside he meets men who plead with him, flatter him or try to amuse him. Later a suppliant actually prays to him as to a god at a sacrifice: 'If ever you are gladdened by the voice of the lamb take pity on the voice of this child' (572). Although there are indications in these lines of a quite undemocratic assumption of the monarch or even the deity, Philocleon's megalomania is cut down by the elements which relate to crime and judicial procedures, in particular by his admission of his own lack of moral integrity. However, the chief impression made by the opening of Philocleon's defence is the glee felt by a poor and powerless man when given authority, and this impression is strengthened by instances of ingratiating behaviour towards him on the part of a distinguished actor or musician seeking acquittal (579-82).

After listing the pleasures of a day spent in the court, pleasures gained from the behaviour of defendants and stemming from their appreciation of the juror's power, Philocleon turns to other aspects of his group's privileged position, firstly their immunity from 'scrutiny' and secondly their influence in affairs of state (587, 590-5).[14] This brings him to the peak of his achievement, the attention paid to him by politicians, particularly by Cleon, who 'takes bites out of everyone else but looks after us and shoos away the flies' (like a monarch's attendant). His son, by contrast, never treated him as these others do but attempts to deprive him of all that he values, actually calling his life 'slavery' and 'servitude' (596-602). This rhetorical climax has a coda, an apparent afterthought of the old man's which takes us back to the narrative frame of the juror's day: 'I forgot the nicest thing of all,' he says, expatiating on the welcome he receives when he returns home from the daughter who kisses him and the wife who brings him a meal (605-12). So to the ending:

> My power equals that of Zeus. People speak to me as they speak to Zeus. If we make a din everyone present says 'How the jurors thunder, King Zeus'. And if I fling lightning there's oohing and poohing from the wealthy and well-bred. You're scared of me too, son, very scared, by Demeter. But I'm damned if I'm scared of you. (619-30)

Let me now try to survey the debate as a whole. If we look at the jury of Wasps who adjudicate this 'case', we may be able to discover indications of the effectiveness of the arguments. The Wasps are not impartial. It is not only that Philocleon is one of them, a brother heliast, whom they feel a duty to support, but that Bdelycleon represents for them a threat greater than his attempts to reform his father would suggest. The Wasps see Bdelycleon as the opposite of a patriot, an 'Athens hater', because, they say, he proposes to abolish the jury system (413-4).[15] They call him a conspirator and an autocrat and suggest that he is creating a tyranny (345, 470, 417, 464). The Wasps here express a genuine sense of outrage at their old comrade's imprisonment in his son's home, but they express it in terms which have degenerated into political slogans or parrot cries, as indeed Bdelycleon points out in his rejoinder to their threats: 'You people find tyranny and conspirators everywhere' (488). The Wasps will not accept that the quarrel is between father and son but insist upon moving it out of the *oikos* and placing it in the public sphere, a tyrannical conspiracy to overthrow a vital feature of Athenian democracy.

To some extent the ferocity of the 'swarm' is mitigated by the Wasps' consciousness of their age and uselessness (540 f) which is relieved by Philocleon's eloquent defence of his occupation as their comment shows: 'He covered everything and left nothing out. Hearing him made me feel great, just as if I were on a jury in heaven' (636-40). Nevertheless anger is their weapon against Bdelycleon as he prepared to speak (644-9), anger which diminishes as they listen so that finally they respond in the judicious tones of tragic Elders: 'Wise was the man who said "You should not reach your verdict until you have listened to both sides" ' (752 f). The alteration in their views is emphasised by their distancing themselves from Philocleon in order to offer him advice, again in the manner of a chorus trying to persuade a stubborn Sophoclean hero: 'Pay heed, pay heed to his words; be wise, be pliant, be malleable . . . accept his kindness' (729-35).[16] A few lines later they claim that their former colleague, still speechless with grief, has seen the error of his ways and will perhaps change his pattern of living, paying heed to his son (743-9).

It is interesting to observe that the Wasps do not comment on what Bdelycleon has said, either in general or in particular, nor do they apply his words to their own situation and question whether they should continue to serve as jurors. Instead they help to narrow the focus again to the old man and his personal unhappiness, leaving aside the political issues of courts, unscrupulous orators, threats to the democracy and the like. These issues are not abandoned for good but surface again in the trial scene and in the parabasis, where, as we have seen, the Wasps advertise the patriotism they once showed in battle and now show again in their service as jurors.

It would be easy, because of the manner of the Wasps' reaction, to accept Bdelycleon's victory uncritically as a successful case against the system as currently operated. In fact the debate takes place on carefully chosen and prepared ground on which an untypical and eccentric juror champions his own desires. Philocleon does not defend the morality and usefulness of courts in general but demonstrates that his membership of a jury brings him power, which he enjoys above all things. Jury service is self-gratification. The picture Xanthias had given of his compulsive behaviour in the prologue is paired with the juror's portrayal here of what it feels like to be that kind of man. Because Philocleon illustrates and describes his enjoyment of power and because he has been introduced as eccentric, his opponent has only to demonstrate that his grandiose conception of his own importance is illusory to win his case. As a result Bdelycleon's criticisms of corrupt advocates and greedy politicians are made to subserve his main, and incontrovertible, argument, that the juror is poor and powerless, more like the despised slave than the monarch.

In recent paragraphs I have not mentioned oratory, the subject of this chapter. After outlining the content of the two speeches and commenting on their style I moved by way of the Wasps' reaction to a consideration of Philocleon's character and personality as dictating the ground on which the battle between father and son would be fought. We are all familiar with the situation in which a politician, asked a question he cannot answer with credit or conviction, gives an irrelevant reply and escapes undetected. The dramatic orator, the poet who chooses to employ set debate as part of his inscenation, must plan and contrive like the wily politician. The speeches, ebullient, vivid, hyperbolic, amusing, are the visible surface of a planned structure. Those particular speeches can only be made, and made successfully in that they persuade the Wasps and isolate Philocleon, because characters and situation have first been created. The play as a whole is a persuasive act in which argumentative speeches, given considerable prominence by their length, brilliance and placing, exhibit the verbal skills of orator-poet in a framework cunningly devised by the dramatist. 'A persuasive act': not propaganda, not an incitement to abolish the jury system, nor to take any other drastic action. In *Wasps* we are shown some of the weaknesses of the system of administering the law, but our viewpoint is not, so to speak, a distant hillside from which we can see the whole scene. Instead we are made to concentrate on the weaknesses of one obsessive juror, an extreme case of power-seeking self-importance. Should Philocleon be a juror? No. Should his 'contemporaries and fellow-members' (728) be jurors? The Wasps would answer in the affirmative, but perhaps the audience, and the jury members among them, will have been persuaded, by direct and by indirect means, to 'listen to both sides of an argument before reaching a verdict'.

Frogs

At first glance it is much less apparent that the agon in *Frogs* is constructed in accordance with the normal pattern, since three characters speak, as if in ordinary conversation. Nevertheless the basic structure *is* observed and arguments are marshalled in an organised way, as the following summaries will show. During the preliminaries to the debate on which Dionysus is to adjudicate, Euripides has expressed his willingnes to open the agon, 'to bite and be bitten' before Aeschylus speaks (861), and now that all is ready he repeats his statement, but not the metaphor: 'As to the nature of my own poetic work, that I shall describe only after I have found fault with *him*' (907 f). Aeschylus cheats the spectators, according to Euripides, by keeping his characters silent on stage and then giving them speeches that are incomprehensible, full of phrases like huge cliffs. As a result (and here Euripides begins his defence) tragedy had become fat and out of condition and needed expert treatment to fit her to compete. Having restored her to health, Euripides made plays which got straight down to business, with clear prologues, and which gave speaking parts to all sorts and conditions of people.

And so he taught the spectators to be mentally alert and agile and more skilful in the management of their domestic affairs.

Unlike his rival, Aeschylus begins with questions, not with a programme, and the first of these, 'Tell me, for what should a poet be admired?', elicits the much-quoted reply, 'For our skill, for our advice, because we make men better members of the *polis*' (1009 f). In Aeschylus' opinion Euripides had actually corrupted the citizens, whereas he himself had taught them to long for excellence in warfare and for victory. In so doing he was both fulfilling a poet's duty and following in the steps of the early poet-teachers, particularly Homer. Aeschylus inspired men to emulate his heroes, whom he created on the Homeric pattern; he forebore to portray evil women or to use stories that were better unpublicised. He maintains, in answer to the charge that his great chunks of verbiage were a barrier to communication, that loftiness of language, like dignified costume, is a necessary concomitant of elevated sentiment and thought. In conclusion he lists the widespread evils for which Euripides is responsible because of the nature of his tragedies (1083-8).

I could have described this scene in such a way as to bring out its comic vitality, its exchanges of insults, the frequency of Dionysus' interruptions, and so on; had I done so, I should have failed to show up the consistency and organisation of the views held by each tragedian. If, as I believe, it is possible to discern a line of argument underlying each contribution, why was it not made more obvious? It seems to me that there are two advantages to the procedure here adopted, in addition to the enjoyment of the trio's vigorous fun and fury. In the first place the comic dramatist wishes to keep his distance from the tragic poets: they are to speak to each other, not to us, and they are to be interrupted and deflated by Dionysus, playing a part like that of the court jester. Secondly, it is better not to set out the differences between the two poets in such a way as to polarise them: Aeschylus and Euripides are to be seen as practising the same art, professing the same altruism and believing in the continuity of tragedy. Their contest is intended to decide which of the two is better at writing plays: their creator cleverly suggests, but only suggests, a much less limited area of conflict where one of them is populist, associated with ordinary men and women and their daily occupations and concerned with contemporary problems, while the other is élitist, interested in warriors and warfare, looking back to a distant past.

Notes

1. The agon, like the parabasis, has a regular structure of which the most important elements are the two speeches, or passages of dialogue, each of which sets out one side of the argument. See further Pickard-Cambridge 1962, 200-4, and T. Gelzer, *Der epirrhematische Agon bei Aristophanes*, Zetemata 23 (Munich 1960).

2. Ovid uses an untranslatable word-play to show that his friend is as much a devotee of the Muses' art as he, the professional poet, is himself. Although, as he says, there is a wide area separating the work of the orator from that of the poet, both ultimately share the same origin, just as streams emerging from one spring may follow different directions. Both poet and orator cultivate their native talent.

3. *Medea* 446-575.

4. C.T. Murphy, 'Aristophanes and the Art of Rhetoric', *HSCP* 49 (1938), 69-113; e.g. D. MacDowell's comments on 546-630.

5. For discussion on Dicaeopolis' speech see L. Edmunds in *YCS* 26, 12; G.E.M. de Ste Croix, *The Origins of the Peloponnesian War* (London, 1972), 239-44, 366.

6. The Lenaean festival of Dionysus was held in late winter, too early for travellers by sea to have made their way to Athens. On the meaning of *trygodia* see O. Taplin, *CQ* 33 (1983), 331-3.

7. The parabasis has most recently been discussed by A.M. Bowie in *CQ* 32, (1982), 27-42. See also G.M. Sifakis, *Parabasis and Animal Choruses* (London, 1971).

8. Too little is known about *Babylonians* to say whether Ar.'s 'criticism' was stated explicitly in the parabasis or expressed by implication in the action, or both. On *Babylonians* see D. Welsh, *GRBS* 24 (1983), 137-50; *CQ* 33 (1983), 51-5.

9. The exact nature of Ar.'s connection with Aegina is unknown: see Sommerstein's note on these lines.

10. For Recognition (*anagnorisis*) in Ar. cf. *Knights* 1229 ff and see Rau 61, 170.

11. The point of the comparison is that, as liquid can be transferred steadily in tiny quantities from one vessel to another by using a strand of wool as a wick, so jury pay, although small, is available with some frequency.

12. And, of course, by pause, gesture, change of vocal tone or speed in actual delivery. The interjections by Dionysus in *Frogs* (e.g. 934, 1036-8) puncture the seriousness of the tragedians' arguments.

13. MacDowell notes the narrative content. For the prologue of *Wasps* see above, p. 9.

14. 'Scrutiny' (*dokimasia*) was the examination of the conduct of holders of office at the completion of their term.

15. The modern reader needs to keep in mind the importance of the courts in the Athenian system of participatory democracy. See, for example, J.K. Davies, *Democracy and Classical Greece* (Sussex, 1978), 115 ff and K. Dover, *Lysias and the Corpus Lysiacum* (California, 1968), 182 f.

16. Cf. S. *King Oedipus* 649, Ar. *Clouds* 87, 90, 110, 119, and see R. Buxton, *Persuasion in Greek Tragedy* (Cambridge, 1982), 117, 143.

3 ARISTOPHANES THE ORATOR: PRAISE AND BLAME

> Criticise me or praise me, as you will,
> It's all the same to me
> > (Aeschylus, *Agamemnon* 1403-4)

> There is nothing invidious in reviling no-goods,
> It amounts to praising good men, if you reckon correctly
> > (*Knights* 1274 f)

Both of these epigraphs show praise and blame in close association, the juxtaposition of polarities being a favourite device of Greek writers. The first is spoken by a defiant Clytemnestra to the Argive elders not long after she has killed her husband and Cassandra: her contemptuous disregard of public opinion is one of the traits which reveal her difference from the typical Greek. My second epigraph comes from the Knights' cheeky but defensive introduction to their wholesale denunciation of the extraordinary sexual depravity of one Ariphrades, the brother of a fellow dramatist.[1] One doubts whether the prefatory apology would have comforted the man here reviled or anyone else in a similar situation; the words, however, have a particular relevance if applied to competitiveness between rival poets, where 'reviling no-goods' is one way of praising good poets, as is demonstrated in a comparatively mild and indirect way in the 'anapaests' of this same comedy (*Knights* 520-40). It is of course because there are recognised categories that the antithesis is effective and divagation from the norm perceived.

To scholars and critics alike, 'reviling no-goods' has too often seemed the main purpose and *raison d'être* of Aristophanic comedy, witness Horace's remarks in Satires One.[2] They select for scrutiny passages attacking individuals, in particular those known or believed to have been real contemporary Athenians and regard the whole play as a vehicle for satirising some aspect of life in the *polis* and as little else. They do not see that Aristophanes is also a poet of praise, a creator of encomia and eulogies for his characters to speak. Moreover, although what he writes has the stamp of comedy, its sources are to be found both in the serious poetic tradition and in contemporary speech-making. In this chapter song precedes speech. Thus songs of praise are followed by lampoons and spoken reproaches ('complaint') by eulogies: the arrangement may help to emphasise the extent to which our poet is 'praiser and blesser'.

It is appropriate to introduce the subject of praise in Old Comedy with the little *epainos* of wine found early in *Knights*. The more austere of the two slaves of Demos who introduce the play objects that no one ever made a good decision when drunk and the other indignantly replies: 'You have the effrontery to denigrate wine as source of inspiration?' and launches into a succinct eulogy: 'What could you find more efficacious than wine? You see? Men drink: riches, success, victories at law, happiness, philanthropy all result. Hurry up and bring me out a jug of wine so that I can irrigate my brain and say something clever' (86-96). One may compare what happens in the contest between the two Arguments in *Clouds*: Wrong says to Right, 'You find fault with spending time in the Agora. I praise it.' On this occasion Wrong fails to develop the theme of praise, contenting himself with the specious interpretation of a verse of Homer in support of his case (*Clouds* 1055 f). We shall note the antithesis of criticism and approval again later in this chapter.

Songs of Praise

It is not surprising that comedies should contain songs which celebrate the hero's success nor that when the poet addresses his audience he should seek to improve his chances of victory by self-praise.[3] During the course of this chapter we shall be looking to see what are the characteristics of these songs and speeches, whether shared or distinct, and to note any affinities any of them may have with an established kind of song or speech. Taking first the theme of success and achievement, it is not surprising to find the comic hero receiving congratulations and compliments after his plans have come to fruition. At these moments he may be, in comic terms, the equivalent of athletic victor, successful general or happy bridegroom and the praise he receives may not only contain elements appropriate to choral celebration of these occasions but may also vary in style from the simple and unpretentious to the dignified elevation reminiscent of praise poetry of the kind commissioned from such poets as Pindar.[4]

The earliest play, as it happens, provides three quite different examples of encomiastic poetry, all occasioned by evidence of Dicaeopolis' prosperity which has come from trading freely in a period of peace. In the first the chorus say, 'The man's enjoying his good fortune. Did you hear how his plans have succeeded? He will bring in his harvest merely by sitting in his market' (836-8). In the bulk of the poem, however, they go on to show how the successful trader will avoid all the usual problems and dangers of the market-place. Thus three lines of congratulation are followed by rather more than three stanzas cataloguing by name men who are public nuisances of one kind or another. Here indeed blaming individuals is a way of illustrating the good fortune of the *laudandus* which was brought about by his prudent counsels.[5] The conclusion of the market episode is marked by a much less colloquial outburst of praise. Once more the beginning, a favourable comment on what has just happened, is followed by something quite different and this time the same procedure is adopted in each of the two stanzas. This splendid poem I shall discuss in greater detail in Chapter 5 where I consider the structure of *Acharnians* as a whole; here I quote only the first of the two complimentary passages which, like our last example, contains a question about perceiving: 'Hast thou seen, O Athens, hast thou seen the man of intellect, of surpassing wisdom, possessing through his truce useful things in his house (including nice hot food)? Of their own accord come all good things to him' (*Ach.* 971-6). As soon as this second encomium ends we learn of the hero's imminent participation in one of the city's festivals and the chorus use this occasion to congratulate him on his foresight and also on his culinary expertise, concluding, 'Have you heard how expertly this *chef-de-cuisine*, this *bon viveur*, this gourmand makes his own preparations?' (1015-17).

At this point it will be helpful to bring in for comparison the congratulatory ode performed in honour of Trygaeus in that scene in *Peace* which shows how the two handmaids of the goddess Peace were received in Athens. It is not just that both songs express comparable sentiments at a time of preparation for festivity but that they resemble each other quite closely in structure. Each has two stanzas, separated by a passage of dialogue, each is written for performance by chorus and soloist, with the opening lines of the chorus evoking a comment or question from the soloist. The form is close to the shared lament of tragedy, the mood and feeling at the opposite pole.[6]

In order to display the features of this type of antiphonal congratulation I quote the second verse of the song from *Acharnians* and then the first verse of that from *Peace*:[7]

> *Cho.* The man has discovered something nice in his treatywine
> – and he's not likely to give any of it away.
> *Di.* Pour honey on top of the sausage; brown the cuttlefish.
> *Cho.* Did you hear his instructions?
> *Di.* Cook the eels.
> *Cho.* You'll make me die of hunger, the neighbours too, with the smell and the sound of your commands.
> *Di.* Cook these and get them nice and golden.
>
> (*Ach.* 1037-47)

> *Cho.* Good luck marks all the old man does, as one can see.
> *Trygaeus* What will you say when you see me as a radiant bridegroom?
> *Cho.* You will be enviable, old chap, restored to youth again, anointed with perfume.
> *Trygaeus* Yes indeed. What then will you say when I hold her breast in my hand?
> *Cho.* You will seem luckier than Carcinus' spinners.[8]
> *Trygaeus* And rightly so. I rode on dung beetle and saved the Greeks and now they all live safe and sound in the country, making love and sleeping.
>
> (*Peace* 856-67)

'See the conquering hero comes': it is as a victor triumphant in villainy that the Knights hail Sausage-seller when he returns from bamboozling the Council and enlarges on his success.[9] In the strophe which follows their first brief greeting, they include the verb which means 'raise the cry of triumph'[10] and refer to his achievement 'in words and in deed far surpassing his words' and emphasise their longing to hear a full report (*Knights* 616-24). At its conclusion they offer congratulations on his good fortune and unscrupulousness before assuring him of their support in the contest still to come (683-90).

So far we have met choruses whose compliments have been warm and unreserved, even perhaps excessive. What if the chorus cannot be given the task of praise? In *Clouds*, at the moment when Strepsiades believes his troubles are nearly over, the chorus preserve an ominous silence and it is left to the principal to perform in his own honour what he actually designates an encomium. Pheidippides, having been educated in rhetoric, is restored to his father whose response is first to insult the audience as ripe to be plucked by clever people like his son and himself and then to declare 'For myself and for this son of mine, because of our good fortune I must sing an encomium'. He goes on with what sounds like an encomium addressed to himself: 'Blest art thou, Strepsiades, blest in thine intelligence and in thy son' but then adds 'This is what my envious friends and associates will say of me when your eloquence in the law court is victorious' (*Clouds* 1201-13). Strepsiades' rejoicing is premature, his encomium ironic, like those happy Sophoclean odes which precede the hero's downfall.[11]

There is a most interesting variant on the encomium at the end of *Wasps* where the chorus, having learned of the scandalous behaviour of the 'reformed' Philocleon at and after the party he has attended, sing two stanzas, the first about the father and the second about the son. I begin with the unequivocal second stanza:

> It is with much praise for his filial devotion and his skill won from me and all right thinking people that Philocleon's son departs. I have never encountered such a benevolent man, never experienced such a flood of wild enthusiasm for anyone else. In each one of his counter-arguments he was superior when trying to persuade his father to take up more dignified pursuits. (*Wasps* 1462-73)

The Wasps speak here both as jurymen who appreciate skill in arguing a case and as parents who admire a son's steady devotion to his father's well-being. This verse is more straightforward than the first, whose subject is Philocleon:

> I envy the good fortune of the old man who has experienced a change from his austere ways. After re-education he will in

truth find a great change in luxury and comfort. But perhaps he will not be willing to change, since abandoning one's long established character is hard. All the same it has been a common experience for men to change their ways as a result of other people's influence and advice. (1450-61)

As a piece of congratulation this is markedly defective, even inappropriate to the actual situation. The conventional early mention of 'envy' and 'good fortune' fails to lead to the usual laudatory exclamations and the second part would seem more in place in the kind of tragic choral utterance one might unkindly label 'fence-sitting'. Perhaps the Wasps' hesitancy is meant only as foil to throw into relief the assured certainty of their praise for Bdelycleon.

Finally let us turn to the end of *Frogs* and the chorus's comment on the result of the contest between Aeschylus and Euripides. By contrast with the poem just discussed, the first of these two verses is unequivocal in its praise of the man of good sense, while the second describes someone who lacks that quality. It is interesting that this song departs both from the direct address of the encomium proper ('Blessed art thou') and from the specificity of the Wasps' praises to use the generalising technique almost without exception ('Blest is the man who . . .'). Nevertheless, although they do not name names, it is clear that the Initiates praise Aeschylus at Euripides' expense when they sing of the man whose intelligence is rewarded by his return from Hades 'for the good of Athens, for the good of his own kin and friends' and when they show by contrast the faults of his rival, who consorts with Socrates and has discarded music and the grandest aspects of tragedy (1482-99).

One ingredient of these little songs, makarismos, is also found in spoken passages, used semi-humorously. When Strepsiades calls himself 'blest', he is adopting a form of address more usually associated with religious occasions and personages (and familiar to us from occurrences in Euripides' *Bacchae*).[12] If Strepsiades is serious, the slave in *Wasps*, uncomfortable after receiving a beating, has his tongue in his cheek when he applies the formula to the tortoise: 'O tortoises, blessed are you in your skin and thrice blessed for having a roof over your ribs. How thoroughly and cleverly you have covered your backs with tiling to keep off blows' (*Wasps* 1292-5, cf. 429-39).[13]

Lampoons

In this makarismos there is a wry, but unexpressed, contrast between the happy associations of the formula and the feelings of the slave who has no shell to protect his body. In the songs we are to examine now, if praise has any place it is in an incongruous or disconcerting prelude, as later becomes apparent, to lines which mock, ridicule, attack or caricature some glutton, pervert, coward or politician. Whereas encomia, as we have seen, arise from and make comments on what has already happened to the hero, for the most part the victim of these lampoons is not an important character in the play nor even obviously concerned with the issues raised therein.

It is easy to guess that the comic poet wanted to poke fun at an individual who was in the news, or to state that such attacks were required by the conventions of Old Comedy; easy also to assume that the audience (apart from the victim and his friends) enjoyed hearing such songs (which may even have become temporary 'pops'). It is less easy to answer questions about the motivation and placing of these songs and about the choice of victim, particularly in those instances where he is not a Cleon or a Hyperbolus, not a major figure but a man about whom little or nothing is known. Why, we ask, does Comedy A contain much ridicule of individuals and Comedy B almost none? Why gibes at X rather than at Y? The problems of reference in Old Comedy to a named individual are not peculiar to choral songs but they are there presented in an acute form.[14] If full, reliable information became available, we might know why X and not Y was selected for ridicule; we would still lack understanding of the function of lampoons in the comedies. What does seem clear, however, is that the use of a name provides a valuable focus; the 'animus of animosity' is increased when directed at Messrs Reprobate and Disgrace rather than at the average sinner. In the audience the anonymous nobody is safe from attack.

Taking just *Acharnians*, *Knights*, *Clouds* and *Wasps* we find songs of this type in the second parabasis of all but *Clouds* (whose second parabasis consists of one single speech admonishing the judges). In addition *Knights* contains a song about Cleon sung while the rival politicians, Paphlagon and Sausage-seller, are off-stage (973 f). Beginning ('sweetest light of day') as if to hail some happy occasion, the Knights unexpectedly continue 'when Cleon's done for'. Next they mention a wry remark they've overheard to the effect that Cleon, for all his faults, at least gave Athens two serviceable utensils, pestle and spoon. In the second verse, after 'admiring' his 'musicalpigity', they tell how Cleon is supposed to have behaved when learning music as a boy. The point of the verse is the implication, expressed in a pun, that Cleon has always taken bribes, but the recollection of boyhood puts the verse in the class of anecdotes told of the famous (or infamous) when young.

Returning to songs found in the second parabasis, the chorus of Acharnians declare that they have a bone to pick with a choregus who, they say, had failed to provide them with the customary meal after a performance at the Lenaea (1150-70).[15] This song is relevant, therefore, to the comic chorus as such in a part of the play in which expression of their feelings is permissible. Moreover, its content foreshadows the opening of the subsequent scene, the 'tragic' recital of the accidents which had befallen general Lamachus during his expedition. In form the song consists of two verses cursing the stingy Antimachus: they pray that he may himself understand the meaning of hunger and experience frustration when a dog snatches the food he's about to eat and secondly that he may be mugged and unable to defend himself. Where the first verse pictures, with circumstantial detail, the actual moment of deprivation, the second recounts a train of events as frustrating as those occurring in dreams: Antimachus is going home, he's attacked, needs a stone to throw at his assailant, picks up a turd instead, throws, misses the mugger and hits an innocent party. It is worth observing also that the passage is amusing as an anecdote with a satisfying shape whether or not an actual Antimachus had treated a chorus ungenerously; in addition it is clearly advantageous that the subject of a tale of this kind should have a name, even if he and it are the poet's inventions.

In *Knights* both songs in the second parabasis are again about hunger, the former about the hunger of a poor man, Thumantis, the latter that of the greedy Cleonymus (1264-73, 1290-9). The first verse begins like an epinician ode 'What fairer way to begin or end our song . . .?' and is in fact quoted from a Pindaric song in honour of two goddesses, while the second has an opening reminiscent of tragic reflections, 'In nocturnal considerations have I oft been engaged and in seekings . . .'.[16] There is no doubt that part of the attraction of these songs is the way in which the tone of the opening is contradicted by what follows, through a form of playing with genres like intentional bathos: begin lofty and end common, begin, as it were, with part of Beethoven's *Missa Solemnis* and continue with an advertising jingle.

From the second parabasis of *Wasps* one song has been lost; the opening trochaics which survive (1265-74) offer a mock congratulation to yet another poor hungry man, one whose cleverness has enabled him to achieve a kind of success. This time the chorus begins by referring to their past reflections on their own cleverness and we might think that we were to hear further praise of 'waspishness', but the initial self-praise is here only foil to sarcastic 'praise' of Amynias the pauper.

Before leaving the subject of sung attacks on individuals (or types), I want to mention two further examples, from *Acharnians* and from *Frogs*. Earlier in this chapter we saw that the chorus of Acharnian elders congratulate the hero on three separate occasions, on one of which 5 iambic lines commending his well-deserved prosperity were followed by 27 commenting unfavourably on seven men whose absence from Dicaeopolis' market is one of its blessings (*Ach.* 836-59). The obvious advantage of this technique of listing absentees is its flexibility: here only two of the victims are treated at length, but, as in an epic, catalogue elaboration and inclusion of additional names is limited only by the author's sense of discretion. In this encomiastic context one might be reminded not so much of lists of warriors as of enumeration of heroes whom the blessed individual might be fortunate enough to meet in some Elysium: in comedy he is fortunate *not* to meet them in the Agora. Very likely most of the men named here were already notorious; nevertheless the song is informative on the subject of their individual demerits.

My final example differs from the others in that the victim is anonymous (not that his identity is in doubt). The makarismos of Aeschylus at the end of *Frogs*, already quoted, comes from a song which has for its second verse an attack on anyone who doesn't exhibit the good sense which results in success and the betterment of one's fellow citizens, friends and kin.[17] This verse initially sounds like its predecessor but almost immediately turns to the negative (cf. *Knights* 1264 f): 'It is a gracious act NOT to sit by Socrates chattering, rejecting the Muses' arts and abandoning the features which give tragedy its greatness. Moreover passing one's time unproductively in conceited talk and frivolous superficialities is a sign of the man who lacks sense' (1491-9). These reflections on mental attitudes and capacity hit at Aeschylus' adversary whom they present as a traitor to his art. The generalising is authoritative and didactic: anyone who acts like Euripides is crazy. So don't join the Socratic circle but cherish traditional poetry and tragedy.

This song ended, Pluto recites some anapaestic lines in which he bids Aeschylus farewell and asks him to deliver various messages when he gets back to Athens: 'Take this (a token of some kind) to Cleophon, these to the Revenue Gatherers, this to Myrmex, to Nicomachus, to Archenomus. And tell them to come here to me quickly and not to linger. If they don't come with haste I will brand them and fetter them, by Apollo, and together with Adeimantus, I will send them swiftly down below earth' (1504-14). Of all the material directed at individuals this must have been the most disquieting for the recipient to hear.

The Complaint

At this point we turn back from song to speech and from attacks directed against a single individual to complaints made, at least ostensibly, about the behaviour of some group or other. These complaints are often signposted by the use of the verb *memphesthai*, 'reproach', and for the most part occur in parabases.

It is characteristic of old men, in Aristophanic comedy as elsewhere, to grumble and reproach their juniors, to complain that during their lifetime everything has changed for the worse, to lament that they themselves have lost their youthful speed and stamina. Any student of Greek tragedy will recall in this context the entrance song of the *Agamemnon* where the Argive elders vividly expound what it has meant to them to be forced by age to remain at home during the ten-year absence of the fighting men at Troy.[18]

The old men from Acharnae are in the same tradition. Once swift-moving and vigorous and still retaining their patriotism and fervour of spirit, they have no doubt of the justice of their complaints against a city which allows their lives to be made a misery by prosecutions and the fear of prosecution. Their parabasis (*Ach.* 665-718) begins with a song invoking the aid of a strong and fiery Muse and thus emboldened they describe what it is like for people who cannot hear or speak as clearly as in their youth, who cannot walk without a stick, to be assailed, made to look foolish and reduced to penury as a result of the exertions of keen but unscrupulous young prosecutors. They make an effective enough plea just by their account of their wretched situation, but they also reinforce it, as often in complaints, by pointing out its injustice; they fought for their country and chased away the enemy but now they are in turn under attack from verbal missiles (686) or even trapped and torn like hunted animals (687-8). Justice demands that a new system be adopted whereby there will be separate law courts for young and for old. It is typical of these valiant and tough characters that their reproaches should end in a positive, if bizarre, proposal for reform.[19]

This topic of receiving one's just deserts returns in the Clouds' parabasis speeches, as the opening lines make clear: 'You who are watching, give us your attention. We have been unfairly treated and blame you for it' (*Clouds* 575 f). The goddesses next give the grounds for their complaint, that unlike other divinities they receive no sacrifices although benefiting Athens by their vigilant protectiveness. They offer instances of their care, but what they say develops almost imperceptibly into an attack on the demagogue Cleon and on the Athenians' folly in electing him to office. The Clouds say, in effect: If you propose a silly campaign we send thunderstorms. When you elected Cleon not only did we produce violent storms but there was an eclipse of moon and sun. In spite of these warnings you persisted.

In the corresponding speech (607-26), the Clouds turn from their own discontents to relay the grievances of the Moon, acting as her representatives. Once more the blessing conferred by the benefactress, in this case moonlight, is set against the wrong done by the Athenians in reforming their calendar and so depriving the gods of the sacrifices expected by them on a particular day. This speech ends with a reference to another demagogue, Hyperbolus, who, in consequence of divine punishment, will, they say, know better in future that he should observe days in accordance with the lunar calendar.[20]

The next complaint, also directed against Hyperbolus, is

refreshingly different because of its use of fantasy. The Knights, in the parabasis whose songs about hungry men we have recently discussed, rather than grumbling on their own behalf recount in the second of their speeches a piece of gossip they claim to have heard about a meeting of triremes. They tell how the 'old lady' among them opened the meeting by asking 'Girls, don't you know what's afoot in the city? They say we're being required to go to Carthage, a hundred of us.' The other triremes were shocked by this news of the demagogue Hyperbolus' proposals for a naval expedition and one of them, so far 'unmanned', protested that she would rather grow old and decay with woodworm than be under his orders. Another suggested that they should all 'sail' into the city and take their places as suppliants in the Theseum or by the shrine of the Eumenides. They will refuse to aid Hyperbolus in his arrogant exploitation of Athens: 'he can launch the containers in which he used to display his lamps and sail off to perdition!' (*Knights* 1300-15).[21]

Let me put the gist of this fanciful grumbling as it might be put in the assembly by an opponent of Hyperbolus' plan: 'The proposal to mount a naval expedition to Carthage at this juncture is rash and ill-considered. Far from commanding general support, it is a piece of political opportunism likely to meet with popular resistance, especially from those required to take part in such a venture.' The poet transfers the reluctance to fight which might in reality be voiced by crews and soldiers to the triremes: the warships themselves know better than to comply. (In a play in which people are for the most part corrupt, vicious or gullible, triremes and horses become models of truly patriotic behaviour.) And, because the word for trireme is feminine in gender, the ships can express themselves with the outrage of virgins resisting rape or forced marriage. Thus a proposal to attack Carthage somehow approximates to a threat of sexual violence. Moreover the suggestion that the girls take refuge in the Theseum brings with it an allusion to the great Athenian hero and protector, Theseus, while the image of a band of female suppliants is in itself a potent one with tragic and pitiful associations. If the device here employed is humorously appealing, it is also shrewd: Hyperbolus has been mocked and his plan opposed, but only by the triremes, not by the Knights *in propriis personis*. Thus these few lines, manufactured to sound like gossip of a fantastic kind, make us look afresh at a proposal and its advocate. In manner they could not be further from political oratory but their message is just as clear.

A reproachful note is frequently also heard in the 'anapaests' of the parabasis and its occurrence in the poet's address to his unappreciative audience in *Clouds* makes a link between all three speeches (525, 576, 610). On this occasion he develops this motif no further, choosing rather to dwell on his past success and the individuality of his plays, but in *Wasps* we find a more extended treatment. 'The poet now wants to reproach the spectators. He says he is treated unfairly, although in the past he has often conferred benefits upon them' (*Wasps* 1016 f). There now follows an account of these benefits, both seen and unseen, culminating in a longer passage dealing with his war against Cleon. Finally he comes to the recent past when, although 'he is still fighting' on behalf of the audience (1037), they have failed to reward him with the success he deserved, that is, he did not receive first prize in the previous year's competition. He concludes as follows: 'Although those of you who failed to recognise immediately the merits of his comedy disgraced yourselves, nevertheless the poet's reputation will not be diminished in the judgement of the wise' as a result of a failure caused by over-ambition. 'In future, love and cherish more thoroughly men who try to say something new and inventive . . . if you do, your clothes will smell of your right thinking' (1051-9).

Eulogies

I began this chapter by assembling some examples of praise in choral lyric, most of them on the subject of the comic hero's achievement, and I now begin this section also with compliments paid by the chorus, this time to participants in formal debate. In general these are polite but judiciously worded, as when the Clouds say to Right at the end of his speech 'How pleasant is the chaste bloom of your words' (*Clouds* 1025). If the chorus side with one of the contestants they are naturally more effusive, like the Wasps who in complimenting Philocleon on the completeness and clarity of his case actually liken the experience of hearing him to being jurors in the halls of the Blessed (*Wasps* 631-41). Even this is mild by comparison with the praises lavished on Sausage-seller by his partisans, praises which are not just effusions of pleasure but have the purpose of encouraging him to further exertions against his adversary. At the end of the first contest their congratulations begin with a pun on his trading in meat products: 'O noblest flesh and most excellent spirit, you have appeared as a saviour to the city and to us. How well and with what subtlety you have defeated his arguments. How could we find words of praise to match our feelings of delight?' (*Knights* 457-9). If this hyperbolic address to the huckster turned saviour would be more properly directed to a cult hero, their second goes so far as to forecast that he may eventually have power like that of Poseidon: 'You who have appeared as mighty benefactor to all mankind, I envy your eloquence. Continue thus and you will be the greatest of all Greeks, sole ruler of Athens and the allies, and with your trident you will cause the land to tremble and bring forth riches' (836-40). Could flattery go further?[22]

During the course of an agon which is composed of set speeches, rather than of a hail of abuse or insolent questions, one could see a place for a reasoned commendation of some quality or principle, perhaps as part of a defensive speech. In fact a degree of exaggeration approaching that we noticed in encomia or the Knights' flattery marks Philocleon's account of the power he enjoys as a juror and the blessings of his way of life (*Wasps* 549-630). In *Clouds*, too, Right's account of education in the good old days contains material which could be utilised in a Praise of *sophrosyne*, but its manner is too expository, its tone too restrained and its purpose too explicitly didactic to encourage its categorisation under the head of eulogy (*Clouds* 961-1023). If we turn finally to *Frogs*, whose agon Sir Kenneth Dover compares in some detail with that of *Clouds*, we may at one moment suspect that Aeschylus will deliver a full-scale *epainos* of poets, or at least of his own tragedies and their didactic virtues, but in the event a good deal of fault-finding with his adversary's productions accompanies his praise of his predecessors and of his own heroes (*Frogs* 1013-55).[23]

It is now time to recall my earlier mention of self-praise by the poet desirous of winning the contest. Self-praise, obviously useful to the writer of comedy, does not make its first appearance in the Theatre of Dionysus. The comic poet was following a tradition established in serious lyric, particularly in the epinician odes where praise of the victor and his family is seen to be interdependent with the esteem in which the poet is held and where the athlete's exertions before and during the Games have their counterpart in the struggles of the poet to perfect his art. The comedies were not, of course, like the poems of Pindar, Simonides or Bacchylides, commissioned by a private patron, but nevertheless the comic poet expressed his longing to achieve lasting esteem from the audience just as Pindar desired to be his patron's *philos*, his established friend.

The reader may be surprised that I am associating the self-advertisement of a comic writer like Aristophanes with the dignified and conventional praises found in epinician odes. I believe that there is one passage which clearly shows the poet himself making the connection. In the parabasis of *Wasps* just before his final exhortation to the spectators, he speaks of himself in Pindaric terms as a charioteer and says: 'If, in overtaking his rivals, the poet has crashed his invention, his reputation among the discerning is not diminished' (1051). Here the play is seen as a chariot whose driver's keenness to win has allowed him to take risks; some lines earlier there had been a more fleeting instance of a similar image in the passage in which the poet alludes to the stages in his career as a dramatist, in the last of which 'he took the risk of entering the contest openly, having bridled the mouths of Muses who belonged to him, not to another man' (1022). Not only are poet and charioteer equated in this metaphor, but the Muses are introduced as the horses which pulled the play to victory; not only is the dramatic competition likened in general terms to a chariot race in athletic games, but the fact that the charioteer was usually not the owner of the team and thus not the official winner is also brought into the field of reference. Aristophanes' hearers could not fail to be reminded of epinician when they heard these lines, reminded of the 'chariot of song' which celebrated the victor's achievement.[24]

In earlier chapters I have tried to show that a parabasis speech can be read in more than one way, as personal narrative, for instance, or as oratory of a defensive kind: now I am concerned with praise and with the traditions lying behind eulogy. In discussing *Acharnians* I emphasised three elements that were combined in the 'anapaests', the poet's assumption of the role of teacher, his condemnation of flattery and his casting of the passage in the form of a defence against the charge of 'making a comedy' of Athens. The third of these points is relevant to my present subject in that it was thought proper that a defendant's self-exculpation should include self-praise, and the second point is also of interest because the line dividing praise and flattery can easily be crossed and it would hardly do for the poet to be seen to condemn and practise flattery simultaneously.[25]

This last problem recurs in *Peace*, where the actual label 'eulogy' is applied to the 'anapaests', but only after the chorus leader has declared 'if any comic poet praises himself in the theatre the steward should beat him' (734 f). He continues, with dubious consistency, to invoke the Muse as follows: 'But if it is proper to honour, O daughter of Zeus, a man who has become the best and most famous comedy producer in the world, our producer claims that he is worthy of a grand eulogy' (736-8). In the lines thus introduced the claim is backed up by instances of the poet's endeavours to elevate the comic art (739-50); then he adduces the fact that he had attacked, not mere private citizens, but a monster (easily identified as the demagogue Cleon) (751-9). My summary contained the verb 'attack': the passage itself is full of verbs which have politico-military connotations. The man here praised 'alone put a stop to' (739), 'first deprived of civic rights and drove out', 'dismissed from office' (743); after 'removing' these evils he set about 'building' and 'fortifying' (749) before 'attacking' (752). The exploits of a warrior are recalled even more markedly in the section about Cleon. Because he is pictured as a legendary monster of a grotesque kind with fearful and nasty attributes like the snake-flatterers encircling his head, his stench and his camel's backside, the poet too becomes a legendary hero, a Heracles who champions the helpless against such terrible creatures.[26] Just as the epinician poet was accustomed to illustrate and magnify the victor's qualities by reference to myth, so the playwright utilises epic tradition to aggrandise his patriotic achievement.

The concluding message is, of course, that the audience should repay the blessings the poet-hero has conferred on them by ensuring his success:

in return for all these benefits both young men and old should be my allies. We advise the baldheads too to unite energetically for victory, because, when I've won, everyone at the banquet and at the symposia will say 'Pass Baldy the fruit bowl and don't let the noblest of poets go short of anything'. (769-73)[27]

I shall have a little more to say about this opening section of the parabasis after bringing into play the third and last conventional element in Aristophanic praise. To do this I turn to the paired speeches of *Knights'* parabasis. In Chapter 1 I discussed, under the heading of description, the paired speeches (and song) in which the Wasps characterised themselves as doughty fighters and true patriots, presenting traits for the most part likely to win general approval.[28] Much of their material has thematic connections with the passages which we are about to examine, and the reason for this link will become clear. The Knights, young, wealthy and well-born opponents of the demagogue called Paphlagon, as members of the cavalry have a natural devotion to Poseidon who is lord of horses as well as of the sea and its creatures, and so in the first of their two songs they invoke his presence on this occasion just as in their second they call on Athene who shares with him the guardianship of Athens (551-64, 582-94).

The note of patriotism sounds again in both speeches which, like the odes, address themselves to distinct, but related, topics. Each is signposted as eulogy by the use of the verb *eulogeisthai* at or near the beginning. In the first the Knights praise their fathers, 'men worthy of this land', for their courage and steadfastness in battle and for a patriotism, which like that of their sons, asked for no reward (565-81), while in the second they record their debt to their horses, not just for their endurance in fighting on land but for their courage, enterprise, adaptability and initiative when required to travel by sea for a battle at Cornith.

Earlier in this chapter I drew attention to the practice of slipping criticism of an individual into a passage purporting to be generalised reproach. Here we have a variant in which a disparaging allusion to Cleon just ripples the surface of praise. In the course of their commendation of ancestors, the Knights, making a conventional contrast between then (good) and now (bad), remark that none of the former generals would have asked Cleaenetus for entitlement to meals provided by the state. The Knights imply that such official privileges can now be gained by ingratiating oneself with those who have influence with the politician currently in power, for example by approaching Cleon through his father, Cleaenetus (573-6). The praise of horses which I now quote in full ends, probably, with a similar indirect allusion.

> We wish to acknowledge what we owe to our horses for they deserve to be eulogised. Together with us they have endured many troubles, both attacks and battles. Their achievements on land are not so marvellous, however, as the occasion on which they leaped on to the transport ships with manly courage, first equipping themselves with water-flasks, garlic and onions. Then they picked up their oars, just like human beings, set to and neighed 'Gee up, crew, who will row? Take hold. What are we doing? Nag from Corinth won't you get going?' At Corinth they leaped off. Then the young horses, using their hooves as tools, scooped out resting places and fetched bedding. Instead of clover they ate crabs, pouncing on any that crept up out of the water, however deep. Theorus actually reports that a Corinthian crab said 'How terrible it is, O Poseidon, if I can't escape the knights by land or sea or in the deep'. (595-610)[29]

Why praise horses? And how would the audience react to such praise? If in epinician odes poet, competitor, chariot and horse were all closely connected, in heroic epic also the association of warrior and horse had been clearly established. The key passage is the invocation in Book Two of Homer's *Iliad* (761-2): 'Tell me then, Muse, who of all of them was best and bravest, of the men and of the men's horses, who went with the sons of Atreus?' These horses shared the courage of the warrior, but those which belonged to Achilles were much more remarkable: they knew and could express human feelings. After the death of Achilles' comrade, Patroclus, their grief was such that they resisted blows and entreaties, unwilling to return to the fighting but

> still as stands a grave monument over the mounded tomb of a dead man or lady, they stood there holding in its place the fair-wrought chariot, leaning their heads along the ground, and warm tears were running earthward from underneath the lids of the mourning horses who longed for their charioteer, while their bright manes were made dirty as they streamed down either side of the yoke'. (*Iliad* 17. 426 f)[30]

Later (19. 397 f), when Achilles himself makes ready to go at last into battle, he reproaches the horses for abandoning Patroclus and one of them is granted speech not only to refute the charge but to predict the imminence of Achilles' death.

In *Knights*, although there is naturally no mention of death in battle and although the hardships of campaigning are presented in novel light, the identity of interest between man and horse is just as clear as in the epic. In what ways do these cavalry horses resemble men? They can speak to exhort their fellows; they can use their hooves to hold oars, to dig and to scoop up crabs – and we may smile as we visualise these unlikely manoeuvres. Aristophanes has done no more than describe, in realistic order, preparation, embarkation and landing, absolutely routine activities in any campaign, if performed by men. Yet performed so eagerly and unforgettably by horses, these acts become exemplary, a model of ingenuity, initiative, courage in unfamiliar surroundings and adaptability; and the effect of all these virtues is to elicit from a crab a tribute to the ubiquitous power of – the Knights.

The secret is out: *laudatores* and *laudandi* are identical. In praising their forefathers and in praising their horses the Knights are praising themselves: ancestors and steeds alike manifest qualities properly belonging to these young cavalry officers. Even the songs imply that they are favoured by Poseidon and Athene, whom they invoke. Moreover, read the two speeches consecutively and it will be seen that they make sense, formally, as parts of a long, unwritten eulogy, a eulogy of cavalry men. It hardly needs saying that eulogy is not normally self-directed: the orator or encomiast mentions himself only at certain conventional points, particularly in his proem, either, as often, in modest disclaimer of his own merits or in the confident assertion of the validity of his assessment of the achievements of the *laudandus*. Traditionally, of course, even if *laudandi* are plural the *laudator* is not (though his words may be composed for performance by a group of singers). What happens in *Knights*? The plurality of cavalry men here gives group support to the views of one man, the dramatist, just as they have previously backed their protégé, Sausage-seller, against Cleon. The praise of the poet, by his own fictional creatures, in the 'anapaests', as one who 'hates our enemies and bravely utters the right views' (510) is appropriately followed by speeches in which, for all the fantastic wrapping, those same 'right views' are promulgated.[31]

We have returned, by a circuitous route, to our starting-point, oratory. The poet, or his chorus, can call upon the conventions of oratory and not only of oratory heard in court or assembly. There is a third category, the epideictic, or display, speech; sometimes examples of this species are composed as the name suggests, just for fun, but for the most part those which survive are suitable for delivery at communal gatherings like the pan-Hellenic festivals.[32] For Aristophanes' *Knights* the relevant occasion was the yearly memorial ceremony held in honour of Athens' dead, at which a laudatory speech, the epitaphios, was delivered. The epitaphios commemorated the deeds and virtues of the dead, exhorted the survivors to emulate their achievement and offered consolation to the bereaved. It is the commemorative section that most concerns us, beginning, as it does in the best-known example of the species, Pericles' Funeral Speech, with mention of the fathers of the deceased and going on to illustrate the qualities they themselves had displayed in battle and to emphasise their love of country. In praising the dead the speaker was also partly praising the living and their city, partly exhorting them to emulate those who had died for them.

The paired speeches in which the Knights eulogise their fathers and their horses are an adaptation, for the purposes of comedy, of material from the epitaphios, and would have been immediately recognised as such by an audience regularly presented with examples of this kind of speech. Moreover, those parabatic addresses in which the poet's benefactions and his heroism are asserted and exemplified are also based on the conventions of the epitaphios (and contain verbal indications of their origins). It may be objected that the funeral oration has no place in comic drama, that reminiscence of it would be at the very least unseemly; all very well for Euripides to adapt the epitaphios for use in his *Suppliants*, a tragedy performed within a year or two of *Knights*, but impossible for comedy.[33] After all, the praise of horses is amusing, isn't it, and must have been written as a rather childish piece of fanciful humour. No. It is because the horses are funny, because their eulogy comes so unexpectedly after the praise of fathers, that we are startled into thinking about what deserves praise: is it the qualities displayed by Athenians of earlier generations and now by the Knights' horses, or is it those so depressingly manifested elsewhere in this play – greed, self-seeking, corruption, bullying? And Aristophanes, famed for his censure, deserves also to be celebrated as encomiast and eulogist. In the words Rilke used of Orpheus:

Praising, that's it! As a praiser and blesser
he came like the ore from the taciturn mine.[34]

Notes

1. The necessity for discrimination in praise is voiced by the sophist Prodicus at Plato, *Protagoras* 337 a-c. For blame as necessary concomitant to praise see A. Miller on Pindar's Second Pythian (*TAPA* 111 (1981), 135-43). See below, p. 53.

2. Horace, *Satires* 1. 4. 1-6.

3. Some of the parabasis' functions are nowadays the responsibility of publicity agents: a degree of 'hype' is common to both.

4. For the encomium in tragedy see E. *Heracles*, ed. G. Bond (Oxford, 1981), 637-700 and H. Parry, *AJP* 86 (1965), 366-74.

5. Words like *laudator, laudandus*, 'foil' have become part of the vocabulary of students of praise poetry as a result of the work of E.L. Bundy, *Studia Pindarica* I, II (California, 1961-2).

6. For the form cf. S. *Oedipus at Colonus* 510-48.

7. The corresponding stanza, at *Peace* 909-23, includes features typical of praise poetry, like the word 'worthy', and the chorus address Trygaeus as 'deliverer' and 'second only to the gods'; see below, p. 130.

8. 'Carcinus' spinners': the allusion is to the sons of the tragic poet Carcinus, noted for their rapid pirouettes, cf. *Peace* 289, 781 and *Wasps* 1530.

9. For the reporting of his triumph see below 156 ff.

10. On the cry of triumph (*ololuge*) see J. Haldane, *JHS* 85 (1965), 33-41.

11. See for example *King Oedipus* 1086-109, *Women of Trachis* 633-62. Strepsiades' encomium is discussed by C.W. Macleod, *Phoenix* 35 (1981), 142-4 (reprinted in *Collected Essays* (Oxford, 1983)).

12. E. *Bacchae*, ed. E.R. Dodds (Oxford 1960), 72, 902-11 with notes on these lines.

13. Cf. *Peace* 715 where the Council is 'blest' by the advent of Theoria.

14. Nor are the problems confined to one genre: witness the variety of interpretations of the function of the names in Alcman's *Partheneion* (*PMG* 1). On references to named individuals in Ar. see S. Halliwell, *CQ* 34 (1984), 83-8.

15. This song is well treated by Moulton 18-24.

16. Pindar fr. 89a (prosodion to Leto and Artemis); cf. for reflective openings E. *Hippolytus* 375 f, Rau 120; A.E. Housman, *Fragment of a Grek Tragedy*.

17. See above, p. 51.

18. A. *Agamemnon* 72-82.

19. For the characterisation of the Acharnians see above, p. 11 f.

20. The angry silence of the goddess Peace ends when she confides to Hermes her complaints against the Athenians and he conveys them to the spectators (including the word *momphe*) (*Peace* 657-67).

21. For similar gibes about the demagogues' trades cf. *Knights* 128-43 with

Sommerstein's note about the 'alleged new breed of shopkeeper-statesmen'.

22. Compare the Pericles-Zeus of *Ach.* 530 f, Cratinus fr. 71 etc., and the self-elevation of Philocleon at *Wasps* 619-30.

23. See below, p. 114.

24. See particularly K. Crotty, *Song and Action* (Baltimore 1982), Ch. Three. Pindar speaks of trusting the hospitality of a patron who 'yoked the chariot of the Muses' (*P* 10. 64-5): see W. Mullen, *Choreia: Pindar & Dance* (Princeton, 1982), 32.

25. See Thuc. 6. 16-18 for Alcibiades' use of self-praise.

26. Lines 752-9 of *Peace* are almost identical with *Wasps* 1030-7, the play produced a year earlier.

27. There are other joking allusions to Ar.'s alleged baldness, e.g. Eupolis fr. 78.

28. See above, p. 13 f.

29. An associate of Cleon was named Theorus. Probably the main point of the lines is to emphasise that the crab's reaction is a piece of fantasy. The name Theorus is apt for one who acts as emissary.

30. The translator is Richmond Lattimore (*The Iliad of Homer* (Chicago 1951)).

31. Few epideictic speeches survive: of fifth-century examples the best known is probably Gorgias' *Encomium of Helen*.

32. It requires only slight adaptation to bring out the resemblance of the opening of the 'anapaests' to the proem of a formal speech: 'If anyone else had asked me to speak on this occasion he would have found it difficult to persuade me, but I cannot refuse X since he and I are fighting the same opponents and he has the courage to say what is true and to withstand the storm . . .' (*Knights* 505-11).

33. The epitaphios is treated fully in J.E. Ziolkowski *Thucydides and the Tradition of the Funeral Speech at Athens* (New York 1981). Rules for eulogy may be found in (Aristotle) *Rhetorica ad Alexandrum*, Ch. III and XXXV. The funeral eulogy of Amphiareus is recalled in the context of praise of the victor in Pindar, *O.* 6, 12. For the epitaphios and tragedy see C. Collard on Euripides, *Supplices* 857-917 in *BICS* 19 (1972), 39-53. Collard convincingly denies that parody is intended here. *Supplices* was produced a year or two after *Knights*. I have not been able to take account of N. Loraux, *L'invention d'Athènes* (Paris, 1981).

The incorporation of praise in the lament is prescribed at A. *Ag.* 1547 and seen at e.g. *Ag.* 445-9, 'And they lament, eulogising one man for his knowledge of fighting, another for his noble death amid the carnage . . .'

34. *The Sonnets to Orpheus* by Rainer Maria Rilke, trs. J.B. Leishman.

4 DIALOGUE

Shall I make one of the usual jokes,
The kind that always get a laugh?

(*Frogs* 1 f)

Continuous speech (or speech with occasional interruptions), which has provided the basis of this study so far, accounts for a rather small portion of each play, and preponderance of dialogue in comedy is a feature which distinguishes it from tragedy in an instantly obvious way. My previous chapters have been concerned both with function and with mode of discourse. I have aimed, for example, to look at the task fulfilled by exposition in a play, at its function in the drama, and also at the form and style of the speeches which narrate or describe. In Chapters 2 and 3 I have examined the occasions on which an adversary is to be outargued, an attitude defended or a change of view effected as well as the persuasive, hortatory, abusive or laudatory forms of expression by which such ends are achieved. Where the continuous speeches of Aristophanic comedy differ from those of tragedy, is not in their expository, descriptive or oratorical function but in the tone and diction which stamp them as comic.

It hardly needs saying that monologue is not the only dramatic means available for setting out situations and arguments, nor that the change from sustained speech to rapid dialogue is a device employed in all kinds of drama (as in some 'real life' occasions which may be transferred to the stage).[1] What may become equally obvious, I fear, is that writing about dialogue, and about scenes composed of dialogue, is much more difficult than describing and analysing a single speech, particularly when the dialogue has the inconsequence and jokiness typical of Aristophanic comedy. In the case of a continuous passage one can summarise content and then quote selectively in order to suggest flavour or to underline the most noteworthy feature: in the dialogue précis may be nearly impossible, or irrelevant, and selective quotation may require so much preliminary explanation of context or extra-dramatic circumstances as to lack interest and point when it finally appears. And what is to be done when the point is mainly verbal, a pun or witticism which disappears in accurate translation?

Having availed myself of the orator's plea for indulgence in one of its guises ('it is difficult, members of the jury, to speak about . . .'), I shall like him announce what I propose to try to achieve in this chapter. My assumption throughout is that the dramatist's primary need is to prevent the audience from becoming bored and that to this end he exploits techniques of structure as well as language and that he makes what is seen as well as what is heard varied and memorable. I am aware that this programme sounds insultingly over-simple and trite, but I believe that the circumstances of the dramatic contest make such considerations unavoidable and in any case I hope that as an approach it will be found to work. I have limited myself fairly strictly to three plays, dealing selectively with *Acharnians*, still more selectively with *Clouds*, and then rather fully with *Knights* in the latter part of the chapter. Thus there will be a progress from the passage or scene taken in isolation towards the assembling of scenes into larger units and this will make the chapter into a link with Chapters 5-8 which are more concerned with continuity of story and theme.

Acharnians

I begin again with the beginning of the earliest play, taking up at the point where Dicaeopolis, his long wait ended, listens to the first speaker to address the assembled Athenians. This is an ambassador whose duty it is, at the conclusion of the mission undertaken by himself and his companion, to report on the way in which it has been conducted. His report naturally assumes narrative format but in tone is somewhat defensive. Later in the play, in the parabasis of the comedy, as we have noted, disapproval of deceitful and flattering foreign ambassadors is expressed, but here an Athenian envoy, himself less than sincere, comes under scrutiny. What he has to say is significant both for this scene and for the whole play and the technique of presentation underlines its significance. In speaking of the envoy's report I may have led the reader to think of a monologue, a text delivered without interruption. A glance at the relevant passage seems to contradict this impression (65-92):

surely what we have here is dialogue, albeit the kind of dialogue in which one speaker has by far the bigger part. Appearances are somewhat deceptive: the envoy's speech *is* a monologue, except at one place where he answers a question put by Dicaeopolis (84), and it can be read as a continuous account of the living conditions the envoy's party experienced while travelling, of their eventual arrival at the court of the Persian Great King only to find him absent, of his homecoming and the subsequent feasting and finally of their return accompanied by a Persian dignitary. In order to clarify form and function I have made this summary as colourless as I could. The ambassador, in trying to defend his long and luxurious absence, adds plenty of detail, but he elaborates in such a way as to produce the opposite effect to that he intends: 'we were compelled to drink out of crystal and gold goblets wine that was undiluted,' for example (73-5). He also exaggerates throughout, notably in the lines about the King's defecatory campaign (81-4).[2] The envoy's recital, of itself sufficiently transparent, is further shown up by Dicaeopolis' comments, which have two main purposes, first to point the contrast between the prolonged luxury enjoyed by envoys and the hardships experienced by ordinary people in wartime and secondly to impugn the veracity of the report, especially by showing up the envoy as an *alazon* (76, 87).[3]

One may conjecture that this format was chosen partly because the playwright did not want another chunk of monologue so soon after Dicaeopolis' expository speech. I do not know whether to view the lack of contact between these two as symbolic, but it is clear that Dicaeopolis' role as dissatisfied onlooker during these proceedings does more than provoke him to making peace on his own account: it shows up the remoteness of such as the ambassador.[4] Non-communication is not common in the comedies but it is among the more striking devices available to the composer of passages shared among two or three participants.

A little later in the play, at the beginning of the long movement concerned with the Acharnians' hostility to the peacemaker, there stands an impressive example of interchanges at their most formal (302-34). The passage is framed by a pair of songs, each of them shared between Dicaeopolis and the Acharnians, and consists of five exchanges of couplets followed by three lines split between the participants (*antilabē*). After a further couplet Dicaeopolis goes off to fetch something that he needs and the chorus deliver three lines to cover his absence. Finally there is one more couplet apiece. There are few occasions in Aristophanic comedy which adopt the Aeschylean pattern by which a scene is shared between single actor and chorus (or its leader), as, for instance, when Clytemnestra confronts the Argive elders (Aeschylus, *Agamemnon* 264 f); in *Acharnians* greater impressiveness is added by the use, not of the ordinary dialogue metre, the iambic trimeter, but of the trochaic tetrameter, found also in the parabasis of the play.

When Dicaeopolis leaves the stage, it is to obtain a 'hostage', which he threatens to kill if the Acharnians persist in their refusal to listen to the reasons why he made a peace treaty (326 f). The couplets and the half lines preceding his exit thus demonstrate the failure of his persistent attempts at appeasement, attempts which combine vehemence, patience and even a touch of humour (321). The Acharnians' argument is that the peacemaker is a traitor whom they should punish by stoning forthwith, but their couplets are so framed as to enable them to give vent to their loathing of the Spartans and to force Dicaeopolis to shift from the defensive position he has initially taken up, his reasons for making peace, to trying to exculpate the enemy. Any attempt at summarising the argument inevitably runs counter to the all-important symmetry of the passage, and has no more than an introductory function.[5] The sound of blow met by corresponding blow is what counts here, and the realisation of the repetitiveness of the pattern. Yet there is also a forward movement and an increase in tension, brought about largely by the angry iteration of certain keywords like 'Spartans' (304, 305, 309), 'truce' (304, 306, 307) and 'listen' (302, 306, 322, 323, 324):

> *Dic.* Sure I know the Spartans we loathe
> Aren't to blame for ALL our woes.
> *Ach.* Not for ALL, you dare to utter,
> Shameless, and get off unscathed?
> *Dic.* Not for ALL, again I say it,
> Show you *they* are wronged as well.

> (309-14)

Acharnians is a play in which extended monologue is confined to the prologue, to Dicaeopolis' defence, and on a much smaller scale to the messenger's report of General Lamachus' wounding (1174-89). I began with a description of two passages of dialogue which differ greatly in form, degree of contact and intensity of feeling; now I wish to touch on ways in which the later succession of iambic scenes manages to avoid the danger of monotony. The inclusion of a visit to Euripides, for example, allows the distinctive language and tone of tragedy to mix incongruously with homelier remarks ('Euripides, please give me a tiny basket that's got a hole burnt in it.' 'Thou wretch, what need hast thou of wickerwork?' 'No need at all, I just want it.' (452-5). When Dicaeopolis' market opens, traders come from Megara and Boeotia. Not only does each speak his own kind of Greek, but the Megarians' daughters when disguised imitate the noises made by piglets (780, 801 f) while the Boeotian has an escort of pipers whose music is not to Dicaeopolis' taste (862-9).

This same scene illustrates also how the sound and tempo of ordinary conversation can be varied by including a list, here of merchandise from Boeotia, in which assonance and alliteration are regular features (874-80, cf. 545-54). The list culminates in the mention of a great delicacy, the Copaic eel, at which Dicaeopolis launches into high-flown apostrophe: 'O thou who bringest glad savour to mankind, allow me to greet the eels thou bringest' (881 f). The listening ear is sensitive not only to changes of tone but also to alterations in the established distribution of speech between participants. Finally, in the last part of *Acharnians*, Aristophanes sets up an antithesis between warmonger and peacemaker which relies on sound as well as sight. Most obviously this is the case right at the end of the play when tragic lament and victory song produce their contrasted music to match the contrasting fortunes of the two men, but both here and earlier great scope is given to Dicaeopolis the mimic with the result that most of what Lamachus says or sings, in solemn or woeful tones, is followed by a mocking echo (1097-142, 1190-end).[6]

In this brief and selective return to *Acharnians* I have focused on two aspects of Aristophanes' art, which I can best express by imagining the experience of a blind member of the audience: he would be keenly aware of the change from speech to song and of the tonal and rhythmic characteristics of individual song, but he would also perceive more clearly than the sighted member of the audience changes occurring in the spoken parts of the play:

differences in metre, tempo, regularity of dialogue, accent, dialect, linguistic and vocal register.

Secondly, imagine the tasks which remain for the author once he has decided on the theme or issue he wishes to explore and on the outline of his story: how is he to flesh it out, how embody it in separate scenes, how make one scene memorably different from the preceding one? To draw an analogy from music, if a tragedy resembles a nineteenth-century symphony in its sustained onward flow and its spacious development of a theme, then comedy is like a suite of dances written a hundred years earlier, its components quite short and strongly varied in tempo, metre and mood, some courtly, others more popular in origin.

Clouds

In the last section I drew attention to the way sound contributed to the contrasting of Lamachus and Dicaeopolis as well as to the mockery of the former by the latter. I might well have said that added pungency is given to the ridicule by the difference in status between the elected general and the ordinary citizen, a difference enhanced by the way Lamachus is described and presented, with his plumes and his Gorgon shield, his hauteur and pomposity.[7] It is the theme of contrast betwen the two participants in a dialogue which I wish to pursue a little further now, in connection with *Clouds*. This comedy offers us the chance to observe the interaction of teacher and taught, learned and ignorant, priest and novice, Just and Unjust Argument, old and young, father and son.

The prologue of *Clouds* is longer than that of the two earlier plays (considerably longer also than tragic prologues in general, even those which, as in *King Oedipus*, subdivide into two or three parts).[8] The second section of its prologue is set at the entrance to Socrates' school and fulfils an introductory function, in that during the course of the dialogue we learn a good deal about what goes on in the school and moreover are prepared for the entrance of the Teacher himself, a climactic event. In answer to Strepsiades' summons there appears no ordinary servant to go through the standard grumpy doorkeeper routine, but a graduate student or Senior Prefect who takes full advantage of the opportunity to make Strepsiades feel the complete outsider

(*Clouds* 133-43).[9] Towards the end of the section the candidate for admission asks questions about some of the apparatus he can see, the final item being a map.[10] In order to appreciate the situation we need to realise that a person unfamiliar with maps may be disconcerted by the difference between a map and a picture or between the scale used and real distances: the interchanges are built on the basis of Strepsiades' ignorance of such matters, but the resulting structure does not remain unadorned: 'Look, there's Athens.' 'Can't be. There aren't any juries to be seen.' 'Here's Euboea, laid out all along here.' 'Of course. Under Pericles we laid her out.[11] Where's Spartan territory?' 'Where? Just here.' 'So close? You must find a way to move it much further off.' (206-8, 211-16). If the pupil of Socrates adopts a condescending tone, at least he does so from ground level. Socrates' opening words, heard a minute or so later, like his position aloft, establish the distance between him and the ordinary man: 'Why callest thou me, thou creature of a day?' (223). The loftier the tone of one participant in a conversation, the easier it is to deflate, as we discover when Socrates begins to invoke the Cloud chorus so that Strepsiades can meet them. We notice at once that the metre changes from that of ordinary conversational dialogue to longer anapaestic lines, no doubt intoned rather than spoken, as Socrates hieratically invokes Air, Aether and Clouds. In answer to his prayer the voices of the Cloud chorus are heard singing their opening stanza. Before their second verse Socrates in a few lines acknowledges that they have indeed responded to his invocation. In all this section, apart from the identity of the gods addressed, there is much that belongs to traditional religious utterance in manner, language and form, and if we had only the Clouds' song and Socrates' prayers the tone of the whole passage would be consistently elevated and serious (264-313). However, Strepsiades does not altogether observe the ritual injunction to preserve a holy silence. Instead, as soon as he hears the Clouds summoned, he calls out 'Not yet, not yet, not till I've huddled down to avoid being drenched. I was a damned idiot to leave home without my rainhat.' This time Socrates takes no notice and continues: 'Come then, esteemed Clouds, manifest yourselves to this man.' But Strepsiades' next remark is treated differently: Socrates turns and asks whether he has heard the Clouds' voices and the thunder and he replies: 'Yes and I do honour to you, esteemed ones, and I want to fart back in reply to your thunderings.' Socrates' immediate reprimand to his disciple reminds us what kind of drama we are witnessing: 'You're not to poke fun or do the things these comedians do but you are to keep a holy silence, for a great swarm of divinities is on the move.' And, when the laughter dies away, the spectators hear the Clouds' praise of Athens, the home of the Mysteries, with its high temples, sacred processions, and its festivals at all times of the year, and especially now, in the spring, this contest in honour of Dionysus (311 f).

After a passage in which the poet's mastery of bathos and of recovery from bathos is so brilliantly demonstrated, I move on to the conversational scene in which Socrates interviews his would-be pupil (478-509). In these situations it is normal for the person interviewed to be represented as somewhat nervous and for the dramatist to exploit his anxiety so as to create amusement at his tactless and maladroit answers. Here, however, Strepsiades is confident, no doubt because of the encouragement he has received from the Clouds, and he begins to act the fool. For the most part Socrates conducts the interview seriously and with patience, asking questions about Strepsiades' intellectual ability and powers of memory and attempting to use his answers, however silly, to further the dialogue, but once or twice he comments sharply ('The man's an ignorant barbarian'). Strepsiades' creator, on the other hand, cleverly judges his act so that he never quite goes too far: so that he can eventually be expelled he must first be admitted! One ploy is to fail to understand metaphors, as when Socrates mentions (educational) 'machinery' (479) or tells him, 'When I throw you a scrap of meteorological lore mind you gobble it up.' 'You mean I've got to eat my training just like a dog?' (489-91).[12] Towards the end of the scene he does show signs of nervousness as the moment of his entry into this extraordinary institution approaches, but his nervousness seems largely put on.

This scene exemplifies the technique of the comic with his 'straight man' or stooge, although here the serious character is the superior in intellect and position and takes the initiative almost throughout. It makes an amusing end to the long section which began with Strepsiades' arrival at the Reflectory (132) and it shows another side of the relationship between teacher and taught, not, as previously, that Socrates is clever and learned while Strepsiades is ignorant and stupid, but that pupils can gain an ascendancy of their own by the way they behave and the attitudes they adopt to those in authority. By his clowning Strepsiades cuts Socrates down to size.[13]

Not all exchanges in *Clouds* are marked by such strong contrast between the participants. To conclude my examples from the play I turn to two passages of verbal sparring which precede formal debate: in the earlier of the two the sparring partners are the two Logoi or Arguments, in the latter, Strepsiades and his son (890-934, 1321-44). In each case, as the subsequent debates show, the opposition between the views of one generation and its successor, between old and young, is vitally important, but in the preliminary scenes it is the fact of opposition that counts and its translation into words and threatening gestures. Scenes of this type may contain, at the simplest and lowest level, exchanges of abuse: 'You're an X.' 'And you're a Y', etc. Lines of this kind usually occur only after the characters have had time to infuriate each other and may continue until the chorus-leader intervenes to keep the peace. In *Clouds* the Better Argument flings insults in the usual way, but his opponent, for a change, pretends that the insults are compliments, with such sarcastic replies as 'You're garlanding me with lilies' (911). His pupil, Pheidippides, remembers the gambit when quarrelling with his father (1328-30).

Little scenes of this kind consist of brief remarks or questions, quick jabs as it were, rather than developed argument or piled-up phrases. When the two Logoi are sparring the shortest contribution is a single word (893) while the longest takes only a few seconds to deliver (920 f). The anapaestic metre may indicate that there is more activity here than in the iambics used by father and son: certainly the later passage, concentrating on the rights and wrongs of father-beating, is more predictable than its predecessor whose personages, ideas and potential for victory are as yet unknown. Just as in tragic stichomythia we can observe here the way in which initiative is made to pass from one Logos to the other and back again, the vital moments being those at which one of the two 'kills' the current topic.[14] These scenes appeal because of their speed and liveliness and the way they build up expectancy; in addition it is agreeable to see the dignified older man scrapping with the young.

Knights

In *Clouds*, as in *Acharnians*, the opening exposition of the hero's situation is carried out by means of monologue; in *Clouds*, as we have seen, dialogue is used to provide information about the Reflectory. *Knights*, however, actually opens with conversation between two people, although in *Knights* (as in *Wasps*) one of the two eventually expounds the situation more fully to the audience (*Knights* 35-79; cf. *Wasps* 44-135). Expository dialogue is naturally less concentrated than monologue; it invites us to observe not one but two characters and the interaction between them and it is often self-consciously 'jokey'. However, the most interesting feature of the prologue of *Knights* is perhaps its calculated slowness in imparting information. Two slaves, companions in misfortune, emerge from the house, sore and aggrieved at the frequent beatings inflicted on them by a third, 'the newly purchased Paphlagonian' (2). How to escape? Should they run away or look for sanctuary somewhere? (21-31). After some further lines Slave A confides more fully in the audience, beginning by describing their master, previously unmentioned, as 'a typical rustic, munching beans, irritable, Demos of Pnyx, an old chap, cross and deafish' (40-2). So the master, we deduce when we hear his name, must be a representative figure, the personification of the Athenian people ('Thepeople' in Barrett's translation). Slave A now begins to enlarge on the characteristics and behaviour of the new slave and at once it becomes evident that the 'hide-tanning Paphlagon' is none other than the demagogue Cleon (44). A little later, as an instance of Paphlagon's habit of presenting the results of other people's work as his own, Slave A relates how the bully had seized a Spartan cake he himself had made in Pylos (54-7).[15] Now the cast is complete: the master of this household is Demos, his three slaves are first Cleon, secondly the General associated with Pylos, Demosthenes, and thirdly, by implication only, another general, Nicias, known for his piety and self-denial. The third identification is helped by recalling that it was he who had earlier suggested turning to the gods for help (30).[16]

The action resumes when the picture of Cleon is complete. The slaves continue their conversation searching for a way out of their troubles. Nicias suggests suicide. Demosthenes, more sanguine, proposes that they try undiluted wine as a stimulus to productive thought. Nicias' disapproval prompts the passage in praise of wine quoted in Chapter 3 and Nicias is dispatched to filch some wine unobserved by Paphlagon. One drink of this wine and Demosthenes has the germ of the idea which is to generate much of the play: Nicias must go thieving again, to obtain oracles from Cleon's private stock (80-111).

In the last paragraph I have used the characters' names as often as I could, in order to suggest that one is now very conscious of their identity. In addition I suppose that the spectator has been startled into reassessing the opening, into reflecting upon the validity of the analogy between *oikos* and *polis*, and into asking which of the two is, or will be, more important for the interpretation of the play: is this, in other words, to be a play about politics or a play about private lives? The reader, however, may well wish to object, arguing that, while laughing at an actor impersonating a thirsty slave, the spectator has little time or inclination to speculate on the deeper significance of what has already passed. Maybe not; but the process I envisage is more like the recognition of a *double entendre*, the quick perception that all is not quite what it first seemed to be, followed by increased and keener appreciation of what has passed and more alert curiosity about future developments.

As compared with the scenes we reviewed in *Clouds*, the prologue shows only a minor degree of differentiation between two participants who share both rank and situation. In this respect it is prophetic. The rival demagogues whose struggles are to occupy the bulk of the remainder of *Knights* also resemble each other rather closely, save that one holds the position to which the other is encouraged to aspire. For the dramatist, therefore, there is no scope for exploiting difference in status, as when beggar confronts general in *Acharnians*, or Trygaeus in *Peace* meets the god Hermes, nor can he use arguments of the kind that arise from the tension between father and son or between husband and wife. Aristophanes has at his disposal for this 'contest in shamelessness' no one but Paphlagon and his challenger, a sausage-seller by trade, Demos and the chorus of Knights.[17]

Knights has only five individual characters with speaking parts, two of whom occupy the stage for much of the play's duration, whereas its predecessor, *Acharnians*, lists 23 speaking participants among its characters, bringing them in ones or twos to face the individual round whose fortunes the play revolves. Since there can be none of the variety and interest provided elsewhere by the entry of a new person, perhaps strikingly costumed or accompanied by a distinctive retinue, perhaps sounding in vocal quality or accent quite unlike anyone else in the cast, the writer must devise dramatic and theatrical means by which interest in a limited issue played out by a few characters may be sustained (and which will not demand impossible feats of resilience and staying power from the three actors, especially the man playing Sausage-seller). *Knights* does not lack variety, but it is variety produced in a confined space, comparable (in this respect) to those modern plays which often generate considerable tension from concentrating on the relationship between two people in one room. The solution for the difficulties caused by the restricted situation of *Knights* was found in the employment of the third actor. Reducing matters to their simplest, A and B are first presented in combat, challenging and insulting each other, then shown adopting postures of quite another kind in their attempts to influence C. Now the spectators no longer look continually from A to B and back to A, as at a tennis match; again and again they focus attention on C, even if he keeps silence, to note his reaction to the words and movements of A or B. The behaviour of A and B may change purely as a result of their awareness that they are observed, or, as in *Knights*, the act they put on may have the positive aim of influencing C in addition to concealing their true natures. In our play the three-cornered scenes involve the two rival demagogues, and at the apex of the triangle, the old Athenian, Demos. Before we look in detail at the scenes for three players, we need to examine the ways in which the earlier scenes develop in order to make the contrast as clear as possible.

At the end of the prologue Demosthenes explains to Sausage-seller how his low birth, and lack of education, together with his experience in the cooked meat trade, are precisely the qualifications needed if he is to succeed as a demagogue; he further encourages him by promising that he will be supported by the Knights (178-226). When Paphlagon bursts in, characteristically but rightly suspecting a conspiracy, Sausage-seller at once expresses his need of support and the Knights ride in to the rescue. There is no response, however, when Cleon calls on *his* supporters, the jurymen. From this moment on the director can show, if he wishes, the imbalance of forces, by his positioning of the Knights in relation to their protégé. In fact, right at the beginning it is the Knights who attack Cleon directly (247-73). As the scene approaches its end, however, we hear the first regular exchange of abuse and threats between the two contenders, including such lines as 'I'll shout you down' and 'I'll outcrow you' (286 f).

There follows the first agon, which like the second is too fragmented to be entitled 'formal debate'.[18] In so far as there is any coherence in this sequence of accusation and counter-accusation about theft, trickery, bullying and shamelessness as practised by each participant, it is given by allusions to the different trades each has followed, for instance in Sausage-seller's recollections of stealing meat when he was a boy (417-20). But for the most part the vigour of their emotions and variety of their metaphors drives the agon forward until at its end they come to blows, Sausage-seller receiving exhortations from his allies, the Knights: 'Hit him like a man. Beat him with your tripes and sausages, meat punishment for him' (453-6).

The little iambic scene which precedes the parabasis is linked to this agon by congratulations from the Knights to 'the noblest flesh and best spirit in the whole world' whom they hail as Saviour of the city (457-60). Soon Cleon leaves to report to the Council the conspiracy which he accuses his opponents of making at home and abroad. The Knights urge Sausage-seller to follow him and Demosthenes, who has taken very little part in proceedings since the parodos, advises him to prepare for the encounter like a wrestler or a fighting-cock (490-7).

The parabasis is composed, as we have seen,[19] of hymns and eulogy and it and the subsequent account of the council meeting provide a valuable change of tempo and temperature after the insistent angry exchanges of the previous section. No sooner are both the rivals present again than a further bout begins, in the form of an iambic scene initially full of threats and curses but later quietening down as each man boasts of the extent of his influence over Demos: 'I'll drag you before the demos to get you punished.' 'And I'll drag you there, charged with more crimes.' 'He won't take any notice of you, you wretch. I've got the old fool just where I want him.' 'You really do think the demos belongs to you' (710-4).[20] Soon Demos emerges in response to their wheedling and from now on the contest ceases to be a trial of strength and effrontery in which one seeks to destroy the other and becomes instead a competition aimed at winning over Demos.

The presence of Demos does not put a stop to the antiphonal nature of the exchanges between the two but rather changes their tone and direction. Essentially the demagogues adopt the role of lovers. This allows them both to assert the strength of their devotion to Thepeople and to demonstrate it by presenting him with gifts. In a rather static and visually unexciting play, the gift scene is welcome; it is also important as keeping alive the fictional Demos, the old man whose household is dominated by Paphlagon, while the words of love tend to be addressed to the demos regarded as citizens in assembly. It is both amusing and salutary to watch the younger men wooing the old; amusing because it grotesquely reverses the normal pattern of mature *erastes* and handsome adolescent *eromenos*, salutary in suggesting the lengths to which politicians will go to gain ascendancy.

The ambiguity of the theme is visible from the first: Paphlagon complains to Demos that he's being assaulted by his rival and the Knights 'because I care for you, because I'm your lover'. Sausage-seller's riposte counters this with the assertion that he is a rival lover of Demos, unable to prove his devotion because Demos, in the manner of boys who are pursued, favours low traders like Paphlagon in preference to respectable men of good birth like the Knights (730-40). A few lines later they agree that Demos should hold an assembly to decide which of the two is to win his favours, Sausage-seller vainly protesting against the Pnyx as site of the meeting, since there the old man's wits invariably desert him (752 f)! This dig at the folly of decisions reached in assembly tips the balance of the scene away from the personal and domestic level and towards the political in preparation for the second agon which now begins (756-926).

This time Paphlagon's case rests on his past services to Thepeople. Sausage-seller, without previous experience in public life, can only counter Paphlagon's recollections by promising future devotion of superlative kind and by questioning his rival's motives and achievements. When it is Sausage-seller's turn to adduce proof of his love, he gives Demos shoes, tunic and some soothing ointment while attempting to enlighten Thepeople as to the true causes of Paphlagon's behaviour, namely ambition and self-seeking. This section gives the appearance of natural three-cornered conversation, quite unlike those examples of formal debate in which one participant sets out his views unaffected by any interjections that may occur, with the result that it is easy to overlook the structural planning which brings about Sausage-seller's dominance. In fact Sausage-seller speaks twice as many tetrameter lines as his rival, because his early contributions are longer and because, unlike the other two, he is always engaged in conversation with one party or the other. Demos' spoken part amounts to little more than a fifth of the total: his importance lies not in what he says or does but in the attention paid to him by the others, directly or indirectly. To illustrate the direct approach, take the short exchanges which end the tetrameters in which Paphlagon offers to pull out Demos' white hairs and make him look young and Sausage-seller offers him a hare's tail to serve as a handkerchief. Paphlagon goes one better: 'When you've blown your nose, Demos, wipe your hand on my hair.' 'No, on mine', is the rejoinder, as the toadying pair abase themselves (908-11). Earlier Paphlagon's complaint when out-smarted by his adversary is turned against him with the acknowledgment that he himself is the source of any 'monkey business'. Paphlagon then defiantly takes off his cloak and offers it to Demos who rejects it on the spot because it stinks of the tannery. Sausage-seller profits from Demos' rejection of the cloak by explaining that Paphlagon actually meant to choke him, just as on a former occasion when, he pretends, Paphlagon had engineered an abundance of a savoury but indigestible food so that the jurors would kill one another by farting (887-98). These few lines show that the initiative passes from Paphlagon to his would-be successor in the matter of jokes as well as of gifts and political achievement, so as to make Demos and Sausage-seller partners in a short comedy routine, silencing Paphlagon:

S. You know silphium was cheap then?
D. Yes, I do.
S. He rigged the market on purpose . . . so that the jurors would kill one another by farting.
D. Yes, by Poseidon. A chap from Shittingham told me just that.
S. And didn't you all go brown from the farts?
D. Yes. It was a ploy worthy of old Brownjohn.
P. [*trying to get in on the act*]. You scoundrel! You really are

trying to stir me up with all your fooling about.

(894-901)

Again and again in *Knights* Sausage-seller overcomes the disadvantages of having, as it were, to return Paphlagon's service. The experienced demagogue takes the initiative and the novice has to adapt his game accordingly with all the quick-witted versatility he can command. It is possible to read this differentiation of the two men as characterisation, primarily intended to point up Cleon's rash confidence.[21] While not ruling out this function, I think it much more important to see the variety of ways in which Sausage-seller solves problems, escapes from traps, counters arguments, ridicules, distorts, in short, turns to his own advantage whatever his enemy impetuously dispatches. At the end of this agon, for example, Paphlagon uses what is probably his favourite type of utterance, the threat. The respondent may in these circumstances answer threat with threat, as on previous occasions, or, as here, he may explicitly choose a rather different course: 'I'll not threaten you, no. Instead this is what I pray.' And he goes on to envisage Paphlagon choking himself on hot squid through his greed (928-39). In the following transitional passage it is Paphlagon who reverts to the subject of oracles, preparing for the scene in which each man seeks to out-oracle the other. In the next chapter I shall consider the thematic significance of this scene: at present I want to continue exploring the theatrical and dramatic possibilities of this example of writing for three characters.

The entire substance of this longish episode (997-1097) is provided by the recital and interpretation of oracles (and finally of a vision apiece). The introductory lines, which establish the quantity, source and subject matter of each collection of oracles, rely on competitive exaggeration for their humour: 'I've got another box full,' Paphlagon boasts; 'And I've got houses full' comes the reply. Throughout Demos is interrogator or pupil of the 'experts', sometimes naïve, always eager to hear predictions about the glorious future awaiting him; although he has much less to say than either of the others, all their remarks (along with much of the spectators' attention) are directed towards him. If the scene, the opening entries once made, is static, interest and variety are provided by what is heard, chiefly by the contrast between the rhythm and diction of the oracular quotations and those of ordinary conversational iambic verse.[22] It is harder for the literal translator to show the change of metre than the change from lofty to lowly words and phrases, but for contemporaries the rhythmical differences were as immediately obvious as those now distinguishing calypso, say, from regimental march. But it is not just that oracle stands out from comment: the oracles themselves may take the form of command (1015 f), prediction (1037 f), warning (1080 f) or promise (1087 f) as well as incorporating in the oracular manner material evidently foreign to the genuine article:

> P. Yea, there is granted to me a winged word prophecy
>   o'er you,
>   That thou art destined to be King Eagle, Lord
>   of the whole earth.
> S. Yea and to me it is said you shall reign o'er
>   th'Indian ocean,
>   Persia besides 'neath your sway, O juror,
>   who nibbles at French fries

> (1086-9)

There is variation too in the patterning of the scene: basically quotation of an oracle elicits from Demos a puzzled question or comment, which is answered first by one demagogue and then rather differently by the other. The second interpreter now quotes one of *his* oracles, and so on. The basic pattern is repeated several times, with Paphlagon presenting himself as Sacred Dog or Lion defending Athens and as Hawk preying on the Spartans, while Sausage-seller casts him as Cerberus, as a criminal fit for the stocks, as a drunkard and as a wily fox. Oracles and interpretations alike become more and more incredible, although Demos is quite happy to believe that he will rule the world. Finally, when Paphlagon pretends to have seen in a dream the goddess Athene ladling good things over the people, Sausage-seller administers the final blow: he too had seen in a dream the goddess Athene, but this time she was pouring ambrosia over Demos' head – and pickling brine over Paphlagon.

In the last round of this prolonged struggle Demos is once more the focus of attention, as recipient of a number of gifts brought to him by the contestants in turn. Although this scene closely resembles its predecessor in design, its theatrical effect is quite different because of the amount of movement it contains and the variety of 'props' it requires. Offering presents to the beloved is one way of gaining his affection, so that through this action a link is created with the earlier picture of Demos as *eromenos* ('I'll sulk if my lovers aren't really generous today' (1163)). That is not how the scene begins. We left Sausage-seller describing his vision of Athene: Demos' reaction is to entrust himself to the meat-trader for schooling as to a tutor. Paphlagon will not yet admit defeat but promises to supply Demos with his daily bread. In response to a counter-offer from Sausage-seller, Demos announces that he will hand over the 'reins of the Pnyx' to whichever of them treats him better (1096-109).

After the song shared between Demos and the Knights, the politicians reappear, heavily laden.[23] As usual Paphlagon is first to speak, pretending that he has been there 'for ages and ages and ages' already. Sausage-seller joins in the simple game, with even greater exaggeration and so finally does Demos: 'I've been waiting for the pair of you for thousands and thousands and thousands of ages, fed up for ever and ever and ever, Amen' (1152-7). After such an opening it is natural to show the suitors engaged in a race to be the first to provide chair and table for Demos. Paphlagon's first offering, a 'poundcake pounded from grain got from Pylos' is his umpteenth attempt to cash in on Cleon's part in the capture of Pylos.[24] Sausage-seller, lacking any record of military success, manages to outdo his rival by calling in their patron goddess (again): 'I bring you finger rolls rolled by the goddess's own ivory finger' (1166-9). This allusion to the great chryselephantine statue of Athene is the first of a series connecting the goddess, or one of her cults, with successive gifts of food. The ingenuity of the passage is such that Athene's services to her people are gradually recalled: she protects the city (1173 f), fights for them (1172, 1176), takes care of the oarsmen on whom naval power depends (1181 f) and is celebrated in the great Panathenaean festival (1180). Moreover, the conventional theme of the divinity providing men with what they need (Demeter's corn, Dionysus' wine being the chief examples) is here elaborated comically so that Athene supplies a fish fillet or a portion of meat stew and expanded so that she takes part in the actual cooking, baking rolls and stirring soup.[25]

Here I should like to explore, though it is not strictly relevant to this study of three-cornered scenes, the reasons why Demos, who had previously received cushion, shoes, etc. (784, 872, 881), is now offered food and not more lasting gifts. Paphlagon's undertaking to provide for his daily needs (1101) may recall both the regular pay made to jurors for their service in law courts and the occasional distributions of corn promised by politicians who desire popular support: in any case, it is implied that the people's favour is to be won by such means. Additionally it is in keeping with Sausage-seller's line of business that he provides dishes made of various kinds of offal to enliven the basic diet and by so doing we are reminded once again that a rogue whose trade can be represented as despicable is to be the new demagogue. Finally the presentation of food and drink to Demos is *Knights'* approximation to the conventional feasting of other comedies which occurs after the solution of the hero's problems. In this play the motif has been moved back, as it were, to generate the substance of the last round of the contest, since the playwright has a novel idea in reserve for the conclusion of the play.

The movements in the first part of this scene follow a pattern underlined by the words: A advances towards C, displays and presents an item, retires. B does likewise. C comments. This routine occurs five times, with only minor variations. As my translation of the opening lines attempted to show (above, p. 000) there is a good deal of word-play, partly because of its usefulness as a linking device in formally constructed dialogue. For instance, to emphasise the protective role of Athene, there is echoing by Demos of a phrase just used by Sausage-seller:

> S. O Demos, clearly the goddess watches over you
>   And now she holds over you a bowl full of bolognese.
> D. Certainly. Do you suppose the city would survive
>   Unless she'd manifestly overheld her bowl?
>
> (1173-6)[26]

Punning occurs when Paphlagon offers a kind of cake to help the oarsmen because the Greek words have three initial letters in common; in English a similar effect can be gained by changing the food: Demos is to eat roes to help the ships' rowers (1182). A little later Demos asks Sausage-seller how he is to use a gift of entrails and receives this answer: 'The goddess sent you these just so that you could use them in the *tri*remes' innards. She visibly watches over the fleet. Now accept a drink, *tri*ple strength' (1184-7).

In the last two sentences a new word-play has begun, with 'triremes' and 'triple': it continues for three more lines of which the last acknowledges that Athene *Trit*ogenes *tri*pled the wine's strength. The flexibility of the verse can be illustrated from the final exchange of this section, since for once the word order can be maintained in (clumsy) English:

> *P.* Take now of lardycake from me a slice.
> *S.* From me entire the lardycake just here.

(1190 f)

At this point the pattern is broken. Paphlagon boasts that he can provide a great delicacy, hare's meat. Sausage-seller, unable to match the offer, distracts Paphlagon's attention, seizes the hare and presents it to Demos as his own gift, thus doing himself just what he had criticised in his rival in the previous scene: 'Beware the cur Cerberus who gulps down your dinner while you gaze in the other direction' (1031 f). Naturally enough this leads to a brief altercation between the rivals at the end of which Paphlagon finally realises he's likely to be outclassed in shamelessness.

Now Sausage-seller turns to Demos to suggest that it's time for him to decide between them. In the ensuing dialogue Paphlagon remains silent and motionless, and in this way the stage picture shows that he has in fact dropped out of the action. The significance of the moment is further marked by Demos' reference to the audience in the theatre who will judge the wisdom of his decision.[27] Sausage-seller clinches matters by encouraging Demos to examine the food containers belonging to himself and Paphlagon: his own is empty, its entire contents having been given away, while that of his opponent is brimful (1218). Sausage-seller, after turning his lack of provisions to such good account, points the moral: Paphlagon is behaving as he has always behaved, enriching himself while acting the generous benefactor. The moment of truth is at hand; the oracle that had predicted the demagogue's expulsion will shortly be fulfilled.

In the following chapter I shall try to draw together some of the strands in this play. In the present section I hope I have been able to demonstrate the careful stagecraft and verbal dexterity which together shape individual scenes and bind into one the successive bouts in the politicians' fight for supremacy. As a brief postscript to this chapter I should like to make a comparison between two comedies on the face of it quite dissimilar, *Knights* and *Frogs*. It might be said that one is political, the other literary, one coarse and crude, the other subtle and refined, and so on. Yet one feature they certainly share, the problem of making a prolonged contest interesting.

If we put the literary contest in *Frogs* beside the part of *Knights* which lies between the entry of Demos and he discomfiture of Paphlagon, we see that in each the agon is followed by further competitive scenes involving the same contestants (*Knights* 728-1229; *Frogs* 905-1411). In the earlier play linguistic variety is provided by the inclusion of oracular language but neither contestant is required to sing, whereas in *Frogs* not only is the language of tragedy imported, in spoken and sung examples, but the quotations are delivered by the tragedian who did not compose them, thus allowing the actor to use scornful mimicry. *Knights* exploits the possibilities of three-actor scenes much better than *Frogs*, particularly in matching words and movements so skilfully. Whereas Dionysus' function in the contest lacks consistency and even interest to such an extent that, when forced to decide, his uncertainty fails to register as it should, Demos, although an ambiguous figure, holds the centre of the stage quite convincingly. One reason for this may be that, unlike *Frogs*, *Knights* gives a feeling of progression to a climax as Demos frees himself step by step from domination by his former steward. The move from one topic to another in *Frogs*, from preludes to choral lyric to monody to poetic 'weight', has no more animation or impetus than the succession of chapters in a critical handbook.

Similar problems are tackled in ways that, as I have indicated, differ in dramatic structure and in stagecraft. Nevertheless, a reading of the comparable sections will reveal some unexpected resemblances too, not least in the traits manifested by the contestants. Not only do two demagogues, like two tragedians, have much in common with each other, in spite of what divides them, but Paphlagon and Aeschylus, Sausage-seller and Euripides are to some extent variations on a stock type.[28]

If we consider, as I believe we should, that the craft of the playwright is a subject that deserves and repays study, then I hope that following the lines of enquiry I have suggested in the preceding pages will be both profitable and interesting. Whether or not I am right in my simple assumption that the dramatist who wanted to win first prize for comedy consciously strove for variety as episode followed episode, it seems to me that the hallowed method of 'compare and contrast' is a valuable approach to understanding comic dramaturgy. I have suggested a few of the ways in which scenes vary: many more remain to be explored. Because I have had to be selective, for reasons of clarity and of space, I have probably given a distorted picture: it is of course not true that only *Acharnians* is interesting to the ear, that only *Knights* shows proficiency in writing material for three actors, or that *Clouds* above all the other plays exploits the humour and significance of strongly differentiated characters.[29] Moreover, in seeking to point out what seem to me to be essential features in a single episode, I have not done justice either to the comic and dramatic range of the particular scene or to the ebb and flow of amusement, scorn, interest or hostility experienced as it proceeds. Selection and emphasis tend to replace the dynamism of the theatre with the static quality of a blackboard diagram.

Nevertheless, even if analysing formal and linguistic aspects of Aristophanes' art leads to some temporary distortion, it will at least have shown that this writer of comedy, no less than 'serious' poets, is a master of many voices who shows his skill, as he himself claimed, by presenting new ideas (and novel stage-pictures) all the time.[30]

Notes

1. Perhaps the best-known instance of expository dialogue is that which opens S.'s *Antigone*.

2. There is a touch of the 'traveller's tale' in these lines too, with their mention of local customs and features.

3. The range of meaning of *alazon* cannot be conveyed by a single English word: an *alazon* is not sincere or straightforward; he may well be charlatan or braggart, always with an eye to his own advantage. This envoy's modern counterpart complains to his unemployed acquaintance about the expense-account lunches he is forced to consume.

4. D. Bain, *Actor and Audience* (Oxford 1977), 87-99 and see D. Mastronarde, *Contact and Discontinuity* (Berkeley and Los Angeles, 1979).

5. *Acharnians* contains indications that there will be an agon between Dicaeopolis and the war party but these remain unfulfilled since neither the Acharnians nor Lamachus is given an opportunity to make a case in due form.

6. See on *Ach.* 1097-142 *BICS* 26 (1979), 95-8.

7. In Lamachus Homeric touches are superimposed on the democratically elected general.

8. *Clouds* 1-262, cf. S. *King Oedipus* 1-150.

9. For doorkeepers cf. *Ach.* 393 f, *Peace* 180 f, *Frogs* 460 f, Plato, *Protagoras* 314c9-e4. These scenes are discussed by A.P. Burnett, *Catastrophe Survived* (Oxford, 1971), 81.

10. See G. Brumbaugh *YCS* 22 (1972), 213-21.

11. The allusion is to the elongated shape of the island. The Athenians under Pericles had suppressed a Euboean revolt some 20 years earlier.

12. For Strepsiades' literal mind see L. Woodbury *Phoenix* 34 (1980), 108-27; see also P. Green *GRBS* 20 (1979), 15-25.

13. See below, p. 180 f, and cf. the scene between Dicaeopolis and Lamachus (*Ach.* 582-92).

14. One of the best examples in tragedy occurs in E.'s *Bacchae* when Dionysus wrests the initiative from King Pentheus, e.g. at 810.

15. An allusion to the campaign waged successfully at Pylos the previous year. Demosthenes' claim to have achieved the victory for Athens was denied by Cleon.

16. On the characterisation of Nicias and Demosthenes see Sommerstein's introduction to his edition, 3. On the stylistic characterisation of Nicias' speeches in Thucydides see D.P. Tompkins, *YCS* 22 (1972), 181-214.

17. In the first agon the keynote is 'shamelessness' (277, 322, 383, 385, 397, 409, 638). One may contrast the commendation of *sophrosyne* by the Better Argument in *Clouds* (961-1023).

18. See above, p. 37 ff.

19. See above, p. 62 ff.

20. In passages like this, play on the two meanings of demos is freer when heard than when seen on the page: you can't (usually) hear capital letters.

21. Cleon's self-confidence and resilience make his fall the more effective. One may recall the Oedipus of the early scenes of *King Oedipus*.

22. Oracular utterances were transmitted in dactylic hexameters, the metre of epic, which stand out from the surrounding single-short iambic verse. My translation of 1086-9 is an attempt to convey the rhythm as well as the manner of the pseudo-oracle.

23. This lyric dialogue (1111-50) is discussed below, p. 101 f.

24. Pylos: see above, n. 15. In my translation of this section I put accuracy second to showing the presence of a pun in the original.

25. For imagery from cooking see Taillardat 348 f.

26. Athene is regularly represented as a warrior with a shield, here replaced by a pot. The lines also recall a passage of Solon (fr. 4): see Sommerstein's note.

27. References to the audience by a character near the end of the play are uncommon: *Knights* presumably stirred partisan feelings in the supporters and opponents of Cleon.

28. e.g. Paphlagon and Aeschylus share forcefulness, Sausage-seller and Euripides dexterity.

29. *Acharnians* has a great deal of visual interest throughout, in dress as well as in action and movement; it also contains scenes for strongly contrasted characters, e.g. Euripides and Dicaeopolis.

30. The expression *kainas ideas* ('new ideas', *Clouds* 547) probably indicates the importance Ar. attached to visual inventiveness.

5 ARISTOPHANES THE MYTH-MAKER

I too will something make
And joy in the making
   (R. Bridges)

These are fascinations of the fabulist's art, these lurking forces of expansion, these necessities of upspringing in the seed.
   (H. James, Preface to *The Portrait of a Lady*)

In modern usage one of the meanings of the word 'myth' is 'a traditional tale which conveys a deeper truth or meaning': in ancient Greek the word *muthos* conveyed, amongst other things, 'story' and 'plot'. My chapter-heading labels Aristophanes as it does because of the range of meanings that can be suggested: it is intended as a kind of pun. An Aristophanic comedy tells a story invented by the dramatist, a story which has to be shaped into a kind of plot in order to be staged, a story which owes some of its shape, and often some of its incidents, to traditional tales, and finally a story whose significance goes deeper than the mere narrative outline would indicate. It is necessary to explain here why I wrote 'a kind of plot' and not just 'plot'. Because of what Aristotle had to say about plot in the *Poetics* and because of the way comedy developed in the centuries after Aristophanes, most people expect a comic plot to display features which are not present in the plays we are studying. As a result I use the term very sparingly when talking about Old Comedy, not wishing to suggest that the structure of the plays resembles that of their successors. If one takes farce as the terminus of the important, elaborate, artificial plot, then Old Comedy must stand very near the beginning of the line, since much of the substance of the action is not engendered by the requirements of the plot. (Therefore it is usually inappropriate to castigate Aristophanes for the weakness of his plots.) I use 'plot' in the present context to refer to the result of the process of turning a story into drama, that is into a series of scenes written for actors to play, not to imply the presence of a complicated substructure of conflicting aims and interests, intrigues, deceptions and chance events involving a number of persons.

The picture of the audience as ears and eyes which I gave in the previous chapter enabled me to underline one aspect of the comic dramatist's craft, the provision of visual and aural variety during the course of the play. I saw the poet as concerned with the play as process, not product, bearing in mind that in the theatre drama is an experience in time: it is not until after its completion that the spectator can regard it as a whole. The play once over, if the spectator goes beyond the expression of approval or disapproval and of personal likes and dislikes, he will probably describe it in terms of story, character or theme rather than structure. Let us suppose, for example, a man returning from the theatre after a performance of *Wasps*: a housebound relative enquires about the play. What will he be told? That the parabasis came rather late in the action? Or that the chief character was an old man crazy about serving on juries? Or that the theme was the misuse of power by demagogues? If, however, the respondent were himself a professional writer talking to dramatists, it is very likely that his answers would develop on rather different lines. Listening to him one might become aware of the connections between story and character or between story and theme, that is of the structure of the whole in the broadest sense. The playwright might be able to suggest reasons for approaching the political issue via conflict between father and son or for including a mock trial or for the course taken by events in the latter part of the play. In this chapter I shall be concerned with structural elements in the comedies and with the ways in which they are combined, attempting to discover the problems facing the playwright as well as to assess the end-product, the play which is not experienced in the theatre moment by moment but is recalled in the memory or studied from the text.[1]

Just as Greek poets could convey their understanding of the forward movement and continuity of a poem through the image of the 'path of song', so they could express their sense of the splendour and perfection of the whole by likening it to a building, seen and admired from afar because of its grandeur and magnificence.[2] At the beginning of this book I used a related metaphor in order to make the distinction between the building materials used by the writer, his working drawings and the finished edifice. We have now looked at some of the materials (different modes of discourse, different types of scene, variation in style and tone) and at one or two of the constraints on their placing in the structure; what remains is to examine the whole and to examine it from more than one viewpoint.

It would, I believe, be unhelpful to abandon the chronological framework altogether, so I shall continue to treat *Acharnians* first and shall also for the most part discuss elements of the individual plays in the order in which they are placed before the spectator. Moreover one of my subjects, narrative, of necessity emphasises continuity, awareness of time and the creation of a sense of expectancy.

Acharnians

'I envy you for the excellence of your planning and even more for the excellence of the feast you are preparing.' The compliment paid by the chorus to Dicaeopolis may well be applied to Aristophanes' art by all admirers of this marvellously organised and bountiful play (1008-10). *Acharnians* begins with a man who remains in Athens against his will, longing to return to his home in the country. It continues with the return to Athens of an envoy whose stay abroad has been selfishly prolonged, but who does not come back without visible results of his mission.[3] When Dicaeopolis, impatient with the delay in discussing peace, decides in the midst of the meeting of the Assembly to make a private treaty with Sparta, he does not go himself but sends an intermediary, Amphitheus. This negotiator, who departs from Athens just after the envoy and his train have been invited into the Prytaneum for the official reception (130), returns to Athens with the visible results of his journey as soon as Dicaeopolis has brought the meeting to an abrupt close (175). During his absence the Assembly had received the report of a second official envoy, just back from Thrace. There are two ways in which Amphitheus acts as a link (in addition to his actually bringing about some degree of contact between two states at war). In Greek drama a new stage in the dramatic action is often initiated by the return of an emissary dispatched in the previous scene: here Amphitheus' departure results from the hero's dissatisfaction with the workings of officialdom and his decision to 'go it alone', while his return, with the peace-wine, makes the beginning of the demonstration both of the blessings of peace and of the

Acharnians' opposition to it. Thus from the structural point of view Amphitheus' return acts as a kind of pendant to the Assembly scene in which the return of envoys to Athens is the major organisational factor, and by its positioning the contrast between the posturing and doubtful benefits of official embassies and the real achievement of the private negotiation is emphasised. Moreover, there is a second contrast between protracted journeys followed by lengthy reports on the one hand and on the other the swift economy with which the comic hero's plan is effected.

I shall come back a little later to the importance of contrast as a linking device in this comedy. Meanwhile something needs to be said here about the story element in *Acharnians*, although, or even because, it is less substantial than in *Wasps* and *Frogs*. The germ of this story, as of so many others, is the quest. Dicaeopolis' sufferings result from the absence of peace. Peace must be acquired. If one were writing an epic or novel based on Dicaeopolis' peace campaign, one would surely wish to include an account of the hero's journey to Sparta, of the difficulties of engaging in negotiations with Athens' enemies and of the dangers he faced from such as the patriotic charcoal-burners. In short, Dicaeopolis himself would be at the centre of this part of the story and the consequent expansion of this section would inevitably be accompanied by changes in the Assembly scene designed to give less space to reporting the official envoys' doings and also to present them only as a means of showing the hero's state of mind and explaining why he took action. In other words both content and point of view would be markedly different. Two observations may be made here. It does not matter much if the solitary reader is angered by material he finds offensive, but if many of the spectators in the Theatre of Dionysus were outraged by the presentation of negotiations at Sparta the consequences for a competing dramatist could have been grave. It is prudential considerations in fact which dictate some of the play's silences. Just as it would not suit Aristophanes' purpose to give an opportunity for a proponent of continued war to voice his opinions, so here it is best for him to avoid inflaming the more bellicose among the spectators.[4] Secondly, the unrealistic compression of this episode gives prominence, as well as space, to the subsequent illustration of the principal's achievements. The story does not lack growing-points: instead the shoots are rubbed out before they can develop.

In those cases where the dramatic action closely follows the shape of a narrative, causation and chronological ordering are prominent and in addition there is no possibility of altering the sequence of deeds and events. The opening scenes of our play are in fact governed, although not constricted, by the logic of the story: longing for peace leads to efforts to obtain it; when the first attempt fails, an alternative is tried, and so on. But what dictates the events and the order of events after the wine of peace has been acquired? Why does the peacemaker celebrate the Country Dionysia before he sets up his market? Look for reasons for the inclusion of scenes (and for their arrangement) in the second half of the play and the lack of narrative compulsion will be obvious. True, it is not entirely absent: to give a minor example, feasting comes late in the play, in its traditional place, partly because the ingredients for the meal were obtained by Dicaeopolis' success as a trader.[5] In the first part of the play, although the quest is complete when Dicaeopolis receives the peace-wine, a feeling of suspense and continuing forward movement is created by the Acharnians' hostility. Normally, in a quest, the hero faces opposition during the course of his journey and has to overcome it in order to obtain the prize: the dragon must be killed, Cerberus given his sop. Here, in this play, the hero is attacked for what he has already done and his defence takes up all that remains of the first part of the play.[6] Thus, although there is little sign of story-telling for its own sake, a means has been found of maintaining the spectators' curiosity about the result of the dispute. Nevertheless the organisation of the material into certain scenes in a particular order is governed by other, non-narrative considerations.

Let us suppose for the moment that we were dealing, not with a play, but with a speech on the advantages of peace. Undoubtedly the orator would mention the ability to enjoy all those things and situations of which the war had deprived his hearers, for example, prosperity, freedom of movement, cessation of military service. Very likely he would strengthen his case by demolishing the arguments of the war party. If I try to sketch a framework for a speech on these lines, I can produce something very like the outline of the relevant sections of *Acharnians*. 'Chief among the blessings of peace is the freedom to celebrate once again, with our wives and families, the country festival so important to farmers . . . And how good to enjoy once more the delicacies that used to come to our city from all parts of Greece . . .' And so on.

Just as Euripides' *Trojan Women* was to display the pity of war by showing the suffering variously undergone by individual members of Priam's family as well as by the mass of Trojan women, so *Acharnians* illustrates the joys experienced by the one man who dared make peace. And his success is complete when others show that they have learned from his example. In their second song of congratulation to the successful trader the chorus point to the heap of feathers outside his door as 'evidence of his way of life'. The short phrase they use, *deigma tou biou*, may be taken as conveying the essence of the play: Dicaeopolis' life provides a pattern and an example for all to follow.[7]

The song in which these words occur is as memorable for its endearing comic earnestness as it is for the vigour of its images (971-99).[8] In it the chorus express their resolve never again to admit War into their homes but rather to unite themselves to the principle of reconciliation and productivity. Although it would be a pleasure to linger over the details of the portrait of War, the drunken comast, the intruder who bursts into a house enjoying tranquil festivity, it is the summary and linking functions of this song which are relevant here. The chorus, formerly hostile to the enemy, not least because of the destruction of their own vines, now understand that it is War who invades their homes, setting fire to their stores of vine-props and spilling wine out of the – vines (987). The terms of peace had much earlier been represented as samples of wine (186-200): now war's devastation is cleverly shown affecting both the cultivation of the land and the security of life in the home. In the second stanza the chorus turn from affirmation to prayer. Where once they had referred pessimistically to the powerless vulnerability of the old, now they look forward to renewed sexual vigour and to planting crops for the future: 'O Reconciliation . . . would that an Eros . . . would unite you and me. Perhaps you think I'm a bit too old? Well, I guess I could still do three things with you.'[9] And in the remaining lines, beneath the description of planting vines, figs and olives, we perceive allusions to aspects of love-making (987-99). The fertility of the *oikos* and its land which now preoccupies the chorus had been the theme of Dicaeopolis' celebration of the country Dionysia (241-79) while their anticipation of festivity serves to introduce the chief concern of the later scenes and is in fact immediately followed by the Herald's proclamation of the Pitcher Feast. Thus the ode strengthens the associations between various elements of the play.

The contrast made here between two powerful opposites, namely the god of War and Reconciliation, the associate of Aphrodite and the Graces, is too obvious to need stating, but because of the importance of this song it is a good starting-point for examining the well-planned use of contrast in the second part of the play. In the dramatic action the human counterpart of Polemos, the god of War, is Lamachus, the elected general who represents the official military policy of Athens; the counterpart of the goddess Reconciliation is, of course, Dicaeopolis. Thus the antithesis between male and female, destructiveness and fertility, which is prominent in the song, has to be replaced by other forms of contrast in the encounters between the two men. Lamachus is present in the play so that he may be defeated and rejected. His first entry, in response to the Acharnians' *böe*, their cry for help, shows him in the panoply of a Homeric hero (566). Stripped of this, he still tries to stand on his dignity, but is completely discredited in the eyes of the chorus when Dicaeopolis says that *he* is 'a decent citizen, no Mr Placehunter, but ever since the war began a Mr Combatant; while *you*, ever since the war began you've been a Mr Wellpaidpost!' (595-7, trs. Sommerstein.)[10] Dicaeopolis has used Lamachus' self-seeking to clinch his own argument against continuing the war: now, as the first part of the play reaches its end, he can set up a market open to everyone else 'but not to Lamachus' (625). In the course of the drama the hero initiates peace, directs and celebrates a festival, speaks persuasively to his opponents (and Euripides), runs a successful market, takes charge of preparations for a banquet and finally wins first prize at the Pitcher Feast. How narrow, by contrast, the role of Lamachus, and how negative! Lamachus' first entry was used to begin the final stage in the Persuasion of the Acharnians (566-622); his second intervention, when he sends his slave to buy expensive delicacies to take to the Pitcher Feast, marks the conclusion of Dicaeopolis' successful trading, and so the refusal to do business with the military commander immediately precedes the Acharnians' rejection of all he stands for: 'Never will I receive the God of War into a house of mine' (979).

It is not until the final section of the play that the contrast

between the two men is fully and generously embodied in action.
In what amounts to an Aristophanic comedy in miniature,
Lamachus' failure and Dicaeopolis' triumph are set out in
parallel. The method the dramatist chose to bring out his
antithesis may be likened to that employed in a piece of
counterpoint, where two themes, announced and developed in
turn, eventually come together and it is made apparent that the
second is actually a variant on the first. So here each man first
receives a summons from a messenger: Lamachus, ordered to
deal with a threatened hostile incursion, begins his preparations
for the campaign; Dicaeopolis, told to hurry to the feast,
performs a series of actions which both mimic those of his
opposite and equip him for his own undertaking (1096-1142).[11]
Then the chorus, as if beginning a complete parabasis, send them
on their different ways, foretelling hardships for one but for the
other the delights of drinking and the services of a pretty girl. At
the end of the accompanying song, which sketches Antimachus'
mishaps, a messenger appears, as in a tragedy, and describes the
mishaps suffered by Lamachus. At this point symmetry returns,
with the entry of the wounded general closely followed by that of
the happy Dicaeopolis. For the third and last time Dicaeopolis
demonstrates the power of ridicule to defeat and diminish those
with pretensions to greatness and rank. His chosen method points
up the wider contrasts that have now been established: on the
one side peace, enjoyment of life's pleasures, acclaim, prosperity,
optimism, achievement based on a combination of persuasiveness
and ridicule typically comic; on the other military defeat, loss of
face, injury, helplessness, isolation, in short all that would make
a Homeric or tragic hero pitiful. But Lamachus' deeds and
sufferings, his stumblings, sprained ankle and sore head, fall far
short of heroic grandeur so that the messenger's sad narrative
and still more the songs of lamentation the vanquished warrior
himself delivers as he limps in utilise the heightened emotion and
the intensity of tragedy to cut the victim down to size and to
clarify the real virtues of comedy. Lamachus returns, not only
without spoils, but even without his helmet-feather; to the comic
hero, however, 'all good things come of their own accord' (976).

Knights

'And they all lived happily ever after.' The creation, in the last part of *Acharnians* and of other comedies, of an atmosphere of rejoicing which extends from stage to auditorium is very persuasive. Although we know that Dicaeopolis' successful new life is in part fantastic, in part exaggerated, we accept the happy ending.[12] There seem to be three elements in our acceptance. On the level of principle we have been brought to understand that peace is preferable to war. Secondly, the action and particularly Dicaeopolis' role in the action have been designed to call forth the kind of response accorded to the hero of a tale. Finally, the thoroughgoing conversion of the chorus dispels any feeling that we might be giving our support to a solitary eccentric. Shared rejoicing assures us of the propriety of the outcome so that we too may affirm, with the poet, 'Right and justice will be on my side' (661-2). Shared happiness at the success of one party and amusement at the discomfiture of the other is the proper end of comedy, we feel. But is it? Of all comedies?

Knights is organised round a simple idea, the struggle for supremacy fought out between a would-be usurper and the holder of power. The comedy acquires its length, and perhaps its interest, chiefly from the prolongation of this struggle into a series of separate bouts or rounds. What is the narrative framework into which this battle is set? Let me state it in terms of folk-tale. 'Once upon a time there was an old man who had entrusted his affairs to a wicked, avaricious steward. The old man still had two loyal servants, who, reduced to desperation by the wicked steward's evil ways, sought to remove him from office, for the good of the whole house . . .' If the story is to have a happy ending, the steward must be replaced by a man of integrity and the master must exercise proper vigilance in future. In order to achieve this result the good servants, at some risk to themselves, will seek a champion to rescue all those oppressed by the villain, who they suspect will one day depose their master. The themes are power, usurpation, revenge, rescue.

At this point I must introduce a factor unsuited to a folk-tale. The rescuer in *Knights* is not a man of integrity at all: he is chosen because he is a rogue. How does this come about? By some novel comic device? Not exactly. In order to produce this surprising turn in events the dramatist borrows another traditional motif from the story-teller's repertoire, the predictions of an oracle. The advantages are twofold. Having heard the prophetic utterance, an audience will want to know when and how it will be fulfilled. At the same time, since in everyday life belief in oracles was far from absolute, the comic poet can make fun of the gullible and of those who exploit superstitions and credulity. To the functions of oracles in *Knights* I shall soon return.

Meanwhile, to begin to relate the narrative elements to the actual play: in the prologue both the initial problem (the suffering of the bullied slaves) and its solution are propounded; in addition we come to realise that the story does not only concern the members of a household but must also be applied to the *oikos* writ large, namely the Athenian *polis*. I originally presented the germ of the story as it might appear in a folk-tale; with slight adjustments I could have made it into a story of a king whose loyal ministers discern a threat to his power. In our play the figure who in days of old, or in more elevated genres, would have been king is Demos, the Athenian people. Head of the household, on one level, he also represents the way the people think and act 'when seated on the Pnyx'. His ministers, the loyal slaves, are two of the elected generals; his steward, Paphlagon, is also a demagogic politician, by origin a trader. Thus our attention is directed almost equally to *oikos* and to *polis* as we try to decode the play, but in addition, and largely because Demos acts the king or tyrant, we are reminded of the distant legendary world of kings and courtiers. In the present world, that of the so-called democracy, as presented in this comedy, the terms of heroic combat are inverted: no longer do we have a duel between the 'best', for now bad must be replaced, not by better, but by worse, in continuous, regular, inevitable descent. Can such a play have a happy ending?

At the conclusion of the prologue, however, our minds are fixed on the forthcoming struggle: will Paphlagon, as the oracle predicts, be worsted by the vendor of cooked meats, one demagogue replaced by another, even more shameless? By now the two slaves have revealed a certain amount about themselves, and a good deal more, deliberately and explicitly, about their effective master, Paphlagon, and also about their nominal master, Demos. There is little more for them to do. Soon their function of opposing the bullying steward-cum-demagogue will be inherited by the Knights who form the chorus and by their protégé, Sausage-seller. It is the arrival of the Knights which most clearly removes the action from the *oikos* to the *polis*.

Nevertheless the slaves have by now so clearly established the *oikos* as the setting of the drama that the fictional household remains in the mind more vividly and forcibly than it would as merely an analogue of the city-state. As an *oikos*, however, it is not quite typical because it lacks wife and children. If the king had a son, a son like Haemon in Sophocles' *Antigone*, there might be a present adviser and helper as well as hope for the future.[13] Worse, the master of this sterile *oikos*, already irritable and deaf, seems likely to decline into complete senility. The future is unpromising. Another strange feature of this *oikos* is the presence in it of a man who is primarily a trader: surely bargaining, sharp practice, money-making, familiarity with the ways of the Agora are disadvantages in a steward who is given charge of the wealth and property belonging to the *oikos*? What is Paphlagon then, steward or intruder?

Thus in addition to our three spheres of action, the *oikos*, the *polis* and the mythical palace, we have also as an intrinsic feature of the tale the notion of succession, of change (for the worse), manifested in the replacement of one man by another as well as in Demos' decline from manly vigour and good sense. The city too had experienced change, first from monarchy to democracy and then in the nature of the democracy itself: in Thucydides' words there came what was 'in name democracy but in practice rule by the first citizen', Pericles. And after Pericles his successors, 'eager for individual supremacy, surrendered the management of affairs to the demos, in an effort to gratify them. And from this . . . there resulted many errors and failures' (Thuc. 2. 65. 9-11).

'O Demos, your power is glorious, seeing that all men fear you as they would a tyrant. Yet you are easy to sway and delight in accepting flattery and deceit. You gawp at whoever is speaking, your mental faculties absent on holiday' (*Knights* 1111-20). This is the comment made much later in the play, when Demos has volunteered to submit himself to the victorious demagogue for 're-education' and has promised to hand over 'the reins of the Pnyx' to whichever of them will provide him with the nicest food (1098 f, 1108 f). Demos rejects the chorus' criticism with the rejoinder:

It's your mental faculties that are missing, seeing that you suppose me to lack sense. I act stupid deliberately. It gratifies me to behave like a baby and cry for what I need. And I want to have a thief in my household, for protection. When he's taken all he wants, I drop him from a great height'. (1121-30)

With these words Demos, Thepeople, condemns the demos, the people of Athens: I write 'condemns', and not 'defends' or 'exculpates' advisedly, since the initial claim to good sense is not supported by what follows. In the circumstances there is little that the old man could credibly and naturally say to excuse his folly, yet it is necessary that there should be some reply to the Knights' candid censure of his tyrannical ways, censure which epitomises the play's main issue.

When the old man has actually handed himself over to the victor, who promises to look after him well (1259-61), another mythical motif is introduced, that of rejuvenation achieved by magical means. The youthening of Demos is carried out with the utmost brevity, in effect through the use, by Sausage-seller, of the single word 'boil': 'By boiling down Demos for you I've made him attractive and reputable,' he says, when explaining to the Knights why he is calling for celebrations (1321). The story of Medea, who gave new youth to her father-in-law by boiling him in a cauldron along with some magic herbs, was so familiar that no more explanation is required.[14] Just as Medea was employing her special knowledge and skill, so was Demos' new tutor, the man who had been producing a variety of cooked meats all his adult life (1241 f). The Knights reply to Sausage-seller's astounding claim not, as might be expected, with a request for details of the process of transformation, but with the question, 'Where is he now?' The answer is significant, since it shows that the real purpose of the rejuvenation of Demos was to reject the present in favour of the past: 'The city in which he lives is the old Athens, the violet-crowned' (1323). 'What is his nature now?'[15] 'As it was in the olden days when his associates were Aristides and Miltiades.' Demos has returned to the Athens of his 'youth' but he is not permitted to forget what he did in his old age. His re-education requires consciousness of his senile failings and this Sausage-seller brings about by giving examples of his foolish susceptibility to flattery. When the pupil is properly repentant, like a tragic hero who has recognised his former madness or folly, he is comforted by the observation that the blame should rest on the deceivers, the unscrupulous politicians, rather than on the deceived. Finally he is encouraged to outline his own improved policy for the future. In return Demos receives, in the form of two beautiful girls, a 30-year peace-treaty, while Sausage-seller is rewarded by an invitation to dine in the Prytaneum (1337-1405). It seems that no happy future can be envisaged without first returning to the past. Reminded of the glory and of the values of the old Athens, when the democracy was young, men may be able to act with integrity once more. Yet only in myth and in the theatre can the present be simply exchanged for the past and instantaneous happiness be achieved: only through the 'willing suspension of disbelief' does *Knights* attain anything like a happy ending.

I have tried to show that the dramatist avails himself of myth in different ways and for different purposes in creating the framework for this play. Near the end a mythical motif, linked to one of the play's vulgar concerns, food and cooking, opens a door to fantasy and the restoration of values lost in the democracy's senescence, while the establishment of situation and setting at the beginning of the play depended on the existence of a traditional story-pattern. Because *Knights* has to be interpreted simultaneously as the story of the old householder and as an indictment of the failings of the people in assembly, any device which links the two aspects will be useful. The oracle is such a device. Furthermore, in the linear development of the play also, particularly as regards Paphlagon, the oracle is structurally important.

At the opening of the comedy, when describing Paphlagon's efforts to ingratiate himself with his master, the slave says: 'He chants oracles and the old chap longs to act the Sibyl.' After this it is not surprising to learn a little later that Paphlagon owns a private hoard of oracles: the two slaves, overwhelmed by their troubles, have turned to wine for inspiration, stealing it from Paphlagon, who, like Polyphemus, is in a drunken sleep. One theft inspires another, and the reason for Paphlagon's vigilant custody of his hoard becomes apparent: it contains an oracle predicting the manner of his own downfall (108-27). The text of the prophecy at this stage seems to consist of a list of vendors of different kinds of merchandise, of whom Paphlagon is the third in line of succession: he is destined, it is said, to be expelled by one whose trade is even less dignified, a vendor of cooked meats (143). And, talk of the devil, who should now come on the scene but a sausage-seller, to be hailed as Saviour of the City (149)?[16]

Some time later Sausage-seller enquires what the oracle says and receives the following reply:

> Nay, but if once the Eagle, the black tanned mandible-curver,
> Seize with his beak the serpent, the dullard, the drinker of life-blood,
> Then shall the sharp sour brine of the Paphlagon-tribe be extinguished,
> Then to the entrail-sellers shall God great glory and honour
> Render, unless they elect to continue the sale of the sausage.
>
> (195-201, trs. Rogers)

Having heard these 'complicated and puzzling' phrases, not unnaturally Sausage-seller seeks elucidation and thus gives the slave the chance to interpret and expound as he will. By this time the slipperiness of oracles has been well illustrated. First there was a paraphrase of the oracle's message, then part of it was quoted, now this part has been explained (202-10): the possessor of an oracle, and of quick wits, can exploit them as the situation requires.[17] In *Knights* the oracle concerning Paphlagon comes true: it comes true because Paphlagon is unaware that it has been stolen from him and because the slaves (men, not destiny, chance or the gods) contrive matters to lead to its fulfilment.

In *Lysistrata* the heroine, faced with insubordination from the women soldiers she commands, and after the failure of other efforts to persuade them to return to the Acropolis, finally has recourse to declaiming a convenient and suitably ambiguous oracle. All opposition ends when she says, 'We shall be disgraced, dearest women, if we do not obey the oracle' (*Lys.* 765-80). Similarly in *Knights*, Paphlagon initiates the contest of oracles only as a last resort. When, at the conclusion of the second agon, he is told by Demos to surrender the ring which is his token of stewardship, he does so with the ominous words, 'Be sure that another will appear more villainous than I' (948-50). Little does he know . . . However, before Demos can appoint Sausage-seller steward, Paphlagon tries one more ploy: 'Not yet, please, master, not before you've listened to my oracles.' 'Mine too,' Sausage-seller instantly adds (960 f).

A choral song in which the Knights joyfully anticipate Cleon's downfall (using for once the real name of the demagogue, not his pseudonym) covers the time the pair need to fetch the chests full of oracles each contestant claims to have at his disposal, on every subject under the sun (1006, 1010). Demos is eager to hear his own favourite, the oracle which promises that he will be 'an eagle in the clouds' (1013), but for that he has to wait some time, the intervening period filled with the recital and exegesis of numerous oracles ascribed by Paphlagon to Bacis and by Sausage-seller to Glanis, a source whom he has invented.[18] The exchange of oracles demonstrates not only the typical vocabulary and mode of expression of these prophetic utterances but also, and more importantly, the ways in which rival interpretations can be used unscrupulously by opportunist politicians who have a gullible or superstitious audience.

Once again, for the last time, Paphlagon has recourse to an oracle. When Demos, who has now realised the extent of his former steward's thefts, is about to deprive him of his garland, Paphlagon says, 'Not yet. I have a Pythian oracle declaring who is to defeat me.' 'Yes,' Sausage-seller replies, 'it gives *my* name, no shadow of a doubt' (1229-31). Now Paphlagon tests Sausage-seller's assertion by a series of questions whose answers increase his reluctant certainty that the oracle is being fulfilled in every particular (1232-48).

This short passage effects the recognition of his destined successor by the unwilling Paphlagon. The point-by-point testing of the truth of the oracle also accomplishes one kind of tragic anagnorisis, that in which identification is brought about by a series of questions whose answers could be known only by the two persons concerned. In tragedy such a recognition often prefaces a complete and disturbing change of fortune. So here. The stubborn hero, to elevate Paphlagon to Sophoclean status, acknowledges and laments his downfall and bids a sorrowful farewell to his garland. Such are his 'dying words'. He says no more (1248-52).[19]

The little scene marvellously juxtaposes the tragic and the everyday. Paphlagon's questions and comments are as close to the tragic as their content permits: the man originally described by the oracle as the noisy predator with a voice like a torrent in full spate (136), whose dependence on vulgar threats and loud abuse has been illustrated all through the play, undergoes not only a change of fortune but also a linguistic transformation. Sausage-seller's answers, by contrast, offered in an unsuspecting, matter-of-fact way, refer to his learning and practising the trade of vendor of cooked meats, to his thefts, cheating and effrontery, even to his prostituting himself. In all innocence he is playing a scene from everyday life in company with a man who has left everyday life for the tragic stage. And meanwhile the author is reminding the theatre-goer that tragic poets, like politicians, can exploit oracles!

The irony of the tyrant's fall, an irony which depends on the complicity of the audience as well as of the parties to his ruin, is much more pointed because of the resemblance to tragedy. It is fitting, therefore, that a story which has been given a tragic shape by the use of the oracle should end in a scene from tragedy. Moreover, although Cleon's expulsion is Sausage-seller's rise to power and the end to which the action of the play has been directed, a flavour of tragedy is not inappropriate given that neither the new demagogue nor the new Demos seems likely to act with wisdom or integrity.

Frogs

In *Frogs* the story element, as the seed from which everything else springs up, is all-important: story and play are coextensive. Yet the story, apparently a simple tale of quest and conflict, is seen to be problematic as soon as attempts to evaluate or analyse *Frogs* begin. In what follows, the two constituents, quest and conflict, will be explored.[20]

While conversing with his half-brother, Heracles, the god Dionysus recollects the moment when, as he was reading *Andromeda*, a longing for Euripides came over him, a longing so intense that he now feels impelled to go down to Hades, 'or even lower', to bring back the poet. Euripides is dead. Dionysus misses him and wants him back. That, in simple human terms, is the motivation for the quest. Once the beloved is restored, the sense of loss will vanish and all will be well. (What I have just said is true, but it is not the whole truth: other versions must be added.)

Early in their conversation Heracles had asked the reason for Dionysus' peculiar costume (45-8), a question not finally and completely answered until much later (108 f). The bantering tone of this and subsequent questions helps to hide the expository function of these lines under a cloak of teasing humour, as when Heracles asks his visitor about the size and nature of the longing he has just mentioned and it emerges that Dionysus wants neither a woman nor a boy nor a man but the dead Euripides, and that he wants him as much as the gluttonous Heracles wants soup (53-67). In the context Dionysus' longing can be interpreted as a sexual aberration, in keeping with his oddity in dress. In this version the motive for the quest is erotic: where Demeter had felt the compulsion of maternal love in her search for Persephone, and Orpheus that of affectionate desire for his wife Eurydice, the comic counterpart is less conventional. But, whatever the nature of Dionysus' longing, it will be satisfied by the mere fact of the beloved's return.

Later in the scene Dionysus offers a different account of the motivation for his quest for Euripides: 'I need a good poet. The good ones are dead and the living bad' (71 f). This is not the voice of the bereaved lover: is it the god of drama speaking, or the theatre-goer who will never again see a new play by Euripides? At any rate, needing a poet is by no means the same as longing for the dear departed. After some comments on the deficiencies of living poets, Dionysus gives a further reason for his choice of Euripides: 'Because he's got no scruples Euripides wouldn't mind trying to escape' (80 f). The question of the tragedian's moral character is to be important later in the play: here the remark is significant as suggesting, not the heroic quest, but an escapade somewhat on the lines of the abduction attempted by the legendary Theseus (to whom there will soon be a reference).[21] Again some lines about living poets intervene which Dionysus concludes by saying that none of them is really 'creative' (*gonimos*), none can produce a 'truly noble phrase' of the kind he's crazy about (96-103). Here Euripides' distinctive quality is neither his dramaturgy nor his lack of scruple but his capacity to produce original and striking sayings (or, in Heracles' view, 'garbage'). No more will be said about the purpose of Dionysus' journey until almost the end of the play (1414) and no more about Euripides until the second prologue (758), soon to be analysed. What features of the quest have so far been suggested? Chiefly that on this occasion it is motivated by desire or need and not imposed by some external authority: unlike Heracles, Dionysus has no taskmaster.[22] There has also been a suggestion that leaving the realm of the dead is audacious; apart from that nothing has been said about the difficulties and dangers associated with quests, especially in the final stage when resistance must be overcome.

In the preceding paragraphs Heracles has been depicted as fulfilling a role in the expository process by asking questions which show his surprised amusement at what he sees and hears. A second look at the scene will reveal other aspects. Dionysus has cast Heracles in the roles of Helper and model. It is the arrival of the god of drama wearing a lion-skin on top of his saffron robe and carrying a club that provokes Heracles' first question: eventually it appears that Dionysus regards himself as adequately disguised for his purpose of re-enacting Heracles' Descent and that he has come to consult the person who knows most about travel underground (108-15).[23] Heracles had traditionally employed his strength and courage to help the oppressed: now it is his ability to offer practical advice based on his own experience that fits him to be Helper. Although Heracles the Helper does not appear again after the conclusion of this scene, he is in a sense present as model all through the first half of the play, a model frequently recalled but imperfectly copied. Dionysus, or rather the traveller who appears to be a hybrid between two immortals as disconcerting as Aeschylus' 'tawny cock-horse' (932), is in fact, whether he knows it or not, a coward, quite the reverse of his model. Viewed as an actor, the god of drama seems to have some difficulty in getting into the skin of his part.

The subject of misleading appearances, which is connected with the problem of establishing reliable criteria for making decisions, had been introduced in the first lines of *Frogs*, during the dialogue between Dionysus and the slave who shares his journey. The god thinks it wrong that he should walk while the slave is riding on a donkey 'so as not to be carrying the luggage'. 'So I'm not carrying the luggage?' 'You can't be carrying it when you're being carried' (23-5). How to decide whether the slave or the donkey is 'really' carrying the luggage? What are the criteria for such decisions? The simple joke, occurring amongst others just as childish, nevertheless foreshadows more serious questions later in the play, questions about choosing people, and plays, that are genuinely and provably good and valuable.

The shared journey will provide examples of these difficulties as material for humour, when the coward boasts of his courage or exchanges his identity at quite the wrong moment. While Dionysus is imperfectly playing Heracles, the comic poet is also engaged in an indirect form of mimesis, in attempting to represent on the stage material more tractable in a narrative mode and first treated in epic.[24] But where epic would have been expansive in its illustration of the hero's valour and endurance, the comedy most economically indicates Dionysus' cowardice: no sooner has he laid claim to pugnacity than he falls victim to imaginary fears; no sooner does Xanthias perceive his weakness than he exploits it for comic effect, pretending to see a monster.[25] At this Dionysus abandons both his roles and begs protection from his own priest seated in the front row of the theatre (283-97). Fortunately, as Heracles had foretold (143 f), after the monsters and criminals in Hades they are now to see 'sacred bands rejoicing in myrtle-groves'. In the remaining scenes, the journey over, Dionysus encounters people who have cause to remember Heracles' Catabasis and who believe that they see Heracles before them now; some of them are hostile while others seek to detain a welcome guest. First of all, in a scene which mirrors his visit to Heracles, Dionysus knocks on a door which is opened by Cerberus' keeper (464 f). Appalled by his abuse and threats, Dionysus persuades Xanthias to exchange identities with him. When Xanthias is greeted by a friendly girl, Persephone's servant, Dionysus naturally arranges a second exchange, only to be met by hostility from a woman defrauded by Heracles. A third exchange effected, Cerberus' keeper returns, intending to punish 'Heracles'. Xanthias rightly protests that he has never before visited Hades and nobly offers his 'slave' for torture, to prove the truth of his denial. A further complication is now introduced by Dionysus, who claims first that as an immortal he should be exempt from trial by torture and secondly that he is in fact not Heracles after all but Dionysus, son of Zeus. In the upshot both master and slave are whipped, until finally Cerberus' keeper, unable to distinguish which of them is divine, takes them to Persephone and Pluto who will be better able to recognise them for who they really are. And before long, in their parabasis sermon, the chorus of Initiates tell us to make use of the genuinely good, tried and tested citizens and not of worthless upstarts (721-6).

Having enjoyed the slapstick of this scene which is the climax of the first half of *Frogs* and having appreciated the contrast between coward and brave man, master and slave, god and mortal, self-image and reality which makes us laugh, we may not pause to wonder why, in fact, Dionysus dressed up, and particularly why his 'disguise' was incomplete. In earlier comedies disguise had been used in the hope that it would completely conceal the identity of the wearer, in order to enable him to travel incognito on a dangerous mission or to facilitate fraud; in most cases the character's disguise was assumed under the gaze of others and before the audience. The incongruity of Dionysus' appearance results from his combining the lion-skin and club which are Heracles' trademarks with the soft boots and the saffron robe which are his own.[26] Strangely enough, the question of his identity does not occur in the scene with Charon the ferryman and the Frogs: the latter, who actually mention their worship of Dionysus (215 f), address him only as 'meddler' (228) and the former calls him 'fat-belly' (200). When terrified by a monster, Dionysus craves anonymity (298-300). The residents of Hades, however, take him for Heracles, although the Hostess asserts that his soft boots are meant to disguise his identity (556-f)! When Dicaeopolis put on the dress of a beggar, he hoped to acquire simultaneously the beggar's insistent, wheedling persuasiveness, but Dionysus would be reluctant to admit that he stood in need of courage: perhaps for him the club and lion-skin were a talisman.

A moment's reflection would reveal to him the dangers of his undertaking: inevitably Heracles would have made enemies in Hades both because of his mission and because of his own immoderate nature. Not only had he stolen Cerberus but he had alienated those affronted by the gluttonous, thievish Heracles of satyr-play. In short, the dramatist has created in Dionysus a figure whose motives make sense but whose plans will not bear scrutiny: it made sense to consult Heracles but not to impersonate him. Acting Heracles is dangerous for all who lack Heracles' might and confidence, and his ability to brazen his way out of difficulties. If Dionysus has nothing to gain by his impersonation of Heracles, what, if anything, does the first half of *Frogs*, or indeed the whole play, gain from it? In order to answer this question let us imagine that Dionysus went on his journey without club and lion-skin; he could still hide timidly behind his more resolute companion when danger threatened, or even change places with him. The main loss would be the incongruity of cowardice combined with the Heraclean attributes. It seems as though making a new myth, the Descent of Dionysus, was insufficient: in addition to creating a mythological burlesque centred round a strange figure who was god of drama and son of Winejar (22) and who had a certain desire for adventure, there was a need also to enact an incomplete and sketchy drama which could perhaps be entitled 'Heracles revisits Hades'. As a result, Dionysus and Xanthias (who fulfils the role played in the Heracles legend by the god Hermes) become victims, as it were, of Heracles' reputation. Dionysus had made two decisions before the play began: one was to fetch Euripides, the other to dress up as Heracles; as a result of the second choice he leaves the stage at the mid-point of the comedy dressed as a slave and suffering the effects of the beating he has just received.[27] The chorus of Initiates, after one of the exchanges of dress, had offered the following observation on Dionysus' versatility, with an irony that does not become wholly apparent until the final reference to the notorious turncoat, Theramenes: 'The experienced voyager who has common sense will always change to the most favoured position and not stay fixed in one place like a graven image, adopting an unchanging appearance. Adroit people turn right round to find a comfortable place – people like Theramenes' (534-41).

Thus the difficulties encountered during the journey are not connected with the quest for Euripides as such. How will Dionysus behave if, as one would expect, the powers of Hades refuse to release the tragic poet? In the event this is not the problem with which he is faced: instead of taking the initiative in deed and word with the aim of restoring Euripides, as the play changes from its expected course his role alters so that he becomes in fact third actor, the part resentfully taken by Xanthias in the play's opening scene (87, 107, 115). For the new play there is provided a new prologue whose function is to introduce 'The contest of Aeschylus and Euripides'.

In this prologue, like the first, Xanthias is one of two players, his partner this time a fellow-slave (and his recent tormentor). Cerberus' keeper, well informed about events in Hades, explains to the newcomer the reason for the shouting and abuse he can hear: there is unrest among the dead because Euripides has laid claim to the throne of honour occupied until now by Aeschylus, as Grand Master of the art of tragedy.[28] He tells how, when

Euripides came down, he made speeches to all the riff-raff in Hades and 'they went really crazy about him' on hearing his rhetorical tricks; 'then he got above himself and laid claim to the throne where Aeschylus sat' (771-8). In response to popular demand there is to be a *krisis* to choose which of the two is superior, or if not a *krisis*, an *agon* or *elenchos* (785 f); we note that there is some uncertainty as to the proper terminology. In the course of this procedure, we learn, the art will be weighed and measured by various devices, since Euripides has declared his intention of testing the tragedies bit by bit (802).[29] As Xanthias guesses, Aeschylus' reaction to the proposal has been unfavourable: 'he glared like a bull, head lowered' (804).

Let us first look back at *Knights*. In both plays there is a usurper and someone who clings tenaciously to his position: unlike Sausage-seller, Euripides draws his support from the ordinary people, the demos, who encouraged his attempt on the throne; unlike Paphlagon, Aeschylus holds his power because he has been judged to deserve it and there is no question of his abusing his authority.[30] In the circumstances, therefore, he could well argue that there was no case for him to answer and that the agon had been wished on him. If in the end Euripides succeeds, he will 'reign' unless and until dispossessed by another (786-94). As we have seen, stories of this kind may have a happy outcome, if the usurper is a good man who replaces a tyrant, but tragic variations on the theme, such as Aeschylus' *Seven against Thebes*, where brother kills brother in a dispute over the throne, and *Prometheus Bound*, whose hero is condemned to long torments for infringing the prerogatives of Zeus, show the darker possibilities. It is interesting to conjecture what would have been the reaction to *Frogs* had Euripides, like his predecessor in *Knights*, ousted his adversary.

The use of the word agon in the second prologue, as well as hinting that there is a set debate to come, allows us to view the proceedings as a contest like those held at the Games between athletes or musical performers; this aspect is favoured by the presence of spectators and the appointment of an umpire.[31] It might have been expected that dramatic victories would be decided in Hades, as in Athens, by means of a vote, and this might have been the case, but for the lucky arrival of Dionysus. Xanthias had asked: 'Who (singular) will decide?' 'That was a matter for dispute because the two of them found there was a shortage of trained men' (805-6). So, unless the outcome of the competition is self-evident or one contestant admits defeat, the onus of deciding will be on Dionysus.

There is a third analogy to add to our list, one suggested by the word *elenchos* in particular: the contest is an adversarial debate or trial at the end of which the loser will stand condemned. The validity of this analogy is to some extent impaired by the use of a single judge rather than the large jury of most Athenian legal processes, but it is supported by some of the material of the formal debate, as well as by legal terms (908, 1006, 1016).[32] Moreover, there is no doubt that the introduction of Euripides as orator-politician or demagogue seeking and obtaining the favour of the mob, in contrast to the paucity of Aeschylus' supporters, gives the confrontation a political slant. Thus Aeschylus may be regarded as appealing to, and backed by, the aristocratic minority (and open to condemnation as 'élitist' in current usage), while his rival is popular with the uneducated masses. Thus, before the literary contest even begins, Cerberus' keeper has defined one poet in terms which condemn him. And indeed a survey of modern discussion of the agon and subsequent scenes shows that some scholars, whether consciously or not, have in fact read the contest as an account of the trial and condemnation of Euripides on charges of corrupting the people with his modernistic poetry and music and his decadent plays.

The idea that the two poets somehow represent opposing groups is linked with the final model suggested for the contest, that of single combat, that is, an attempt to decide an issue without full-scale battle. The warlike language of the choral odes with which the contest is prefaced and interspersed turns the setting into a field of battle and in some cases specifically indicates that a duel is envisaged (814-29).[33] Not only, of course, is the language warlike; it is frequently reminiscent of Homeric epic. One of the best-known instances of single combat occurs in Book Three of the *Iliad*, where Paris and Menelaus fight a duel to decide whether or not Helen should be restored to her husband. Before they fight, Greeks and Trojans offer a preliminary prayer to the gods, as do the poets and Dionysus in *Frogs* (885). In the case of Paris and Menelaus the outcome is inconclusive because Aphrodite removes Paris miraculously from the field of battle, whereupon Menelaus claims victory for the Greeks. Soon general fighting breaks out again (4.221). In

Aeschylus' *Seven Against Thebes*, the 'drama full of Ares' (*Frogs* 1021), a single combat was deadly: when Polyneices, with an army of Argive supporters, came to attack his native city, Thebes, whose throne his brother Eteocles would not relinquish to him as he had previously agreed, the issue was settled by single combat between seven warriors from each side. It is in the seventh and last duel that both Eteocles and Polyneices die. The throne of Thebes passes to Creon.[34]

During the formal debate Aeschylus propounds the values of the warrior and athlete, demonstrates their importance to Athens and places himself in the poetic line which descends from Homer and other great teachers. He charges Euripides with deliberately breaking away from inherited tradition, with despising the warrior ethic and with seeking to replace it by the elevation of speech and argument to the position formerly occupied by deeds, by acts of heroism performed by men who became models for all to emulate (1010-88).

What of the outcome of this contest? Will it be self-evident, as in a race or a duel in which one combatant is slain? Will Dionysus' task thus be simplified, limited to announcing the victor? Or are there objective criteria he can use, tools for assessing the worth of poetry? So far our Dionysus has been characterised neither by the courage and tenacity admired by Aeschylus nor by the intellectual and verbal dexterity preferred by Euripides, although it is the latter which had originally fascinated him. He came down to fetch Euripides, and by rights should have returned with him, having overcome the powers of Hades. The contest which displaced the expected struggle left him in uncertainty (*aporia*), having found no way of distinguishing the merits of different poets. Aeschylus sets off for an Athens he will hardly recognise, while Euripides' position is like that of Philoctetes in Sophocles' play, expecting to be taken home and then disappointed. One play wins, another loses: the reasons for popularity and success are too complex for the critic to unravel.

To return to the folk-tale for comparison: the quest in *Frogs* concludes like those stories in which the hero sets out to gain a certain princess for his bride but returns with her sister. In the folk-tale the story usually develops in such a way that the unexpected ending is as satisfactory to the audience as to the prince: the ending of *Frogs*, however, has continued to puzzle even those who believe that Aeschylus' supremacy as tragedian and political adviser has been demonstrated beyond doubt in the preceding scenes. The disease from which the drama suffers has usually been diagnosed as lack of unity: *Frogs'* bipartite structure, more distinct than that of *Ajax*, for example, the shift of focus from Dionysus to the tragedians, and the management of the ending have all been regarded as symptoms of the same disease.

In his book about the poet Tennyson, Christopher Ricks writes:

> Literary criticism since Tennyson's time has become more aptly flexible in its ideas as to artistic unity, less committed to a narrow or mechanical idea of such unity. But it has also become more skilled at imagining some such unity where it may not exist, and (a natural consequence of professional academicism) more skilled at exculpating works of art which in fact deserve the higher compliment of not being whisked away into the irreproachable.[35]

Frogs is intrinsically and unalterably bipartite because the element of conflict has been allowed to expand so as to fill half of the play and even more because in that conflict the original hero has lost the central position he should by rights occupy. In the narrow and mechanical sense, therefore, *Frogs* is not a unity. If it is less satisfactory as a whole than the admirers of the brilliance of many of its parts would desire, then a reason must be sought elsewhere. What *Frogs* needs is the restoration of Dionysus as protagonist in a scene long enough to give the decision-making the space it requires. In other words, Aeschylus and Euripides must leave the stage so that Dionysus can be liberated from the ill-matched roles of umpire and buffoon and return as his former self, the questor. No problem, then, if he were to announce a change of heart, a verdict which dismays his former choice.

The establishment of unity as supreme desideratum in Aristophanic drama is mistaken. Unity is often recognised in the 'well-made play', the carefully proportioned, neat comedy: the freedom to condense or greatly expand, to juxtapose extremes of mood and style, to change direction, which is a characteristic of Aristophanes, is more likely to be allied with a taste for variety. That is not to say that the plays lacks coherence, that they are as disconnected as a modern comedy show made up of separate acts; their coherence does not depend on 'unity' or uniformity: it allows considerable freedom in the development of components of the action and aspects of the theme as well as of the wide range of tone and language in respect of which Aristophanes' versatility is admired.

Notes

1. Information about structure in the narrow sense, which is not my concern here, may be found in Pickard-Cambridge 1962, 194-229.

2. E.g. 'path of song', *Od*. 8.74, Pindar *O*. 9. 47, *Birds* 1374; 'building', Pindar *O*. 6. 1-4, *P*. 7. 3., *Peace* 749 f.

3. 'Returns', originally material for epic, became an important theme in tragedy also; here the envoy returning from a journey adopts the tone of the warrior back from a long, hard campaign.

4. Among the bellicose would be Cleon, on whom Thucydides commented that in time of peace he would be 'more manifest in his villainies and less credited in his calumnies' (Thuc. 5. 16).

5. Preparations for a feast begin e.g. at *Peace* 1039 and *Birds* 1579.

6. For *Ach*. 284-346 see above, p. 70 f. See also *G & R* 29 (1982), 35-41.

7. For *deigma* cf. 642. The seriousness of the play is questioned by D. MacDowell, *G & R* 25 (1983), 143-62.

8. On *Ach*. 971-99 see Moulton, 86 f, Newiger in *YCS* 26, 224, and M. Silk in *YCS* 26, 140.

9. The age and decrepitude of the Acharnians had been made clear in the Entrance song (210-22) and parabasis (676-718).

10. It is the contrast between Lamachus' successful career and the disadvantages experienced by the elderly Acharnians that finally tips the scales in Dicaeopolis' favour.

11. The pattern is: Messenger A – Messenger B – preparation scene (mimicry) – parabasis – messenger speech – returns (mimicry). For the preparation scene see *BICS* 26 (1979), 95-8. For the parabasis song see above, p. 53.

12. See F. Kermode, *The Sense of an Ending* (New York, 1967).

13. S. *Antigone* 683-723.

14. The rejuvenation of Iolaus by prayer is reported in E. *Children of Heracles* 847 f. Through her knowledge of herbs Medea effected the rejuvenation of her father-in-law and the death of Pelias, the latter at the hands of his well-intentioned daughters. In each case the patient was boiled in a cauldron, see M.L. West, *The Orphic Poems* (Oxford, 1983), 160.

15. The audience might well expect a full narrative ('messenger speech') at this point.

16. See Taplin 1977, 137 f.

17. There is a comparable uncertainty about the wording of oracles in S. *Women of Trachis*.

18. Bacis' predictions had become famous during the Persian Wars. Sausage-seller calls his oracle Glanis for the sake of the echo.

19. Cleon's ignorance is amusingly different from that of the tragic hero. 'The point of misleading oracles is normally that they cause the recipient to take the wrong evasive action, or prevent him from realising that he is approaching danger' (M.L. West, *The Orphic Poems* (Oxford, 1983), 957). P. Rau discusses

the function of the oracle motif and analyses the scene in which Paphlagon learns the truth, giving verbal and other parallels from tragedy (Rau 168-73).

20. Whereas the quest for Peace restores something generally agreed to be desirable, the quest for Cerberus results in the arrival of a creature so dangerous it must be returned forthwith. Would the return of Euripides be regarded as generally desirable, as menacing or as negligible? Aeschyius is eventually presented as Deliverer (*soter*) (1419, 1458, 1487-9, 1501 f), so beneficial to the community as a whole. An interesting perspective on quests was given in an article by C. Booker: 'In fact the parallels between *Watership Down* and other stories formed by the Quest archetype run even deeper. It is a misconception, for instance, that the essence of Quest stories is that they simply describe a long journey towards a distant goal. In almost all the best-known stories of this type, the journey itself only accounts for a part of the tale. The worst ordeals all await the hero and his companions when they have already come within sight of the goal, and lie in the difficulties which still stand in their way of winning it and securing it for the future. The whole of the second half of the *Aeneid* is taken up with Aeneas's battle to secure his new home in Italy against the tribes who already live there, the same is true of the Jewish Exodus (the Battle of Jericho etc.). Jason's fiercest tests await him when he has already arrived in the neighbourhood of the Golden Fleece in Colchis, just as Odysseus's arrival in Ithaca before the final great battle with the suitors occurs scarcely halfway through the *Odyssey*. And it is here that we can also see, in almost every instance, what is the real nature of the goal of the Quest story. What matters is not mere arrival at a goal, the winning of a treasure, or whatever, so much as the securing or establishing of a Kingdom, and usually, simultaneously, the winning of a Princess into the bargain.' (Christopher Booker, Spectator, 14 July 1979.)

21. Heracles rescued Theseus from Hades. The Attic hero's descent to Hades (*Frogs* 142), with his companion Pirithoos, had the purpose of abducting Persephone. His return from Hades was mentioned in E.'s first *Hippolytus* and S.'s *Phaedra*.

22. If we wish (vainly, as it turns out) to see Dionysus as a principal of the Dicaeopolis type, it is because of the way in which he describes his own feelings.

23. It is interesting to compare Heracles' role with that of Hermes in *Peace* or of Euripides in *Acharnians*. The motif of peculiar dress recurs at 1036 f, 1066 f. For Heracles' Catabasis see R.J. Clark, *Phoenix* 24 (1970), 244.

24. Descriptions of journeys belong to the narrative modes, witness such narratives in tragedy as Clytemnestra's Beacon-speech (*Ag.* 281-316) and Prometheus' predictions (*PV*. 707-35). Some suggestions of locale are given in the Initiates' songs, 372 f, 441 f.

25. This Dionysus and his adventures would not be entirely out of place in a satyr-play.

26. The process of dressing-up can be made very funny and the result often exploits the contrast between appearance and reality. Dionysus is odd-looking because he lacks items normally associated with him and because his saffron robe, normally worn by married women, contrasts sharply with the 'masculine' club and lion-skin of Heracles.

27. It is interesting that uncertainty about the identity of the two men is the means of bringing the scene to an end (clearing the stage) and thus avoiding the threatened punishments of the dog-thief.

28. In this scene the native resident informs the newly-arrived traveller, cf. 431 f; *Peace* 195 f. On this prologue see E. Fraenkel, *Beobachtungen zu Aristophanes* (Rome, 1962), 163-9. See also J.T. Hooker, *Hermes* 108 (1980), 169-82. For 'noise within' see Taplin 1978, 102 f.

29. The implication is that there are objective criteria for establishing the worth of literary achievements. See *Poetry and Criticism before Plato* (London, 1969),

93-7 and 148 f.

30. Unlike Demos, Dionysus is not open to flattery or bribes.

31. At 1263 Dionysus says he will keep the score by means of pebbles.

32. Some legal processes were still decided by a single arbitrator. On the implications see K. Dover, *Lysias and the Corpus Lysiacum* (California, 1968), 181.

33. Cf. the song in which the chorus (as if introducing a parabasis rather than concluding an agon) praise the audience for their expertise in judging drama: the underlying metaphor is of battle veterans watching a duel between warriors (1099-118).

34. There is a verbal reminiscence of A.'s tragedy when the chorus reflect on the 'magnitude of the strife' between the poets, using the words which are components of Polyneices' name (1099). Did Ar. ever contemplate sending both contestants back to earth and giving the throne to S?

35. Christopher Ricks, *Tennyson* (London 1972), 212. See also E. Fraenkel, *Beobachtungen*, 163 ff, C. Segal, *HSCP* 65 (1961), 207 ff, J.T. Hooker, n. 28 above.

6 FROM MYTH TO PLAY: *DONA NOBIS PACEM*

I set ev'ry tree in my June time
And now they obscure the sky.
>   (Thomas Hardy, 'At Day-close in November')

I'd swear
that men have always lounged in myths
as Tall Stories,

That their real earnest
has been to grant excuses
for ritual actions.
>   (W.H. Auden, 'Archaeology')

Peace celebrates the imminent cessation of the war between Athens and Sparta. Peace (or victory under the guise of Peace) has often enough, no doubt, been celebrated – by religious services, by parties, by concerts, by public monuments; rarely by plays. Aristophanes has created a comedy, a full-length play, to celebrate peace, a theme apparently ill-suited to dramatic treatment. What material can he use? What kind of story or plot can be created on such a subject?

'Men are longing for the return of peace.' Change from lower to upper case and remember the Greek love of personifying, of deifying, abstractions and you have the germ of the comedy. The Peace whom men desire is no longer simply cessation of hostilities, no longer the peacemaking imminent when Aristophanes was writing, but the goddess. And if a man can find the lost Peace and restore her, the drama possesses not only a central figure with potential, but a story-line which can be expanded almost ad lib. The hero sets out upon a quest for a desired object or person. The journey may be difficult in itself; he may encounter enemies or acquire helpers; he may achieve his goal only to meet further problems during and after his return. The pattern is well known, especially in the narrative modes, and Aristophanes himself exploited it, notably in *Birds* and, as we have seen, in *Frogs*.[1]

119

It is in fact instructive to compare *Frogs* and *Peace*. In each play the desideratum is the return of someone who has disappeared, gone to a place above or below our world; in each the quest in itself generates sufficient material for roughly half of the play. One main point of difference is that Trygaeus' motives are more altruistic than those expressed by Dionysus at the beginning of *Frogs*; another is that in the second part of *Peace* we have returned to earth, the quest successfully completed, whereas in *Frogs* the scene all through the play is Hades. In general effect the two plays are very different, *Peace* being more varied and diffuse than *Frogs*, but also more closely tied to Athenian religious and civic institutions.

The journey to the underworld requires preliminary advice from an experienced traveller (Heracles) but is actually staged by walking and rowboat and the dangers encountered 'below' are, at least until after the parodos, purely imaginary. The journey to heaven takes place in spite of remonstration and entreaty; it is staged on the flying-machine, and when the goal is reached Helper and Enemy are encountered immediately.[2] *Peace* is not only more episodic but the action is carried out by several characters, whereas in *Frogs* Dionysus and Xanthias develop what is largely a duo.

The Quest

Let us now examine the prologue of *Peace* in more detail. Its three hundred lines may be divided into two main scenes, the first taking place on earth and the second at Zeus' (former) dwelling, the protagonist's flight linking the two. The play, following the pattern of *Knights* and *Wasps*, opens with 50 lines of dialogue for two slaves, succeeded by an expository speech delivered by one of them. Then their master, appearing on the point of departure, has short exchanges with the slave and his own daughters, interspersed with exhortations to his steed. After this fragmented opening the heavenly section is tidier, being composed of the conversation, or mutual interrogation, of Trygaeus and Hermes and the scene, of similar length, played by War and Uproar.

By describing the prologue so colourlessly I have hoped to make apparent that identity of story-pattern does not produce uniform structure. The opening sequence of *Peace* has greater similarities with those of *Wasps* and *Knights*, particularly the former, than with *Frogs*. In the latter the introductory scene, between master and slave, leads to the visit to the adviser, to whom the master's problem is, briefly, revealed. Thereafter Dionysus' encounter with the Corpse and the Frog chorus are further instances of variations on the quest theme.

Such a colourless description (though serving a purpose) is of course false to both plays. What the audience first sees in *Peace* is an ordinary dramatic activity, food preparation. But the food is excrement, the consumer a beetle, the cooks rebellious.[3] One of them expatiates on the misery of kneading dung for a finicky eater with a large capacity until the other decides that the spectators' curiosity should be satisfied: 'My master's mad . . . he gapes up at the sky and reviles Zeus, saying "Zeus, what are you planning? Put your broom down. Don't sweep Grace away" ' (56 f). At this point the 'madman's' voice is heard from within (like the tragic Medea's).[4] The slave continues his explanation: his master's rage had led him to bring home the beetle after an earlier attempt to reach the sky by ladder had ended in painful failure; the slave has become a 'groom' whose master treats his steed as an epic warrior treats his horse, exhorting him to his great task of flying 'straight to Zeus'. The exposition is brought to an end when the speaker sees that the flight is now actually beginning.

If the prologue, formally analysed and now described in terms of a comic action, seems so far to have little connection with the 'myth' of my chapter-heading and less with the 'quest' which I asserted shaped the play, then that is no accident. Aristophanes here proceeds obliquely. So far there has been no explicit reference to the war (and the suggestion that Cleon will be an important theme is a red herring) (47). The hero's desire to approach Zeus, cited as an instance of his insanity, becomes overtly mythical only when these words of his are reported: 'Noble, winged Pegasean creature, fly me straight to Zeus' (76 f). Dung-beetle being now cast as Pegasus, his rider must be Bellerophon. Previously only an unnamed 'mad master', he has now an ill-fated role (already 'prepared' by his fall from the ladder), that of the tragic figure who in righteous indignation set out to upbraid Zeus.[5]

Our Bellerophon now enacts his myth. The tragic scene, first suggested by the 'voice from within' (62 f), is developed by the use of tragic language, specifically by phrases borrowed from Euripides' Bellerophon, and by tragic situations, like the children's appeal to their 'departing' father (114 f).[6] The staged flight and 'Bellerophon's' song are reminders of Euripidean tragedy. Nevertheless, this flight ends successfully and its dangers exclude tragedy as often as they suggest it. That is, the journey is explicitly presented as a use of stage machinery operated by a 'real' technician and is threatened only by his inattention or the incontinence of men who might distract dung-beetle.

Information about Trygaeus and Zeus has been provided piecemeal; first Trygaeus' request to the broom-wielder not to sweep Hellas away (59), then his intention to visit Zeus (68, 77), then his explanation to his slave 'on behalf of all Hellenes I fly' (93), and 'I intend to ask him what he plans to do about all the Hellenes' (105). Two points to notice here: first the silence about the nature of the trouble threatening Hellas and secondly Trygaeus' pan-Hellenic altruism.[7]

Once arrived in heaven, the hero is met by a flood of abuse from the god Hermes, the porter, whose role here resembles that of the doorkeeper in the *Frogs* (464-78). It is only now (190 f) that Trygaeus is identified, by name, by deme, by occupation ('skilled vinegrower') and by civic character ('not an informer, not a political activist'). The journey safely over, Trygaeus is amazed to be told that the gods have moved home, motivated by rage against the Greeks, leaving Hermes to guard their 'bits and pieces'. War has taken their place, at liberty to treat the Greeks as he will (250 f). 'I don't suppose you'll ever see Peace again' (221 f).

This scene, crucial for the play's development and containing in outline ideas that are yet to be filled out, does not quite exhaust the productivity of the journey motif since later in the play there are two further offshoots. In the later of the two, on Trygaeus' return, his slave asks him about his journey (819-41), while in the earlier Peace, through Hermes, interrogates Trygaeus about recent events in Athens (670-705). Dramatisation of the return journey has no place here, save for the brief 'tidying away' of dung-beetle in an exalted new post (721-4).

Trygaeus has left a Greece embroiled in war only to find that War reigns in heaven, War who is planning to pound the cities (231, echoing 58). War is of course his 'enemy' and would in a heroic quest be confronted directly; in a comedy it is enough for him to be observed and shown for what he is. Whereas the play began with the preparation of excrement as food for a 'monster', so now men themselves become ingredients or utensils in the making of a sauce for War's table.[8] In this scene, although Hellas is no longer spoken of as a whole, the separate cities will not survive except in so far as they contribute individual flavours to the sauce (242-52). For the personification of War and Uproar Aristophanes had poetic precedents reaching as far back as Homer, but the likeliest point of comparison for the audience was surely the presentation of the demagogue as cook and bully in *Knights*.[9]

Nevertheless, the mythical and religious undertones of these two scenes are not to be ignored. The gods who withdrew from their accustomed dwelling through anger with the warring Greeks are not unlike the more irascible among Homeric deities and the contrast and opposition between War and Peace also reflect the Homeric gods' propensity to quarrel. The gods' attitude is interpreted, as in Homer, by Hermes, who tells Trygaeus that the gods moved 'so as not to see you continually fighting or to get out of range of your entreaties' (207-9) and because 'you chose war although they frequently promoted peace negotiations' (211-2). So Peace has become War's victim, cast by him into a deep pit-like cavern with rocks heaped over its entrance (223-5). Herself a divinity she is nevertheless helpless and passive in the face of the determined aggression of War whom the philosopher Heraclitus had described as 'King of all' (fr. 53).

His discovery of the situation of Peace turns Trygaeus' mission to upbraid Zeus into a specific kind of quest, a 'rescue bid', an attempt to rescue a person, often female, who is held by an enemy.[10] In myth, the heroine may be chained to a rock, guarded by a dragon or entombed in a cavern and her rescuer, often her lover, usually has to fight to free her. As already observed, Trygaeus, with his peace-loving nature, does not fight; instead he leads a co-operative, vigorous effort to restore Peace.

War's cooking is broken off for want of a pestle (the Athenian and Spartan generals, Cleon and Brasidas, now dead, are no longer 'pounding' the cities) and it will take time to make a replacement. Trygaeus accordingly uses the interval for hasty excavation, calling on 'farmers, traders, carpenters, craftsmen, metics, foreigners, islanders' to bring shovels, crowbars and ropes (296-9). The chorus, answering his call, are at first too excited by the prospect of peace to begin their task and are then delayed by Hermes' opposition. Eventually, however, they begin to pull on the ropes and finally Peace emerges (458-519). Trygaeus' quest has succeeded.

Peace and Her Image

At this point, and in advance of Aristophanes, I turn aside from the action to discuss the figure of Peace.[11] Peace is a prisoner ('removing the bonds of Peace', 1073), entombed and left to die, perhaps, like Antigone (and others named in Sophocles' *Antigone* 444-87); she is buried below ground and will be raised up; she is female and she is divine. Some of the scenes of the second part of the play grow from seed planted here. Peace is a statue and her excavation is reminiscent of work in the quarries during the early stages of the stonemason's or sculptor's task. The staging of the scene, however it was staged,[12] required the employment of an object, not an actor, and not only for practical reasons, since in the satyr play by Aeschylus on which it was modelled the chorus were hauling a chest out of the sea.[13]

Aeschylus' *Net-fishers* is not the only text relevant to the staging of the emergence of Peace. The scene in the *Odyssey* (11. 25-43) in which the ghosts of the dead come up to the pit where Odysseus has offered sacrifices was well known in itself, much illustrated and staged in a lost play by Aeschylus. Dramatic presentations of deities emerging from below the ground are known to have been enacted, particularly in satyr plays, one of which, Aeschylus' *Sisyphus*, has an additional connection with our play since in it the hero, pushing his stone up out of the underworld, is likened to a dung-beetle rolling its ball of dung.[14]

At another level the statue represents the hoped-for permanence of peace and manifests her divinity. Nevertheless she is simultaneously humanised, as the lost beloved, as the words of the chorus make clear: 'I greet you, we rejoice at your return, dearest one; I have been overcome by longing for you' (582-3). The reunion of kin or of lovers joyfully celebrated after painful and prolonged separation is familiar from recognition scenes in tragedy and forms part of many legends.[15] For this play one group of myths is particularly important, those dealing with the departure of a fertility goddess and her seasonal return, brought back from darkness to light (307).[16]

But Peace is not Persephone. Although she has been stored underground like the seed corn, and although she has an Anodos supervised by Hermes, our deity is much closer to vine-nurturing Dionysus in function.[17] It is interesting to see how late the dramatist introduces the important viticultural aspects of the play. We know Trygaeus' name and profession at 190 and Peace is addressed as 'vine-loving' at 308, but it is not until the farmers succeed in restoring the goddess that her gifts are fully realised. It is possible to suggest a number of reasons for emphasising the connection of peace and wine. In the first place wine links private, domestic celebrations and the state's Dionysiac festivals (at one of which the play is being performed); secondly, the equation of wine as used for libations with peace-treaties is familiar from *Acharnians* and elsewhere. More important, however, is the political implication of the restoration of vine-growing: the destruction of annual cereal and vegetable crops, damaging enough, is less grave than loss of vines. Peace must be made to last long enough for the vines to grow to production, and not only vines but also the associated slower-growing olives, figs and other fruit trees, since all manifest the power of Dionysus and all were commonly grown together in enclosures: 'O day desired by farmers and right-thinking men, I see you and rejoice and long to greet my vines; our hearts are set on greeting, at long last, the fig trees I planted in my youth' (557-9).

The best-known representation of Peace, Cephisodotus' statue of the goddess with her baby son Ploutos, postdates our play, but the association of peace and plenty was familiar and long-established.[18] Peace is one of three sisters, the Horae, or Seasons, daughters of Zeus and Themis; together with Dike and Eunomia she 'protects men's cultivated land' since agricultural prosperity requires 'peace and just administration'.[19]

In the comedy the basic seasonal meaning of the Horae, their dance to the Music of Time, is transmitted in the person of Opora, the 'after-season', the time of vintage, one of the goddess's two 'sisters' and attendants, while the other, Theoria, represents the non-agricultural, civic, state of peace. Of the two, Opora plays the longer, and probably more important, part in the later scenes, as 'bride' of Trygaeus, but Theoria's shorter contribution needs to be understood too.[20]

Theoria's name is difficult to translate by a single word in

English. Connected with the words for theatre and spectator, it suggests presence at a festival, watching athletic or dramatic or musical contests, and in a more specialised sense membership of an official delegation sent to such a festival or to consult an oracle. In each case the desirability of contact between states at a personal or communal level receives emphasis, such contact only being possible during times of peace, or at least of truce.[21] When Trygaeus returns to earth, he proposes to hand over Theoria to the Council and his slave, pretending to recognise her, recalls a scene of revelry at an Artemis festival and tries to stake a claim to her body (871-80). (The slave's reaction neatly underlines both the festival associations of Theoria and her sexuality.) In entrusting Theoria to the Council, Trygaeus explains that now they can engage in a splendid athletic contest, each event of which we must interpret also in a sexual sense.[22] The ingenious obscenity of the lines should not obscure the fact that peace and the great Hellenic festivals require government action to ensure their continuance. And what government could refuse to act, given these enticements (894-908)?

It is obvious that there needed to be living presenters of the erotic and fertile aspects of the nature of peace and that the less decorous parts of the actions and descriptions affecting them would not suit the goddess herself. Opora is precisely the season when fruit ripens, and by extension the principle of fertility and the pleasant intoxication given by wine; with Trygaeus as her bridegroom she will give birth to – grapes. The wedding procession of Trygaeus and Opora develops into something of much wider significance, the return to the countryside, to agricultural production, of farmers prevented by war from cultivating their vineyards and orchards.[23]

The wealth peace traditionally bestows is manifested not in hoarded treasure but in the plentiful prosperity of daily life. The Horae, 'stewards of plenty', as Pindar called them, among them Peace, 'giver of wealth', provide a divine endorsement of a stable, productive country life.[24] The traditional characterisation of the peace-giving deities is found chiefly in choral lyric written for communal religious occasions (and choral lyric is not far from Aristophanes' thoughts at several points in this play). It is possible to gain some insight into the traditional beliefs from surviving poetry like the Paean by Bacchylides which gives a full description of a community blessed by Peace who 'brings forth for mortals mighty wealth and the blossoms of honey-voiced songs'. Peace also restores festivals and sacrifices and 'on the iron-bound shield-grips are spiders' webs and red rust undoes the spearpoint . . . brass trumpets are mute; early-morning's gentle and soothing sleep is not plundered'.[25] At a later date, Euripides had in similar terms composed for a tragic chorus a song expressing the longing that long-absent Peace, 'abundant in wealth and fairest of the blessed gods', return to the city bringing song and revelry: 'Keep from our homes hostile unrest and frenzied strife who takes pleasure in keen-edged iron.'[26] Euripides' invocation had been picked up by Aristophanes for use in his lost play, the *Farmers*, produced three years earlier than *Peace*:

Peace, abundant in wealth, and you my pair of oxen,
I pray that, when I'm free of this war,
I may dig and prune, then take a bath,
eat fine bread and salad, then drink the new vintage.[27]

In this section I have presented a conspectus of Peace, beginning from the visual, staged elements (the statue, burial and excavation, reunion) and proceeding by the associations which these elements suggest to a consideration of the 'literary' tradition lying behind our play. I have described this literary tradition, which in fact goes back to Hesiod, as 'lyrical', since it is represented most importantly by passages of Pindar and Bacchylides and the choruses of drama and because in *Peace* Aristophanes himself uses quotations from choral lyric to launch his own verses, quoting from Stesichorus in the ode and antode of the parabasis. When the farmers associate themselves (and their poet) with the Muse who 'pushed war away' and celebrated festivity in heaven and on earth (774-80), they are establishing the foundation of the post-parabasis scenes. In *Peace* tragedy makes its contribution initially, epic provides ammunition for false and true prophets, Archilochean escapism is condemned (1295-1301), but choral lyric is powerfully pervasive. Peace gives wealth, the poets affirm, she brings about communal celebrations, both musical and athletic and sees the laying aside of weapons and the instruments of war: is this not almost a synopsis of the second half of the comedy? 'Almost a synopsis', but not quite. I quoted earlier the fragment of *Farmers* in which

Aristophanes, as in the parabasis odes of *Peace*, begins by quoting a 'serious' poet but rapidly changes to more mundane affairs, to digging, pruning and oxen. In our play the farmers' idea of peace includes the practical and homely, a way of life which is pleasurable but not sentimentalised, 'hard' as opposed to 'soft' pastoral.[28] There is no doubt that the farmers who had freed Peace were energetic and skilful labourers and that by comparison with the hardships of war agricultural work was desirable: repeatedly Trygaeus or the farmers speak of 'getting rid of' people or things characteristic of war and military service, for example, officers like Lamachus, battle formations or the garlic which was part of the 'three days' rations' the hoplite had to provide (303, 920, 1128-9).[29]

The Aristophanic farmer is no wealthy landowner and cannot just repeat the somewhat aristocratic lyrics of the 'serious' poets. Moreover, the Aristophanic chorus adds an erotic element at a personal level inappropriate to Pindaric or tragic song. If Stesichorus' Muse celebrated the marriages of gods, then Aristophanes sings not only the wedding of Trygaeus and Opora but also the pleasures of casual sex with the slave girl (1138). For the interweaving of human sexuality and agricultural fertility which is so important in the first two peace plays, the songs of the chorus are vital and in them Aristophanes makes use of a language indebted to the literary tradition but also quite idiosyncratic. The erotic element is notably expressed in the song from *Acharnians* which may serve to introduce my discussion on the later scenes of *Peace*. The first stanza of the song presents War as a drunken reveller, smashing things and spilling wine, while the second is a prayer to Reconciliation (*Diallage*), associated with Aphrodite and the Graces: 'If only Eros would unite me with you . . . but I suppose you think I'm getting on a bit? Well, if I had you there would still be three ways I could get something done. First, a big planting of vine . . .' The singer continues to enumerate, untranslatably, feats both sexual and horticultural, by which not only the vines destroyed by war but also figs and olives will be replaced (*Ach.* 971-99).[30] These Acharnians may have reached their 'day-close in November' but given Peace fertility too will come again.

Peace Restored

Trygaeus' quest may be regarded as complete when the goddess has emerged, to the joy of her rescuers, at line 600, rather less than half-way through the play. The next scene follows on very naturally as the chorus conclude their greeting of Peace with a question, addressed to Hermes, about Peace's long absence, but it is in no sense an unimportant coda to its predecessor containing as it does the play's only statement about the genesis of the Peloponnesian War. This statement is made, and I emphasise the point, by Hermes, not, as later, Hermes conveying words uttered *sotto voce* by Peace, but speaking on his own authority.[31] In *Acharnians* and *Lysistrata* the protagonists, Dicaeopolis and Lysistrata respectively, make the crucial long speech which reflects on bellicosity and influences the bellicose; in *Peace*, by contrast, Trygaeus is never given an argument to develop. Which of Hermes' many functions is relevant here? Is he Zeus' messenger or the patron of tricksters? What credence is to be given to his words?[32] He begins, at any rate, in confident didactic tones, to explain why Peace vanished. His rhetoric is vivid: Pericles started a fire whose smoke brought tears to all Greek eyes; vines crackled and wine jars were smashed; Peace disappeared (606-14). Hermes' second paragraph sounds more prosaic: Athens' subject allies took their chance and by bribery induced the Spartans to 'throw out Peace and grab War' (624). So began the farmers' sufferings, described in the god's final paragraph: brought into the city because of the war the farmers became gullible victims of politicians who were 'pushing Peace away with their two-pronged – rantings' (637).

In this idiosyncratic version of events there is a tension between what Peace did of her own volition (disappearing 614, appearing 638) and what the Spartans and Athenian politicians did to her (624, 636) as well as some inconsistency between the content of this speech and the story of War's burial of Peace which Hermes had earlier told Trygaeus (222). At that earlier point Hermes had been a caretaker who could merely report recent events; now his status is obviously greater although his veracity and authority are in doubt.

From Hermes' hermeneutics we move to Hermes as 'loud-speaker' for the goddess, who has so far been preserving an Aeschylean angry silence (657-62). Peace complains that, on her voluntary return after Pylos, she was thrice rejected in the Assembly (thus amplifying one of Hermes' points).[33] She then begins to ask for the latest news of political figures (Cleonymus, Hyperbolus) and poets (Sophocles, Cratinus). Trygaeus' return to earth is prefaced by the presentation to him of the two mute but attractive attendants of Peace, Theoria and Opora.

After the parabasis, preparations for the wedding of Opora are put in train and continue, at least as background, to the play's end. Theoria, however, once handed over to the Council and the presidents, has fulfilled her task: peace has been institutionalised and returned to interstate politics. During and at the close of this section the chorus sing the praises of Trygaeus in language which suggests his heroisation and with which he gladly concurs: 'You have become saviour of mankind.' 'And when you drink a goblet of new wine, what then?' 'We shall ever count you supreme, but for the gods.' 'Yes, for I am worthy . . .' (914-18).[34]

Next the action is centred on Peace herself and the establishment of a cult in her honour, Trygaeus' slave sharing in the ceremonial and sometimes advising on procedure.[35] The scene contains an anapaestic hymn begging the goddess to accept the sacrifice (and not to disappear again like a provocative flirt, in the slave's words). 'Deliver us from battles . . . put an end to our evil suspicions . . . blend us afresh and add friendliness, grant to our spirits merciful forgiveness. Then fill our market with good things . . .' (991-1000). The subsequent listing of imported foodstuffs may to our ears follow oddly on a prayer for moral reform, but the juxtaposition of festivity and teaching is particularly characteristic of the later scenes of this comedy. The prayer does not culminate in the sacrifice of a sheep, as planned, for the slave declares that Peace takes no pleasure in bloodshed (1019). As master and slave begin their cooking, the oraclemonger Hierocles intervenes 'to oppose the peace' (but actually attracted by the cooking smell) (1049-50). This impostor with his ambiguous portentous prophecies is no match for Trygaeus but rather provides him with further opportunities to preach peace: 'What is our duty? To continue fighting?' (1080); and, when Hierocles asks for wine and food, he replies in mocking echo (1106, 1075) that this is not yet dear to the blessed gods; 'first we must make libations and you must depart. Lady Peace, stay with us all our life.' Finally the pseudo-prophet tries to snatch some food and is driven off, having achieved nothing.[36]

At this point a backward glance may be useful. Hierocles has appeared as an opponent of Trygaeus' peacemaking, not in his own right but as a religious figure. Earlier in the play Trygaeus' peacemaking had been opposed by Hermes, in a scene to which I referred very briefly (362-425). From one aspect the earlier scene is to be understood as presenting further, unforeseen difficulty coming at the moment when the quest seems set for achievement. If formally it is predictable yet Hermes' role in it is surprising, as is shown by Trygaeus' initial reluctance to take him seriously, even when he says that by Zeus' orders 'anyone found excavating' Peace will be punished by death (371-2). Hierocles is a negligible adversary: not so Hermes who is unmoved by entreaties, reminders of past offerings and flattery. His obduracy acts as a spur to the ingenuity and inventiveness of Trygaeus, culminating in the presentation to the god of a gold cup, received with the reply: 'I'm always very merciful to vessels of gold' (425). Trygaeus aimed to prevent Hermes from 'telling tales' to Zeus and to gain him as fellow worker in the excavation; Hierocles the interfering busybody he could ignore. Does Hermes share in the self-seeking disguised by the pretence of authority found in many Aristophanic impostors and clearly evinced by Hierocles? Is he 'conning' Trygaeus throughout the scene? At any rate both this Hermes and Hierocles partake of characteristics abjured by Trygaeus when he introduced himself as 'worker in a vineyard, neither sycophant nor busybody' (191).[37]

In the second parabasis, too long to quote, the chorus demonstrate their understanding of the blessings of country peace as opposed to the hardships and injustice which city-based militarists inflict on peasants: 'they wronged me much, those men, acting like lions in the city but in battle like foxes' (1188-90). The description here included of the army officer with his plumed helmet serves as preparation for the scenes played by makers and sellers of tools and weapons, among them the purveyor of crests (1210f). These scenes provide an object lesson on the virtues of beating spears into pruning-hooks; they may also be categorised negatively, as lacking (save by implication) serious religious and moral comment of the kind found in the previous scene; they have no mythical, religious or literary background.

Preparation for these scenes had in a sense begun when the farmers were told to return to the country without the weapons of war but taking the spades and crowbars they had used to dig out Peace (550-5); (indeed farmers who had to cope with the rocky Attic soil were well used to levering up large pieces of stone). Agricultural tools are here set against the weapons of war and this is the first mention of the opposition which generates the later contrasting pair of scenes. There are suggestions earlier still: 'We pray that any man who joins zealously in hauling up Peace may never take up a shield again' (437-8) and then in the libation scene Hermes and Trygaeus curse 'any spearmaker or shieldseller who longs for battles to increase his trade' (447-8). After Peace has been raised up, Hermes pretends to be able to tell what trade is practised by a spectator from his appearance: the crestmaker is tearing his hair but the manufacturer of hoes has just farted at the swordsmith, and so on (545-9). A little later Hermes and Trygaeus comment ambiguously on the appearance of the farmers' chorus now formed up in a 'column close-ranked and compact like barleycake and buffet table . . . their mallets battle bright, their forks gleaming in the sun' (565-7).[38] To return to the traders. The first of these, a sicklemaker, is very pleased with Trygaeus: his trade and that of his friend who makes agricultural containers is now prosperous again (1198-206). Not so the armament business: no one wants crests, breastplates, trumpets, helmets or spears (though Trygaeus makes an insultingly low offer for these latter to use for staking his vines) (1210-64).[39]

As soon as the retailers depart, their pride wounded, the mood changes. The next entrance, from the skene, brings in two boy soloists who are to sing at the wedding (1270).[40] The first of them, not yet identified as Lamachus' son, begins to rehearse an epic passage about warriors and finds it hard to change his tune when chided by Trygaeus, while the other, the son of Cleonymus, performs the opening of Archilochus' famous couplets about the loss of his shield on the battlefield.[41] In this short section, much of it conducted in metre and language foreign to comedy, there is presented the peacemaker's rejection of poetic glorification of warfare and also of Archilochean insouciance.

These are not the songs of the Aristophanic wedding feast which is about to begin, after a brief transitional passage in tetrameters. Trygaeus exhorts a responsive chorus to pursue energetically their task of – eating (1305-15). The concluding songs, although basically hymeneal, have also a clear propemptic element which bids farewell to the countrymen who at long last are leaving Athens to return to the countryside; the two elements are naturally linked by the promise of fertility. In the 'anapaests' with which Trygaeus (the probable speaker) prefaces the wedding song there is a marvellous drawing together of the themes of the moment and of the play as a whole: marriage celebration, return to the farms, expulsion of the demagogue, prayers for wealth and for fertility of various kinds. The prayer to the gods concludes: 'Grant us to gather in again all those good things which we lost; and grant that the flash of weapons cease' (1326-8).

I wrote above of Hermes' idiosyncratic version of the causes of the Peloponnesian War. It may be thought that my reading of *Peace* is at least as idiosyncratic, if not positively negligent or wrongheaded. My *Peace* is not that of its editor, Maurice Platnauer ('It is true that our play has neither the wit of the *Frogs* nor the imagination and fancy of the *Birds* nor yet the *saeva indignatio* of the *Knights*; that it contains a – mercifully short – scene of obscenity unrelieved by wit, and that it ends with one of those tedious *stravaganze*, so dear, apparently, to the hearts of the Athenian groundlings, which tend to spoil for some the finale of so many of Aristophanes' plays. On the credit side may be set some really charming lyrics, a hero more distinctly characterised than perhaps any other personage in the poet's works . . . and finally that hero's journey to Heaven . . .') nor even of Carroll Moulton's recent description.[42] The play interests me as much for what it lacks (much contemporary reference, lively debate and quarrelling) as for what it notably contains.

It has been my contention not only that in the first half of the play the story-line has affinities with myth (and ingredients drawn from tragic versions of myth) but that the play as a whole should be read in the ways in which we read works acknowledged to be mythical, that is that we should look for serious and integrated religious and moral content among the fun. It is a play about prayer, about interaction between gods and men; the divine characters in the play are essential to the plot and present for much of its duration; a large part of the text consists of prayers and religious ritual. On the verbal level the effects of all this are profound: the language is non-rhetorical, lacks argument and insult;[43] on the positive side it gains from the traditions of choral lyric.

Describing the play has not been easy. It seems that it has often been found really memorable only for the flight of dung-beetle (although I would argue for the impact of the excavation scene also). Critics have had recourse to praising Trygaeus (who is actually a mere sketch compared with Dicaeopolis or Strepsiades) or examining the imagery associated with peace and war (as though *Acharnians* were defective in such images). I suspect that some would like to label *Peace* 'boring' if not restrained by a sense of decorum or by reluctance to damn Aristophanes. One thing is clear: Aristophanes did not intend to write a boring play. Since this comedy was accepted for performance and received the second prize it must have had at least some contemporary appeal. If I were required to advertise the play, I should want to stress its merits as an encomium of peace, an encomium designed to instil in men's hearts the desire for enduring peace. I should point to the effect of the successful quest gained by communal effort, believing that the audience might feel almost like participants in the rescue of Peace. I should praise the skill with which the text combines the idea and reality of peace and the image and divinity of Peace, the establishment and festal celebration of cult with the return to the production of crops. I should argue that the success of the quest was reinforced by the fact that Peace was no Aristophanic invention and that Opora and Theoria, whom he did invent, took the places of the other Hesiodic Horae, Dike and Eunomia. The association of peace, festivity and fertility, already promulgated in *Acharnians*, is developed here not only in the concluding meal and wedding celebration but much more importantly in the promise of successive years of vintage and harvest, a promise likely to please not only all whose vines the Spartans had cut down but all wine drinkers. The *Peace* is a celebration of peace: it is a play in which conflict in minimal, in which prayer and praise, traditionally based, inculcate right attitudes, in which the pleasures of life are seen to flow naturally from the ending of war. For all its visual appeal, it is not a play for spectators but for a congregation of worshippers.

Notes

1. See above, p. 106 ff.
2. It should be added that some of the possible dangers of the flight are forecast in the preceding dialogue between father and child (e.g. drowning, 140; injury, 146).
3. I am not aware of any structuralist study of this play, although among the

oppositions set up by Ar. that concerning food, cooking and excrement is particularly striking: dung-beetle, unlike his human master, makes a permanent transition to the realm of the gods, there to eat Ganymede's 'ambrosia' among the steeds of Zeus (722-4), an interesting outcome after the interchange between Trygaeus and his child in which the father's reference to Aesop as authority for the flight to heaven gets this reply: 'Father, father, that's an incredible tale you tell about a foul-smelling creature reaching the gods' (129-32).

4. E. *Med.* 96 f. On the 'voice within' see Taplin 1977, 372.

5. Rau 90 f, 154 f.

6. The children's appeal, in part indebted to E.'s *Aeolus*, may suggest their fear that their father's madness will end in death.

7. Although the slave says that his master 'remonstrates' with Zeus, Trygaeus' own formulation is interrogative: 'What do you mean to do?' (58); 'What will you do to our people?' (62); 'I plan to ask him what he means to do about every single one of the Greeks' (105-6). Whereas flying to heaven and chiding Zeus is hybristic, consulting a god about the future is altogether normal and pious.

8. Moulton, 85 f, rather exaggerates in describing the dressed salad as a feast.

9. Polemos, rather than Ares, is used because he lacked extraneous and unwanted mythical associations. The chief references for the personifications are Homer, *Il.* 5. 593, 18. 535, Heraclitus, fr. 53, and the opening of Pindar's fragmentary Seventh Dithyramb, written for the Athenians. For further discussion see Newiger 1957, 111 f, Moulton, 86.

10. On the motif of rescuing a princess see S. Trenkner, *The Greek Novella in the Classical Period* (Cambridge, 1958), 50 f.

11. In this section I am concerned only with the resonances which are, or may be, produced by the presentation of Peace in this play, not with the conceptual range of peace in the moral or political sphere in the late fifth century (when pacifism, as we know it, was unthought of). For discussion of Greek attitudes to war and peace see A. Momigliano, *Secondo Contributo alla Storia degli Studi Classici* (Rome 1960), 13-27; J. Romilly in *Problèmes de la guerre en Grèce ancienne*, ed. J.-P. Vernant (Paris 1968), 207 f, and with particular reference to Aristophanes, G.E.M. de Ste Croix, *The Origins of the Peloponnesian War* (London, 1972), 183 f, 355 f.

12. The problems of staging this play have not all been solved. I have written nothing about them here, not because I regard staging as unimportant, but partly because I have nothing useful to contribute to the discussion and partly because I wished to concentrate on other, comparatively neglected, aspects of *Peace*. However, since any reading of the play makes certain assumptions about staging, I should say here that I visualise Peace as emerging from below ground level.

13. The fragments of A.'s *Net-fishers* with translation can be found in the appendix, edited by H. Lloyd-Jones, of Aeschylus, vol. 2 (Loeb Classical Library, 1971).

14. A. fr. 385 Mette; see Taplin 1977, 429.

15. Scenes of greeting are discussed by Rau 144 f. The recovery of the lost beloved may be the sole object of a quest, as in the case of Orpheus and Eurydice.

The chorus's unstoppable rejoicing at *Peace* 301-37 is a comic inflation of a motif discernible at, e.g., E. *El.* 596 f.

16. The story of Demeter and Persephone is relevant to our play *qua* story and because Demeter, like Peace, is giver of wealth: see Hesiod, *Theog.* 969, Homeric Hymn to Demeter, 486-9; at Orphic Hymn 40 Demeter, like Earth, is also 'nurturer of young men' (see T.H. Price, *Kourotrophos*, (Leiden 1978), 199 f).

Another legend which gave rise to representations of a female figure rising from the ground was that of Pandora.

17. In the *Origins of Attic Comedy* (Cambridge, 1934), 85, F.M. Cornford wrote: 'Now the scheme of this Anodos ritual is the basis of the first part of the *Peace*. The image of Eirene is dragged up by the chorus of farmers, apparently out of an artificial cave or mound in the orchestra . . . Hermes presides over the operation . . .' In Thrace seed corn was stored in caves.

E. associated Dionysus and Peace in the first stasimon of *Bacchae* (419-20): 'Dionysus loves Peace, the goddess who gives prosperity and who nurtures young men.'

18. The association of peace and prosperity is found in Homer, *Od.* 24. 486, and in an elegiac couplet (Theognis 885-6) the two are addressed as deities: 'May Peace and Wealth keep the city so that I may join in revelry. Evil War is no friend of mine.' Cf. the epithets used in invoking her in *PMG* 1021, Euripides fr. 453, Ar. fr. 109. In E. *Supplices* (488-91) peace is linked with wealth, human fertility and the Muses.

Peace is 'lover of feasts' at *Thesm.* 1147.

19. For the Horae see Hesiod, *Theog.* 901 f and M.L. West's comments on these deities. Pindar (fr. 30) tells how Themis 'brought forth the ladies of golden veils and radiant fruits, the truthful ones, the Seasons'. In a fragment of a Paean (1. 5-10) the Seasons, daughters of Themis, accompany the 'all-fulfilling year' to celebrate a festival of Apollo at Thebes with the 'flowers of right-thinking Eunomia'. On these seasonal dancers see W. Mullen, *Choreia: Pindar & Dance* (Princeton, 1982), 217-20.

Dike and eunomia, prerequisites of peace, need to be practised by ordinary people as well as by their rulers and Eunomia is said by Bacchylides (13. 186-9) to preserve the cities of pious men in a peaceful condition. For the link between communal religion and the 'pattern of the farmer's year' see E.R. Dodds, *The Ancient Concept of Progress* (Oxford, 1973), 145.

Pausanias (5. 17. 1) describes figures of the Seasons (near those of Zeus and Hera and a standing Themis) in the Heraeon at Olympia, and at Athens there was a temple dedicated to two Horae, Thallo and Carpo.

Very little survives of Ar.'s play *The Seasons*, perhaps roughly contemporary with *Peace*.

20. For Opora and Theoria see Newiger 1957, 108 f.

21. During the Olympic Games in 424 there had been in fact no sacred truce and the Athenians and their allies were guarded against possible Spartan attack.

22. On the sexual aspect see J. Henderson, *The Maculate Muse* (New Haven and London, 1975), 62-6.

23. For Opora the following two passages are relevant. In a Nemean Ode (5. 6) Pindar praises an athlete so young that he does not yet show on his cheek the *opora* ('full summer') which brings forth the bloom of the grape; cf. *I.* 2. 5.

In A.'s *Suppliant Women* (edited by H. Friis Johansen and E.W. Whittle) Danaus, warning his daughters, compares the protection of young women with that of ripe fruit (*opora*) threatened by human and animal thieves; the passer-by, over-powered by desire, tries to gain what attracts him (998 f, cf. 1015, with editors' comments).

24. Pindar, *O* 13. 6-8; later he calls the Horae 'many-flowered'. In the myth of the Ninth *Pythian* (61 f) Chiron prophesies that Earth and the Seasons will make the baby Aristaeus immortal when Hermes has carried him to them. Nemean 8.1. associates a singular Hora with Aphrodite.

25. Bacchylides fr. 4. 61-80 (the Paean for Pythian Apollo); at 15. 53-6 the Horae are mentioned. Ar. invented the compound epithet 'most hostile to the shield grip' for Peace (662).

26. E.453N^2 (*Cresphontes*); in the *Suppliant Women* (489-91), written not long before *Peace*, the Herald describes peace as 'most friendly to the muses' arts,

hostile to lament, delighting in human increase, rejoicing in riches'. The association of peace and music is matched by A.'s references to Ares' antipathy to choirs and the lyre (*Suppliant Women*, 681). In the *Prayer to the Fates* (*PMG* 1018 (b)) the poet asks them to send Eunomia and her sisters and 'make this city forget the misfortunes which lie heavily on her heart'.

27. Ar. fr. 109, cf. Ar. fr. 107 (*Farmers*): 'Let's leave the city now for the country. It's time to take a bath and enjoy some leisure there at long last.'

28. In his other play called *Peace* the agricultural element is differently presented: A. 'of Peace, the friend of all mankind I am the trusted nurse, steward, fellow worker, guardian, daughter and sister . . .' B. 'What is your name?' A. 'Farming.'

29. Two recurrent words deserve brief comment: Trygaeus boasts that he has freed Athenians from *ponoi* (920), from hardship in general, but specifically from war, for which *ponoi* was a current euphemism: see A.L. Boegehold, *GRBS* 23 (1982), 147 f. Ar. repeats the word I translate as 'free', 'get rid of ', frequently in the war plays: *Diallage* (Reconciliation) belongs to the same group of words.

30. See above, p. 96 f.

31. Hermes' speech is discussed in detail by A. Cassio, *Riv di Fil* 110 (1982), 22-44.

32. The reliability of the opening section is at once questioned by Trygaeus and the chorus leader ('I never heard that before' 615 f). See below, n. 37.

33. The disappearance of Peace may be compared with Demeter's withdrawal in angry grief for her daughter; in Ar.'s *Poiesis* the heroine, Poetry, who has withdrawn as the result of being wronged, is the object of a search (see H. Lloyd-Jones, *ZPE* 42 (1981), 23 f).

34. See above, p. 49.

35. Plutarch's statement (*Cimon* 13) that the Athenians had established an altar of Peace in 465 is often questioned.

36. See above, p. 106.

37. In a play in which Peace and War are unequivocal, substantial entities and Trygaeus is constant in his devotion to peace, the mercurial, questionable, fickle aspects of Hermes are thrown into relief and his roles exemplify his inconstancy, his lack of consistent principle. 'Hermes is cunning, and occasionally violent; a trickster, a robber. So it is not surprising that he is also the patron of interpreters . . . He is the god of going between: between the dead and the living, but also between the latent and the manifest (god, one might say, of the third ear), and between the text, whether plain or hermeneutic, and the dying generations of its readers'. (F. Kermode, *The Genesis of Secrecy* (Cambridge, Mass. 1979), 1 f). The god is perhaps not unlike the typical Athenian as he is portrayed in Aristophanic comedy.

38. As bystanders might admire the close ranks and gleaming equipment of soldiers marching to war, so Hermes and Trygaeus compliment the farmers in terms partly military and partly, as is appropriate, referring to food: barley-cake is close-textured and the word I translate 'buffet table' suggests an abundance of dishes, a 'good spread'. Xenophon (*Mem.* 3. 3. 14) likens soldiers to a chorus, reversing the Aristophanic image.

39. Cf. the fragment of the *Second Peace* (295) in which someone is ordered to use a shield to cover a well.

40. These young singers of songs from 'outside' comedy, performing just before the play's final scene, balance the children, imported from tragedy, whose pleas precede Trygaeus' flight.

41. Archilochus (fr. 6D) takes the loss of his shield in a matter-of-fact way which is the reverse of heroic and which might be thought congenial to the cowardly Cleonymus.

42. *Peace* ed. Platnauer (Oxford, 1964) viii; Moulton.

Nor is my *Peace* that of Charles Segal in *Tragedy and Civilization* (Harvard, 1981), 51 f: 'Plots like those of *Peace* or *Birds* blur or reverse the distinction between man and god . . . in Aristophanes' *Peace* the hero reaches Olympus on his grotesquely earthy variant of Pegasus and there attains the divine prerogatives of Zeus.' Not so.

43. Even Hermes' abusive address to Trygaeus (182-4) lacks sustained hostility since its main purpose is to facilitate the joke in the following lines.

7 DRAMATISING INSTITUTIONS

Each poet with a different
 talent writes,
One praises, one instructs,
 another bites.
  (Wentworth Dillon)

As soon as Cloudcuckoocity has been established in the sky, a string of visitors arrives seeking gainful employment. They are not, as one would expect in a twentieth-century *Birds*, business men plus a sprinkling of potential civic administrators but, in order of arrival, priest, soothsayer, poet, town-planner, inspector, dealer in laws. These are some of the people the new city, like the old Athens, is supposed to need and I refer to their introduction partly as a reminder that the *polis* and its institutions were very much *sui generis*, that the boundaries between civic and religious, public and private, were not drawn as we should draw them and that the roles of men and women, family and individual, were not defined in a way immediately familiar and intelligible to us. One simple example is comedy itself. In the present age a comedy is one product of the entertainment industry; in our terminology the ancient festivals of Dionysus at which comedies were performed might be labelled either as religious or as civic occasions but in neither category should we quite expect to find competition so dominant.[1] The British Arts Festival, itself a remote descendant of Greek culture, beginning with its cathedral service attended by the mayor and including lectures, competitions for young cellists, opera, plays, brings together but does not combine these separate aspects.

To clarify the focus of this chapter it will be helpful to begin by drawing a contrast between comedy and tragedy. With rare exceptions, Greek tragedy dramatised what were essentially private and personal situations usually involving close kin.[2] My generalisation remains true even when, in Sophocles' *Philoctetes*, for example, the motivation of the play is the Greek army's need for Philoctetes and for the bow he possesses or when, as in Aeschylus' *Persians*, the defeat of a king is the defeat of a whole nation. *Persians*, in dealing with recent history, might be expected to be less unlike comedy, always set in the present, than the other surviving tragedies whose time is the remote past but in fact its account of battle or council does not essentially differ from that of any other Aeschylean tragedy. It is, of course, in the final play of the *Oresteia* that Aeschylus both creates and re-creates a real institution, the Athenian court called the Areopagus.[3] Reducing the concluding section of the trilogy to crude terms, one sees that the existence of the Areopagus offers the playwright a way out of the impasse of interminable revenge, a way moreover which is essentially dramatic in that opposing views about human and divine justice can be acted out in Orestes' trial. As will soon appear, in the *Wasps* Aristophanes was to follow the tragic pattern.

If it is only rarely that tragedy actually 'borrows' from the institutions of the *polis* the means of enacting part of its story (the songs of the chorus quite often adopt existing forms such as hymn or lament), there is no doubt at all of its indirect and often unexpressed links with the wider community. Within the tragedy the repercussions of the decisions of an Antigone or an Agamemnon are felt not only by their kin and by the people in authority in their community but eventually by ordinary men and women: Oedipus' investigation (in *King Oedipus*) was actually initiated because of the sickness affecting the land and people of Thebes.[4] Tragedies themselves affected those who saw and heard them in ways hard to demonstrate but easy to envisage: could an Athenian father and son return home after a performance of *Antigone* without pondering, among other things, the nature and justification of parental authority? Could the audience of 458 fail to debate questions of attribution of blame for war or of pollution by homicide or of the place of chthonic deities in Athenian cult? Like all writers the Athenian dramatists were influenced by the times in which they lived; more than most works of the imagination, their plays have leapt the fence which divides what is past and mythical and concerned with kings and heroes from the real world of fifth-century Athenians engaged in the running of a powerful and important *polis*.[5]

Returning to comedy we find that Aristophanic plays raise directly issues whose immediately contemporary relevance was obvious and whose presentation on the stage involved some impersonation of 'real' men as well as incidental and often trivial mention of features of Athenian public life like festivals, landmarks, historical events, current gossip and so forth. It may well be indeed that this abundance of detail and this insistent topicality distracted attention from the wider and more lasting implications of the dramatised issues, that the Athenians looked at Cleon rather than debating the proper location of power in democracies (and that we have followed suit).[6] Whether or not this is so, what is remarkable (though largely unremarked) is the substantial use made of institutions in creating the inscenation of the play. *Acharnians*, to take the earliest example, includes successively an Assembly meeting, a celebration of the Country Dionysia, trading at a market, preparations for the feast of the Choes (and for the military expedition).

If the reader pauses to ask himself why surviving Old Comedy makes such extensive use of public occasions he is likely to reply: in order to satirise them or hold them up to ridicule. This answer, if true, or partially true, suggests, or should suggest, further questions, such as: Are institutions (or these institutions) ridiculous *per se*? Are some institutions unnecessary and undesirable, others all right? Or if institutions themselves are unexceptionable, is it merely at some times, in some ways, and in some hands that they are open to criticism?[7]

For the moment, however, let us forget the satirist and consider only the playwright. In the *Clouds'* parabasis the poet boasts 'I show my skill by presenting novelties (*kainas ideas*) all the time' (*Clouds* 547): the embodiment of story and of theme in varied and visually striking stage action or tableaux is certainly an important part of his creative skill.[8] This can be illustrated by making a brief summary of the story of one of the comedies as distinct from giving a scene by scene account. A summary of *Acharnians* might run as follows: an Athenian citizen, sick of the war with Sparta, makes and profits by a private peace with the enemy. Accurate enough as a summary but how different from the play as experienced, even by the reader!

In this part of my introductory section I have been suggesting the positive side of the dramatising of institutions, their provision of material as well as setting to a dramatist whose success depended to a large extent on novelty and freshness of treatment. Nevertheless staging institutions may well be problematic. Even granted, as seems likely, that the recreation of trial or ritual caused no offence to cast or audience, technical difficulties had to be overcome (and as we examine specific scenes later in this chapter I shall hope to pinpoint one or two individual problems of this kind).

Oikos and Court of Law: *Wasps* and Other Plays

In recent years a good deal has been written about male and female roles and the relationship of *oikos* and *polis* as revealed in *Lysistrata*, *Women at the Thesmophoria* and *Assemblywomen*.[9] The aspect of family life which I wish to consider here is the relationship of father and son, crucial in *Clouds* and essential in *Wasps*. From one point of view, that of the literary historian, these early examples of a situation which was to become the germ or staple of so many plays and novels must be of interest; the student of Greek drama will also want to compare the comic expression of this kind of family conflict with that found in *Antigone* or *Hippolytus* for example. My own purpose here is rather to ask questions about the ways in which comedy uses (and distorts) the everyday life of the family.

Just as Dicaeopolis appears to have an only daughter, so Strepsiades and Bdelycleon have a son apiece (in the earlier *Banqueters* the father had two sons, one virtuous, the other dissolute). In *Clouds*, to sketch in a situation to be described more fully in the concluding chapter, the father still controls the *oikos*, as best he can given that his authority over his son is not secure. As we have seen, very near the opening differences of attitude, values and life-style between the father on the one side and the mother, son and his maternal uncle on the other are carefully established (*Clouds* 40-78). There are even indications that Pheidippides can disobey his father just because he is sure of a welcome from his uncle (although financially it is upon his unhappy father that he seems to depend). In their quarrel the father interestingly appeals to his son by recalling the physical care he had given him when he was tiny (thus raising a doubt about child-rearing as an exclusively female occupation), but Pheidippides can no longer be moved by sentiment (1380-1405).

A father's care is even more important in *Wasps*, but this time paradoxically it is extended to the father by his son, now in charge of the household. It must be assumed that Philocleon has made way for his son for reasons of age or infirmity (we are not told that Bdelycleon has a wife) but that he, together with his wife and daughter, continues to live under the same roof. In his son's view, the old man is now in his second childhood (or sometimes adolescence) and needs 'fathering' in both senses, loving care and social and moral guidance. This topsy-turvy situation does not prevail throughout, but its serious implications deserve as much attention as its comic aspect.

It is customary for those writing about Aristophanes to make a distinction between the public issue prominent in each play and the personal story whose course shapes the drama. Although to an extent this distinction is a matter of convenience, a useful way of simplifying and organising material for a lecture perhaps, there is a real problem about the relation of public and private in Aristophanic comedy, even a question as to the place of the family-based story in a play largely concerned with what happened in public. At this moment I am looking at a household in which father and son are at variance; in an earlier chapter I described their debate and soon I shall move on to the trial at whose conclusion the son plays a trick on his old father. In the debate the father's personal happiness is the criterion: Bdelycleon's attacks on Cleon and on the abuse of the jury system may as a result be made to appear incidental to his demonstration that his father's present happiness is founded on an illusion about the extent of his power. Described in these terms the public issue of *Wasps* can be made to vanish, to leave behind a conventional 'family comedy'. Let me now try the opposite procedure and give an outline of the public issue as it might be stated in an introduction. 'There is concern and indignation that a politician like Cleon can wield unchecked power over courts and jurors, and in particular that the jurors' loyalty to their "champion" is misplaced. In the play an opponent of Cleon's policies seeks to reform one of his supporters, partly by convincing him that jurors are being exploited and partly by enabling him to enjoy more varied and intense pleasures than he experienced as a juror.' There is no doubt that political discussions on such topics would often take place outside the *oikos* and there is no reason why plays, like Platonic dialogues, could not set fictional debates in the public spaces of Athens where they would really happen. Was it just the influence of tragedy that impelled the playwright to make supporter and opponent of Cleon members of the same family?

Through many centuries of comedy a leading part was to be taken by the young man of good family who kicks over the traces, lives extravagantly, gets drunk and engages in amorous intrigues, all in spite of his father's efforts to guide his conduct. At the end of *Wasps* Philocleon comes home from a party (at which he had behaved disgracefully) bringing a girl with him and drunk enough to fall out with all he meets on the way (1325-479). Although we are not allowed to forget entirely that he is an old man, he is mainly presented as an adolescent, and even addressed as one (1333); it is as the adolescent son of a rich family that the juror, once weaned from his addiction to lawsuits, enters a period of preparation for attendance at symposia, a way of life which is a great change in the direction of luxury and comfort (1454 f), and which culminates in renewed conflict over his unruly behaviour. Thus the play comes full circle when the slave who had initially described the old juror's madness (88-130) sees him dancing drunkenly at the close and recommends a dose of hellebore to cure his mania (1486-9).[10]

What can be discovered from *Wasps* about paternal attitudes and behaviour? The members of the chorus, themselves shown grumbling at their sometimes cheeky young sons (248-57), compliment Bdelycleon on his wisdom and affection for his father and his desire to provide him with a classier way of life (1465, 1471-3).[11] It is reasonable to suppose that a father might well pride himself on such qualities in dealing with a son and in fact Bdelycleon's warmth of feeling towards Philocleon, not fully reciprocated, survives through thick and thin. It may be expressed in physical care as when he provides such home comforts as hot soup and a potty during the trial scene, just as if his father really were a baby, or it may take a more subtle form in the use of the trial itself as a distraction for the old man and as a harmless substitute for attendance at an actual court. Here too, of course, there is a suggestion of adult complicity in a childish game. What are we to make of the trick by which Philocleon is (literally) led to acquit the thief in the home trial? Perhaps it serves only to make the ex-juror receptive to Bdelycleon's promise to 'bring him up nicely, take him about to dinner parties, to drinks parties and to shows, and generally give him a good time from now on' (1004-6). More likely it shows that Bdelycleon, too, can manipulate procedures for his own ends.

In this story of a changing relationship the trial scene marks an important stage. Philocleon, who has already been brought to understand that his belief that jurors are privileged was ill founded, has by no means reconciled himself to a powerless and boring life spent at home. In fact, although he is now better informed, he is no happier than he was at the beginning of the play. It is because the son cares about his father's happiness and comfort that he prepares to set up a domestic law court where the old juror can hear cases at will. However, as we shall see in due course, when the scene ends the father has again been reduced to despair, by unforeseen means.

In Aristophanic comedy it is usually enough to say This is the Pnyx or This is Euripides' house: thereafter the previous scene is forgotten, replaced by the new location. The trial in *Wasps* is an exception: the setting remains the same, the house belonging to Bdelycleon and his father, but it becomes, additionally, a court by a process of 'Let's pretend', a childish game intended to gratify the chief player, a game prefaced by a longish preparation scene. Philocleon is so far a reformed character that he stays at home, entering with ingenious glee into the equipping and rearrangement of the private space of the *oikos* so that it can double as public space and 'house' a court.

Aristophanes is adept at prolonging scenes which lead up to some great event.[12] Here both participants, especially the father, express their impatience for a trial to begin (825, 847, 849, 852, 860) while drawing out the preparation of the court. Thus there are 60 lines of activity, during which articles are variously fetched from inside or improvised, or both; the errand boy, usually Bdelycleon, may be unexpectedly replaced by his father; once the son goes in but the next emergence is that of a slave (832-5). Initially Bdelycleon sends out for basic equipment plus articles provided as home comforts for an old man; potty, fire, warm soup, a cockerel to wake him if he nods off during a defence speech (805-17). Thereafter a shrine and some railings to give the semblance of a court are requested by Philocleon, while such necessaries as legal notices, voting urns and a water-clock (for timing speeches) are supplied one by one.

Unfortunately we cannot recreate the stage setting thus obtained so as to say how far it accurately presents (with its homely and 'truly Attic' improvisations) the layout of the actual court in which the juror had served; the best one can do is to try to establish the disposition and movement of persons and things in such a way that what needs to be seen can be seen and in particular so that the old man, with his paraphernalia, is not masked by the other participants in the trial. Thus it is impossible to say whether the necessities of staging prevented realism in setting (supposing any degree of realism was desired).

We had been led to expect that, the court once set up, a trial would begin, but there now follows another kind of preparation, religious this time. Bdelycleon sends for garlands and incense so that he and the chorus may join in prayers.[13] In their timing the prayers and hymns mark the establishment of a new institution, the domestic court, but their content reminds us, not of the preparations we have just been watching, but of the relations of father and son. This is made clear from the opening anapaests in which the Wasps express approval that father and son have come together 'after their war and strife' (866 f) and in Bdelycleon's later prayer to Apollo for the reform of his father's 'tough, hardhearted character' and for the removal of his ill temper and prickliness in favour of kindness and sympathy and a heart tinged with honey (877-84). The Wasps endorse these words because 'we have been well-disposed to you ever since we realised your devotion to the demos' (887-90). In this way the dramatist has neatly reminded his audience of the results of the agon, of the difference between Philocleon and his former confrères and of the son's benevolence, while also underlining the domestic motivation of the trial.

Apollo does not change the old man's disposition. Almost before the prayer has ended, the juror is displaying readiness to convict, to punish severely, to judge by appearances, to ignore evidence, all in spite of his son's attempts to moderate his behaviour (893, 898, 912, 918-21, etc.). No doubt these remarks made by Philocleon exaggerate the attitudes of typical jurors; their dramatic function is to keep the audience aware of the doubling or trebling of roles in this scene where the father is juror and the son advocate and president, a situation not altogether unlike that of the actor in the theatre of Dionysus, who in the course of one play often had to play more than one role.

It had originally been suggested that a misdeed by a slave, who would no doubt normally be punished by his master without more ado, would provide occasion for a trial within the *oikos* (766-70, cf. 827 f); in the event the theft of a cheese by one of the dogs, occurring opportunely during the preparation of the court, enables a trial to go ahead. The thief, a dog called Labes ('Snatcher') is prosecuted by another dog, Cur (played by the third actor), whose speech, however, is not so much concerned with the accused and his crime as with his own rights and position.[14] He does not care that the cheese belonged to Bdelycleon, only that *he* did not receive his portion from the accused, a selfish solitary eater (923); unless the criminal is punished, Cur will never again bark as a watchdog should (927-30). Various kitchen utensils now enter as witnesses for the defence, but before their evidence is called it is Labes' turn to mount the platform. When, unlike Cur, he is found to be speechless, Bdelycleon undertakes on his behalf a defence based not on innocence but on previous good character with the added excuse of lack of training (950-9). The cheese-grater (not, I think, played by a mute actor, like Labes, but dumb as the statue of Peace is dumb) is now represented as asserting in support of Labes that she had in fact grated the cheese; Labes' advocate concludes by the standard appeal for pity, adapted to suit a dog; his final touch is to introduce Labes' 'children', whimpering, tearful puppies (976-8).[15]

Before turning to the political significance of the trial, it is worth analysing the overt 'doggy' material, both that which relates only to the dogs and that which has a double meaning. Clearly, if it would be odd for a householder to go right through court procedures before punishing a servant, it is absurd to try a dog; similarly, if the conventions and clichés of human forensic oratory raise a smile, they will be more ridiculous applied to dogs. To this basic comedy something more complex is added, mainly in the comparison of the two dogs which itself comes about because Bdelycleon speaks for Labes (thus also avoiding the use of another actor). Labes, he says, is a good dog who chases wolves away and can take charge of a large flock of sheep (952-5); he is also an efficient housedog, always on the prowl and content to eat scraps (957, 968 f). Cur, by contrast, is a stay at home whose position enables him to demand his share of whatever is brought across the threshold, 'or else he bites' (970-2).[16] All of this makes good sense purely as an assessment of dogs: in order to be of use a watchdog must be alert and responsible but also obedient and subservient to his master; both the sheep-dog and the housedog are required to bark when danger threatens. A well-trained dog should not have gone into the kitchen or stolen food, far less have menaced those with right of entry to the house.

Once familiar with the criteria used in assessing dogs, it is possible to distinguish the additional interest given to these passages when they are understood to apply also to men. (And throughout there is no clear line between treating animals or even things as though, like creatures in a fable, they had the human powers of speech and thought and presenting them as men with the characteristics typical of dogs, or wasps.) For example, to call a man a stationary housewatcher suggests that he is deliberately shirking military service, an insult not applicable to Cur (970 f). Similarly Labes is (naturally) speechless: a human defendant may have nothing to say for himself or he may actually be struck dumb with fear (944-9).

Labes' silence allows Bdelycleon, his advocate, to speak unfavourably of Cur-Cleon. Whereas the defendant's command has taken him abroad, Cleon has stayed in Athens, demanding his share of all revenues (and claiming that any offence against him is an offence against the ordinary people) (970-2, 908 f). In his prosecution Cleon objects that he has not persuaded Laches to share the 'cheese' he acquired on his Sicilian campaign (914): Cleon cannot be expected to help people unless and until he gets a reward (915-16).[17] The impression given, by Cleon himself and others, is that he is a thief (903, 927 f), that his services to the state consist of mere loud noise, that he shirks duty abroad and that he frightens others into submission. It may also be indicated that he is greedy and given to yapping or whining (instead of barking) (904). About Laches' embezzlement of booty taken in Sicily little is said: cheese-grater's 'evidence' may be taken to suggest the possibility that he had not actually 'devoured the whole cheese' himself but shared it with the soldiers (965 f).

At the end of the scene interest immediately switches from the acquitted defendant and everyone else involved in the trial to the old juror, again a tragic figure. Formerly he had longed, like the Euripidean Phaedra, to leave his home and escape to a place where he could be happy (753-6);[18] now he has suffered a tragic reversal, having been tricked into voting for an acquittal against his will. Nearly fainting with shock he begs the gods' pardon: 'It was unwittingly and uncharacteristically that I did the deed' (1002). He has indeed learned his lesson, not by attending to his son's precepts, but by what he has experienced.[19] It is one single vote which has decided that the accused will not be punished for the theft he committed; this single vote was cast by Philocleon's hand but the directing purpose was Bdelycleon's and he had also been the presiding magistrate and spoken for the defendant. If there is some slight reminiscence here of the acquittal of Orestes in the *Eumenides*, the Furies have no equivalent: the Wasps have been converted from implacable retribution to benevolent responsibility before the trial begins and take no part in it. Nevertheless the promise made by Bdelycleon to cherish his father henceforward so that he leads an enjoyable and respected life, abandoning his present distress, may faintly echo Athene's conciliation of the Eumenides.

The scene's primary function is to increase, by fair means or foul, Bdelycleon's control of his father. There seems to be no serious criticism of the procedures of courts, here presented (in condensed form) from opening proclamation to final verdict, although forensic rhetorical clichés and appeals for pity are ridiculed. It is difficult to assess the strength of the attack on current misuse of the legal system: a cynic might argue, on the evidence of *Wasps*, that all trials were no more than play-acting, or that jurors were inevitably puppets controlled by prosecutors and court officials. The formation of such an attitude would result mainly from Bdelycleon's final deception of his father. It seems to me that the scene engages the audience's attention at a number of levels simultaneously and that it can do this because the element of pretence is foregrounded. We watch father and son playing at law courts, pretending that dogs, cockerels, even kitchen tools are sentient beings; they remind us from time to time that they are aware not only of their pretence of being engaged in a real trial but also of the real identity of their creatures: what happened in the home corresponded with and may be taken to stand for deeds committed by elected or self-appointed servants of the Demos, Cleon and Laches, in recent history. A dog can be trained to acquire habits which make him useful to man: a man like Cleon may sink without shame to the behaviour of the undomesticated dog, which is made more harmful and more shocking because directed by human intellect. For all the fun of the trial scene, for all its invitation to complicity in fantastic make-believe, there is no escape from the issues of abuse of power, exploitation and trickery.

Assemblies: *Acharnians* and Other Plays

One is tempted to suggest that Aristophanes was fascinated by the challenge of converting meetings into theatre. Twice he used the direct method, in *Acharnians* and *Women at the Thesmophoria*, once the report of a meeting by a participant (Sausage-seller in *Knights*), and in *Assemblywomen* a mixture of representation and report. Surprisingly enough the formal debate, which is a component of so many comedies, is never staged in an institutional setting, and conversely, where there is a meeting of Council or Assembly, there is no full-scale adversarial debate. Let me illustrate this statement: although the first debate in *Knights* between Paphlagon and Sausage-seller takes place before the house of Demos, actually on the Pnyx, in no way does it differ from a normal dramatic agon. Similarly the argument between father and son in *Wasps*, held before jurors, has no hint of the law court. In order to present a clearer picture of Aristophanes' dramatisation of Assemblies, it is necessary to look at scenes from two of the later plays as well as at *Knights* and *Acharnians*. It is paradoxical that the fullest representation of a meeting is the Assembly held by the women celebrating the festival of the Thesmophoria. This scene could be studied from several points of view, among them the treatment of women, the portrayal of Euripides and his art, the use of rhetoric or of humour, but for my purposes in this chapter it is the arrangement and organisation of the proceedings and their contribution to the play that will receive attention.

The plot of *Women at the Thesmophoria* springs from Euripides' awareness that this very day the women holding their festival will decide whether he lives or dies. He explains his offence briefly: 'I put them in tragedies and say bad things about them' (85). The women's decision is to be reached at a debate which is a normal part of the rites of the Thesmophoria. Euripides needs someone to speak for him who can infiltrate the gathering convincingly disguised as a woman; a connection of his finally takes on the task.[20]

The scene changes to the women's meeting-place for the arrival of Euripides' kinsman, accompanied by a maidservant, at the moment when the heraldess is summoning the worshippers to the prayers which open the session of debate. The women sing a hymn invoking Zeus and other gods and then the heraldess lists a number of crimes and offences upon whose perpetrators (including Euripides) she calls down a curse, while bidding her hearers to ask the gods' blessing on all other women (332-51). Again there is a sung response by the women which overlaps the heraldess's words. At the conclusion of this religious observance she makes a proclamation about the Assembly and its business, after which the debate begins.

Before commenting on the speeches made during the debate I should like to consider what might have been in the minds of the spectators at this point. First and foremost, I suppose, they will be curious to see how long it is before the kinsman's female impersonation is detected and whether he gives himself away by some slip. Secondly, they will expect to hear the women's case against Euripides and its refutation by his agent. Thirdly, they will surely be intrigued by the idea of women taking part in an Assembly and in particular by the opportunity of witnessing part of a secret, exclusively female rite, as recreated by the dramatist. In these conditions the male Assembly will function as standard for comparison, not as target.

In this dramatised meeting the essentials are opening proclamation and contributions from three speakers, each speech followed by choral comment. Remove these songs and turn the speeches into prose and the procedure would be much like that of the regular Assembly. The heraldess's proclamation makes clear that the women have a Council, called the *Boule*, like its male counterpart, which arranges and decides on the agenda for the larger meeting. She announces the Council's conclusions, naming the president, secretary and proposer of the motion for debate. The first item on the agenda is to be the proper punishment of Euripides for the *adikia* all agree he has committed. She ends with the conventional opening question: 'Who wishes to speak?' (379).

The wording of the proclamation in effect turns the Assembly into a kind of court of law at which the tragedian is being tried, *in absentia*, but, since Euripides' guilt has already been determined, this 'trial' is to begin where others end, in proposals for penalties. In the event, however, the debate is not so restricted in scope as the agenda suggested.

The first speaker puts on the garland and clears her throat 'as the politicians do' when beginning a long speech (381-2). (She will speak 50 lines without interruption, a 'long speech' for Aristophanic comedy.) The gist of her complaint against the tragedian gives a new slant on the conventional role of the poet as teacher; Euripides, she says, 'has instructed our husbands in women's evil ways' (399 f). As a result they are detected when committing their traditional misdemeanours, of which she lists and illustrates a good number, with apt quotation from the tragic poet himself. She concludes by proposing the penalty of death.

Unlike this practised orator with her conventional phrases, rhetorical questions and other devices, the second contributor is artless and speaks briefly from her own experience. As a widow she has had to support her five children by making garlands. Now that Euripides has inculcated atheism, her sales have been halved. He must be punished. Thus far a convincing if hackneyed case, beautifully undermined by her closing lines: she must hurry off to the Agora to complete an order for 20 garlands (457-8).

Whereas each of these speakers is complimented in song for her skill and intelligence, the reception to be given to the third and last debater is quite the opposite. Euripides' kinsman and defender, in a speech rather longer than that of the first woman, begins by allying 'herself' with those who hate the poet. But, she continues, seeing that this is a private occasion for women, 'why do we get upset if he reveals just a couple of our misdeeds – out of a total of thousands?' (474-5). From her own life and that of the other women she quotes examples of misconduct, concluding in fine style: 'Aren't these our misdeeds? Yes, by Artemis. And do we still rage at Euripides though we suffer less than our deeds have earned?' (517-19).

I hope that I have written a sufficient amount about each of these speeches to show what the Assembly format contributes to the comedy. If the playwright had chosen to use the agon form he would have had to compose one speech defending Euripides and a second refuting the first, with a clear result at the end, whether decided by a chorus or an arbitrator. By incorporating a debate in Assembly he can include speeches of substantial length and formality without being limited to the symmetrical pair of the agon and, although all three of the speeches are concerned with the same broad issue, there is a kind of progression from first to last which I will shortly try to describe. Moreover, there is an easy transition from the end of the final speech through the informal angry exchanges between the kinsman and the first woman to the arrival of the effeminate Cleisthenes to report Euripides' rumoured attempt at subversion which would not have been possible if the strictly prescribed form of the agon had been employed.

The first woman, blaming Euripides for men's new wariness and suspicion in their dealings with wife or sister, inadvertently includes in her account instances that show that their watchfulness is justified. Women do filch goods from the stores they are supposed to keep safe; they do attempt to pass off others' children as their own (419 f, 407 f). This woman, who clearly takes as her linguistic model the rhetoric of the male politician, is made to admit to the faults normally ascribed to women by men in comedy. Presumably the simplest response to this speech would be that of the male chauvinist delighted to hear again both the old charges that women drink, gossip and take lovers and the countermeasures adopted by their husbands and guardians. The next level of appreciation comes from her combination of rhetorical sophistication and innocent revelation of reprehensible conduct: were male politicians thought exempt from accusing themselves out of their own mouths? Finally there is the level at which one becomes aware that this woman has been created by one man for another man to impersonate.

By contrast the simple, short-breathed sentences of the second woman seem to represent her lack of education, and her *naïveté* comes out in her working of the old joke about Euripides' mother: it was because he was reared among vegetables growing wild in the country that his treatment of women is so uncultivated (455 f, cf. 387). How will this woman's children turn out, brought up in the myrtle groves where she gathered materials for her garland-making?

Her little speech is not much more than an interlude before the climax of this act of the drama. What can his kinsman say to defend Euripides without further enraging the women? How can the comic irony of his disguise be exploited? Can any further scandalous examples of women's misconduct be unveiled? The solution found by the dramatist is to provide a speech very like Dicaeopolis' defence in *Acharnians* in its approach. The speaker in each of these plays expresses loathing of the enemy, reminds his audience of the absence of outsiders and then deals expansively with the wrongdoings of his own side or group

(*Thesm.* 469 f, cf. *Ach.* 509, 504 f); each speech contains a passage of narration, Dicaeopolis recounting the events leading up to the outbreak of war and the kinsman incidents from married life (*Ach.* 515-39, *Thesm.* 476-90, 502-16); whereas in *Acharnians*, instead of defending his own peacemaking, Dicaeopolis had shown that Megarians and Athenians as well as Spartans shared responsibility for the war, here Euripides' kinsman 'defends' the poet only in so far as 'she' enumerates female sins he had failed to mention; in fact Euripides' name occurs only three times in 'her' speech (467, 490, 518) and there is only one mention of a female character, Phaedra (497).[21] What the kinsman does triumphantly and gleefully achieve is the further blackening of the female sex with 'her' stories of 'her' own adultery, after four days of marriage, with a childhood lover, and of the tricks played by a childless wife on her husband. If women really acted as the kinsman proudly claims, then the continuity of the *oikos*, so valued by the Greeks, would be a sham. Were there even members of the audience in 412 who went home determined to keep their women more closely guarded having heard the kinsman's admissions? Or was there rather an increasing enjoyment of the even greater risk of detection as the kinsman's disloyalty to the female sex became more and more blatant? At all events, when challenged by the first woman, the kinsman refuses to be silenced, even when threatened, and no doubt he could have developed the theme much further had it not been for Cleisthenes' arrival.

To conclude: there is no reason to suppose that a negative attitude to Assemblies as such underlies this scene; if an Assembly of women is to be held and to make decisions, then naturally it will follow the procedures followed by men meeting on the Pnyx, or so at least we may suppose it seemed to a dramatist who will not necessarily have known exactly how the women conducted themselves at their private festival. The Assembly scene serves the plot well and facilitates the disclosure in breadth and detail of women's sexual and moral offences.

At the private rites of the Thesmophoria, the kinsman is an intruder and the audience an illicit spectator. The opening scene of *Assemblywomen* is a secret rehearsal for a meeting of the Athenian Assembly which women disguised as men are to infiltrate. In the later play the secrecy is conspiratorial, not religious, although the women disguise themselves for the same reason as the kinsman, namely to be accepted as members of the opposite sex. The rehearsal scene has for its climax the leader Praxagora's revolutionary speech in which she proposes that the government of Athens be handed over to women. Although Praxagora admirably takes the part of the male politician skilled in rhetoric, her comrades display an inability to remember that they are supposed to be men and, unlike the women at the festival, an ignorance about the routines of public assembly which provide the rehearsal with most of its humour, particularly given an awareness that young men play the female roles.

The rehearsal includes several good jibes at the Assembly as run by men: it is a talking-shop (129) whose discussions are so crazy that they could not have been made by sober men (137-9). More seriously, Praxagora's indictment of the management of affairs by men shows up weaknesses in the machinery of democratic government (174-208).

At this point the spectators may well expect that they will shortly see the performance in Assembly of what had been rehearsed in the prologue of the comedy. However, instead of enacting the debate, the dramatist eventually provides a report of what had happened, a report all the more pointed for being given by a man. The speaker, just back from an exceptionally crowded meeting engaged in what would now be called a crisis debate, answers his neighbour's questions, finally telling him in detail about the speech of the 'pale young man' who by pointing to men's faults had argued for women's government and had then gone on to outline a 'communist' programme (383-472). Chremes' recital of events could be taken to show that men attended the Assembly only to get their three obols (380 f), that even so meetings were rarely crowded like this one (383 f), that unpunctuality was normal (389 f, cf. *Ach.* 19-26), that a speaker (the dim-sighted Neocleides) could be noisily refused a hearing (398-404) and that when a speech concluded different sections of the Assembly erupted in roars of approval or the reverse (431-3). A little later he remarks that the decision to hand over government to the women was made because it was the only measure that had not been tried before (456). Whether any of this should be regarded as serious criticism of the Assembly must be a matter of individual judgement: my estimate of the tone of the passage is that the weaknesses shown by citizens in conducting the affairs of the *polis* are recognised with tolerant amusement as unalterable and typically Athenian.

It is not a meeting of the Assembly whose proceedings are reported in *Knights* but of the Council. The report given by Sausage-seller takes the form of continuous speech, unlike Chremes' – no doubt because so much of *Knights* is composed of dialogue for the two rival politicians, each seeking to outface and outbid the other. Whereas in *Assemblywomen* as in *Acharnians* the meeting occupies the early part of the play, in *Knights* it is supposed to occur somewhat later, while the chorus deliver the parabasis. Thus it may be seen as a device for clearing the stage of actors through the departure of Cleon and Sausage-seller, the former to tell the councillors about his rival's 'conspiracy' with the Knights, the latter to outmanoeuvre Cleon. As a result Sausage-seller's account follows immediately after the three substantial speeches of the parabasis and it is itself the only continuous passage of any length before the second parabasis. There is a kind of continuity of theme, too, from first parabasis to Sausage-seller's report in the idea of victory and of the fickleness of men's favour, but the contrast of tone between the eulogy delivered by the Knights and the would-be demagogue's boasting is as marked as the implicit difference in moral values.[22]

In brief, Sausage-seller had done no more than announce a glut of sardines. His good news turns the Council in his favour and he further profits by purchasing coriander and onions to go with the sardines. What Sausage-seller actually claimed to have done is of minor importance: it is the length and manner of his recital, with all its circumstantial detail about his listeners' reactions and his own feelings, that is so impressive. It is worth reading the speech with attention to note the management of narrative continuity, of the sharing of attention between the three participants (the Council acts and speaks as one man) and the visualisation of the setting: Sausage-seller's self-revelation needs no emphasis.

In tragedy decisions reached elsewhere are often succinctly conveyed by a herald to those affected, such as Hecuba in *Women of Troy*, while detailed narrative of horrific and disastrous events is entrusted to a messenger. Occasionally, however, a passage of extended narrative may be delivered by a principal, as when Clytemnestra in Aeschylus' *Agamemnon* herself relates her bloody triumph. The lines we are about to examine have stylistic and other features typical of messenger speeches while belonging to the same sub-species as

Clytemnestra's in that Sausage-seller announces his own victorious (and deplorable) achievement. If there were any doubt about the nature of this speech in itself, it must be removed by a glance at the Knights' introductory and concluding words. In fact, as he left to address the Council, the Knights had encouraged him, praying that he might be protected by Zeus of the Agora and return wearing the garlands of victory (498-502).[23] On his return they hail his victory and ask for a full account of his deeds (612-23) and when he has finished this they offer congratulations on his surpassing villainy, wily tricks and verbal deceits (683-7). As regards these features, their compliments are well deserved but the extent of his victory is less clear. Clytemnestra's three blows had indeed killed her husband; she went on to murder Cassandra too. What has Sausage-seller actually achieved? In what does his victory consist? Cleon lives, undeterred and uninjured (save a little in his self-esteem, 722). For all the difference made to the further course of the play, the episode might just as well not have happened. Perhaps we should observe that Sausage-seller has acquired confidence and that he certainly seems to the Knights to have done what was required of him by surpassing Cleon in villainy. Looked at in another way, as we shall see, gaining the favour of the Council foreshadows the courting of Demos enacted later in the play.

If two warriors engage in single combat in the Homeric manner, the object is to kill or wound one of them. Because of the importance of the heroic leader, the Hector or the Achilles, the removal or defeat of one individual significantly affects the watching host. On the other hand, the spectators do not change sides as a result of the combat. In this respect the heroic model is misleading. It remains true, however, that *Knights* is an 'epic struggle' but with values reversed. In myth the hero is supreme until overcome by one better than he: in *Knights*, if not in Athens, a demagogue is supreme until overcome by a rogue worse than himself (683 f).

In fact, as well as the grandiose implications just mentioned, there are indications that the two demagogues are pictured as wrestling, for instance when Sausage-seller is advised to grease his neck so that he can slip out of his opponent's grasp (490 f). The content of the speech on this view divides itself into two rounds, the first consisting of bad news (Cleon's) countered successfully by good and the second of Cleon's recommendation for a sacrifice rebutted by his adversary's extravagant counter-proposals. Defeated and on the point of removal, Cleon finally attempts to win back support by mentioning peace negotiations only to be cleverly outsmarted by Sausage-seller's sarcasm. It is worth noting that, as in an agon, in each round the eventual loser moves first. The object of the wrestling match, as of other athletic events, was of course to win a prize, the intangible reward of popular esteem. In this particular event the wrestlers had a specialised audience, not a chance collection of spectators.

The descriptions I have offered in the last two paragraphs seem to have brought us a long way from the tragic messenger speech.[24] We have seen that nothing much is altered as a consequence of the events narrated and that the nature and associations of the struggle also are incompatible with tragedy. Now the evidence on the other side must be brought into play. First and foremost one notices the fullness of the narrative, the amount of circumstantial detail supplied from the moment of the speaker's departure to his return, and in particular the careful reporting of feelings, as shown in the Council's faces when they heard Cleon and his supplanter, or in Sausage-seller's dismay openly confessed (629-31, 646, 658). At under 60 lines, the speech is on the short side compared particularly with some Euripidean examples, but for the amount of information it has to convey its length and stylistic elaboration reach tragic proportions. The inclusion of direct speech, in prayer and otherwise (634-8, 642-5, etc.), and mention of ominous sounds (639) are details characteristic of the tragic species. If all of this is a deliberate reminder of a form regularly occurring in the sister art, does it give no more to *Knights* than a touch of piquancy, an unexpected flavour to Sausage-seller's boasted knavery? There is no doubt a contrast between report of a wounding and the arrival of a shoal of fish, between thunder and a fart, but there are also tragic parallels for reports of battle or of debate, there is Agamemnon's own account of Troy's fall. The vital factor, however, is the third party, the Council, not just as witness of the conflict but as, in a sense, the victor's prize, like Deianeira waiting while her two suitors were fighting for her (Sophocles, *Women of Trachis*, 25).

For much of *Knights* it is not so much the rivals' quarrelsome striving for supremacy that really counts as its effect on a third party, on Demosthenes, Demos or the chorus, present in the theatre before us. The real spectators watch two characters in contest before a third, characters who are also actors engaged in a competition before them. The audience in the theatre has been directly addressed by the Knights in the recent parabasis (503-6, 518-19) and told not only of the deeds of their ancestors but also of the ingenuity, courage and endurance of their horses. And now the spectators listen to Sausage-seller telling his audience, the Knights, how he bamboozled another set of hearers, the unseen Council. I do not believe that the Knights' horses caught crabs, nor do I believe that Sausage-seller won over the councillors. The dramatist will give us his version of the people of Athens, represented in the apparently gullible Demos; by way of preparation he lets Sausage-seller tell of another of his fictions, the Council, taken in by deceit and open to bribes (what is there to choose between the two organs of the democracy?); the teller of his tale reports his exploits to the amazingly credulous Knights.

We know that the demagogues are game for anything; that goes without saying. The unscrupulous demagogue, however, cannot win unless there are men who are greedy, fickle, gullible, selfish. Such men are found in the Council, in the Assembly, even among the Knights. And in the audience? Does Aristophanes' satire not indict the fickle ingratitude of all his hearers in this complex formed by parabasis and report?

I begin my discussion of the earliest, and in some ways most elaborate, dramatisation of a meeting, the Assembly scene in *Acharnians*, where I ended the previous section, namely with the spectators. Harold Pinter's *The Caretaker* opens with Mick alone on stage; he looks around and then exits. *Acharnians* opens with Dicaeopolis alone on stage; he looks around, fidgets and eventually tells us what is biting him, leading up to it by way of a focusing priamel in which, he, the character in the comedy, speaks of his own previous experiences as a man in the theatre waiting for the entertainment to begin. He had enjoyed watching Cleon (in a comedy) worsted by the Knights, been disappointed at the cancellation of a tragedy by Aeschylus, pleased by a well-known singer, tortured by another musical item (5-14). And now he is still waiting, not for the arrival of some actors or musicians, but for the officials and ordinary members of the Assembly, bitten to the heart by their failure to arrive on time and discuss the restoration of the peace for which he longs (32). And throughout the scene the watcher on the stage, whose name we do not learn until he visits Euripides (406), continues to comment on what he sees and hears (64, 68, 71, 75, 79, 83, 86-7, 90, 92-3, etc.); his comments are sometimes almost indistinguishable from his attempts to participate, to force the presidents to discuss peace. But he, though more conspicuous, is as helpless as the rest of the crowd gathered at this Assembly. For this scene is so staged that the mere spectators, attendants at the Lenaea of 425 BC, become participants in a regular meeting of the Assembly. The audience plays the 'crowd'. If, as I should like to believe, the Herald, Prytaneis (presiding officials) and Archers (who 'police' the meeting) make their entrance down through the theatre, then this method of arrival would help to draw the ranks of spectators into the play. And if the (fictional) presidents really do compete for places 'in the front row' (25), close to the seats occupied by those who actually preside over the dramatic festival, then the envoys and other personages involved in this scene may be enabled to hold the centre of the stage and make their reports directly facing the audience, while Dicaeopolis observes from one side.

To continue with the element of spectacle; first from a negative angle. The importance of what is seen is enlarged by what is not said, specifically by lack of initial announcement of an agenda (contrast the Thesmophoria Assembly) and then of speeches for and against ending the war with Sparta; indeed the scene contains no uninterrupted speech of any length. It is likely that the spectator was surprised by the richness and variety of spectacle in this scene, even by the sheer number of people arriving either in haste or slow dignity. As well as five speaking parts, mute roles include Persian eunuchs and Thracian soldiers and the opportunities for providing strange and elaborate costume and accoutrements are unparalleled in the prologues of the surviving comedies, at least until *Birds*.

For the scholar interested in staging, this scene raises minor but difficult problems which could only be solved by increased knowledge of theatrical conventions in the production of Aristophanic comedy, but about which a director must decide. Where, for example, does Godschild (Amphitheus) go when 'arrested' (55)? He must be able to reappear instantly in mid-line later in the scene (129) to begin his peace mission. More important, how much emphasis is given to the entry of the ambassadors, Pseudartabas, Theorus and the mercenaries? Do words cease while we watch each separate entry the length of the eisodos, or, as seems likely in the case of Theorus (134), is the entry 'covered' by the preceding dialogue? Such uncertainties should not cause us to ignore the originality of the staging. It is normally after the parabasis, and in separate short scenes, that arrivals of this kind occur: evidence can be found to hand in the scenes for the Megarian and his 'piglets' and the Theban with his retinue, later in the comedy (729-978). In the opening scene, before a chorus has entered, there arrive, from the gods, from Persia, from Thrace, envoys of varying degrees of strangeness, all in the space of little more than a hundred lines. (It is hardly surprising if an inexperienced young dramatist was reluctant to undertake the direction of this play.)[25]

There is still a little more to say about the visual aspect of this scene. Although the text provides (and needed to provide) almost no information about the layout and surroundings of the meeting-place, it does contain indications of the appearance of the Athenian ambassadors to Persia and especially of Pseudartabas and the eunuchs they bring back with them (95). These are the people we see with our own eyes and with the eyes of the watcher who sees through them. The point of all this exotic splendour is not to provide visual interest (though it does), not just to contrast Eastern softness and self-indulgence with Greek manliness, but to present an Assembly in which imposture is the order of the day, and Dicaeopolis the unmasker. Such an interpretation at least makes the seen conform with the spoken idea of *alazoneia* (63, 87, 109, 135), that combination of imposture, bragging and bamboozling manifested in comedy by socially respectable characters as well as by beggars and vagabonds.[26] However this clear-sighted, upright Dicaeopolis who indicates how easily others are fooled is himself to act the importunate beggar, and his integrity is undercut even in the Assembly scene by his pretence of feeling a drop of rain, his pretext for demanding the closure of proceedings, and perhaps by mock identification of the eunuchs as the contemporary Athenians, Cleisthenes and Strato.

So far I have been concerned with the play in performance. Now I want to go back to an earlier period in its making, which I think can best be approached from the perspective of our own century. A film-maker who wished to present a fictional public meeting at Athens could show the Pnyx deserted save for one lonely figure, the crowds in the Agora, the disorderly arrival, the opening formalities, religious business, reports from envoys and other officials and as many speeches in the main debate as suited his purpose. Not only can the camera establish location precisely, and range freely from place to place, from crowd to individual; what is much more important is the director's ability to transcend the temporal restrictions of the stage. If he chose, he could make his film as long as an actual meeting or he could compress it into a fraction of its real duration, selecting only those moments significant for his purpose, and ending simply by a shot of a new location. That Aristophanic comedy could not employ a large cast or build elaborate sets does not matter; the real problem is temporal continuity: the dramatist could not simply 'cut' to a new scene.

In *Assemblywomen*, as of course in *Knights*, no difficulty arose; in *Women at the Thesmophoria* proceedings were broken off by the arrival of Cleisthenes and its consequences and not until after a reasonable amount of speech-making. In *Acharnians* debate, or at least a speech in favour of continuing the war, must at all costs be avoided: how is this to be achieved? The obvious solution would have been to include in the opening monologue a carefully-worded account of Dicaeopolis' attempt to get peace discussed by the Assembly. The failure of this (reported, not staged) attempt would allow him to begin what was always to be his 'great deed', making peace just for his own family (128-32). Once the dramatist has decided to dramatise the Assembly meeting, he needs to find a way of ending it before its business is over and luckily a pretext is to hand; Dicaeopolis can pretend to feel a raindrop, a 'sign from heaven'. But Dicaeopolis had emphatically expressed his determination that peace should be discussed. What then could make him change his mind? Impatience. However, if Dicaeopolis' impatience is to be used as a dramatic device, then it must be made to seem natural and justified, not sudden and whimsical.[27] Looking at the scene again, we can trace his reactions: displeasure at Godschild's dismissal, resentment of ambassadorial easy living and anger with the mercenaries who steal his shopping. It is too much: the Assembly must end. And, so that the next stage in the story may follow straight after the meeting, Godschild has already been sent to Sparta, 40 lines earlier (130, 175).

The Assembly scene makes an indirect contribution to the case against continuing the war with Sparta by showing that war's hardships do not fall equally upon all Athenians and that Dicaeopolis' urgent longing for peace cannot be fulfilled without ignoring the assembly's official routine. The effect of this is to suggest that the ordinary countryman, lacking support from the wealthy and powerful, may be forgiven for his overtures to the enemy. In this respect the scene is consistent with the bulk of the rest of the play in its failure to propound the case for peace or against war in formal argument. It would not be too extravagant to claim that the principal function of the Assembly scene is not to make fun of the institution or its meetings but to avoid debate. And when, at long last, Dicaeopolis sets out to defend his action, he still fails to argue against the continuation of war. The blessings of peace are self-evident: to the peacemaker 'all good things are supplied without effort' (977, trs. Sommerstein).

At the beginning of this chapter I placed, without comment, lines which insist on the distinctness of genres: the poet, it is implied, selects and works at encomium, didactic verse or satire, choosing a single genre according to his natural endowment. The label 'dramatist' applied to Aristophanes should be large enough to contain an indication that as a poet he was skilled to praise, instruct and bite.

Notes

1. For the organisation of the dramatic festivals see Pickard-Cambridge 1968.

2. Because the action of tragedy took place out of doors, the distinction between public and private is not made visible in the form of interior and exterior setting and scenery. The enclosed nature of the places where the Council and the courts functioned is brought out in verbal description (e.g. *Knights* 626, 640 f, *Wasps* 104, 552). Of course the conflict usually has wider effects and wider implications, but, with few exceptions, the primary location of the tragic situation is the *oikos*. Even a play like E.'s *Trojan Women*, in which the *oikos* has been destroyed both literally and by the removal of the adult males, is centred on Hecuba and members of her family.

3. A. *Eumenides* 566 f.

4. e.g. *Ag.* 445-51 describes the impact of the war caused by Paris' offence on the families of the bereaved. S. *King Oedipus* 65-77.

5. A strong sense of the past, when shared by writer and audience, facilitates the interpretation of the present in the light of the past and vice versa. The modern reader, living in an age when it is fashionable to despise or, at best, ignore the past, may not appreciate the prevalence of this habit of mind in Athenian culture.

6. The comedies, more than most Greek texts, require elucidatory comment of the kind provided by editors. As a result we are well informed about Aristophanic trees: we now need good maps of the wood.

7. The extent to which *Acharnians* is permeated by institutional material suggests that the author's motives are not satirical. On the general question of Ar. and politics, the article by A.W. Gomme is still valuable (*CR* 52 (1938), 97-109).

8. On this aspect of tragic staging see Taplin 1978, Ch. 7.

9. See e.g. H. Foley, *CP* 77 (1982), 1-21; F. Zeitlin in H. Foley (ed.), *Reflections of Women in Antiquity* (New York, 1981), and in general S.C. Humphreys, *Anthropology and the Greeks* (London, 1978) and *The Family, Women and Death* (London, 1983).

10. T.R. Banks (*CB* 106 (1980), 81-5) points out that the law court symbolises formal, written law and the symposium also symbolises nomos, as informal, unwritten convention.

11. T. Long, *ICS* 1 (1976), 15-21.

12. See for example *Ach.* 448-80, *Lys.* 904-51.

13. The trial is enclosed, as it were, in a domestic frame: for religious ceremony preceding a great or new undertaking cf. *Frogs* 871-94 and (in a single word) *Clouds* 127.

14. In the Greek the dogs are called *Labes* and *Kuon*, 'Snatcher' and 'Dog', after Laches and Cleon. I use Cur for Kuon, partly because it is pejorative, partly to keep the initial sound.

15. The puppies replace children in the standard appeal for pity mocked by Ar. at 568-9; cf. Plato, *Apology* 34c.

16. Cf. *CQ* 32 (1982), 17.

17. In order to demonstrate Cleon's readiness to prosecute on each and every occasion it is best for Cur to have a grievance of his own, Labes' refusal to share his booty. In fact it is the householder (that is, the people of Sicily) who has been deprived of his property.

18. E. *Hippolytus* 208-31.

19. Philocleon thinks himself agent but is really patient; he learns, if he learns at all, from what is done *to* him.

20. Euripides' defender, called Mnesilochus in older editions and in most translations, is here called the Kinsman; the play's title appears variously as *Thesmophoriazusae*, *The Poet and the Women*, *Women at the Thesmophoria*, *Ladies' Day*, etc.

21. See above, p. 31 f.

22. See above, p. 62 ff. On Sausage-seller's 'epiphany' see H. Kleinknecht, *Die Gebetsparodie in der Antike* (Hildesheim, 1966), and W. Horn, *Gebet und Gebetsparodie in den Komödien des Aristophanes* (Nuremberg, 1971).

23. The little song belongs to the class labelled propemptic.

24. For the tragic messenger speech in Ar. see Rau 162-8.

25. See P. Rhodes, *The Athenian Boule* (Oxford, 1972), 54 for discussion of the staging of this scene as well as of procedures of meetings.

26. See above, p. 89, n. 3.

27. Socrates' impatience with Strepsiades is similarly employed in *Clouds* 781-9.

8 CLOUDS

Lots of folk live on their wits;
  Lecturers, lispers,
Losels, lob-lolly men, louts –
  They don't end as paupers.
            (Philip Larkin, *Toads*)

The critical moment in *Clouds* occurs quite late in the play, when Strepsiades rushes out of his house to escape from his son, who has already punched his head and jaw (1321 f). From this moment Pheidippides demonstrates that he is superior to his father in argument as well as in physical strength and Strepsiades, seeing the results of his decisions and realising at last what he has brought upon himself, turns from optimism and confidence to bitterness and the desire for revenge. Thus the play ends, not with the usual merry-making that results from the hero's success, or at least creates a mood of jollity, but with a downturn. If this scene is critical in the shaping of the play, it is also crucial in another way, for it is here that the two elements, of rhetoric and family relationships, come together, or rather collide. In order to understand the nature and repercussions of the impact it may be helpful to trace each of the two elements separately up to this point, taking first the relationship which provides the mainspring of the plot.

Father and Son

Let me begin by looking at the traces of a simple and traditional comedy in which a sympathetic hero moves from anxiety to triumph. It is in fact to a play of this kind that our prologue actually seems to belong.[1] Strepsiades' account of his problem and its causes serves to engage sympathy for himself and to encourage interest in the relationships within this family. The solution he proposes, that his son shall learn the art of successful speaking in order to evade his creditors, is presented in a way that discourages any question as to the morality of defaulting:

sympathy for Strepsiades means sympathy for him as defendant in any suit to recover money owing. We seem to be going to watch a play in which private concerns will be paramount and in which the new rhetoric will be a useful tool for ordinary people to use, not something to be feared and deplored. A closer look at the prologue indicates lines on which the story might develop and how it might be embodied in different scenes: Strepsiades would need to persuade his son to undergo training and take him to a teacher; episodes illustrating his education in rhetoric would lead to a demonstration of his successes against the creditors, to his renown as an advocate and concluding celebrations. In fact, and contrary to what one might at first assume, our *Clouds* contains a good deal of this play or of one very like it. If the play as outlined sounds rather impoverished, or rather lacking in variety, there would be the possibility of exploring the tensions resulting from Strepsiades' marriage 'out of his class' by incorporating, for instance, a scene for Strepsiades, Pheidippides and his wealthy uncle. And, although the prologue does not encourage speculation about the identity of the chorus, we might not be surprised to discover that it was composed of angry creditors.

But our *Clouds* is not a straightforward account of the principal's progress from dilemma to successful outcome, to a life free from debt and an amicable relationship with his son. It is significant that the first downturn, placed before the prologue ends, prefigures the final, climactic downturn: Strepsiades fails, first and last, to impose his will on his son. Pheidippides will not go to school.[2] Strepsiades, 'old, forgetful and slow', resolves to go in his place. If Strepsiades were to succeed, if he were to acquire eloquence and skill in argument, then he might not only evade his debts but be enabled to impress his authority upon his son and solve all his problems. In the event, Strepsiades fails and the play picks up again, as it were, with the situation obtaining at the end of the prologue (as though all the subsequent scenes were to be ignored), and the young man embarks upon the training he earlier refused (124 f, 814 f). Thus, the second downturn, Strepsiades' expulsion, sets in train the events which will lead to the final catastrophe. Where the father had been deemed a failure, the son succeeds: 'Blest art thou, Strepsiades, for your own wisdom and for your son' (1206-8).[3] But the young man has learned his lesson only too well. Now that he can win any argument and now that he values winning above everything he cannot even agree with his father at the dinner party held to celebrate his graduation. As a result, the final reversal immediately follows a time of hope and confidence.

In composing a play of this kind, a comedy without a happy ending, the dramatist has adapted but reversed a pattern found in some tragedies at this period, a pattern which avoids complete and final disaster and permits the hero to escape from his troubles, at least for a time, while frustrating the hopes of his enemies. A tragedy which ends happily may well please the audience, if not the academic critics, but, when a comedy leaves its usual path in favour of one which leads to disappointment and unhappiness, contrary to the expectations of the spectators, there is the risk that the failure to provide a celebratory atmosphere at the end may lessen the chance of victory in the contest. On the other hand, there are advantages in avoiding the obvious and boring.

Clearly changing the pattern necessitates altering the normal comic structure since, to begin with the obvious factor, the play cannot end with scenes demonstrating the success of the hero's scheme. In fact the structural abnormalities of *Clouds* are quite considerable, and this can be shown by suggesting the form the 'simple' play might have taken and contrasting the result with our *Clouds*. If Strepsiades' plan had succeeded, the training in rhetoric would have been completed before the parabasis and the remainder of the play would have contained encounters with creditors followed by preparations for feasting. And even if an element of conflict between father and son were to be included, their agon could precede Pheidippides' entry to the school, in which case the parabasis might well occur rather late in the play. Our *Clouds* contains two agones, two parabases and a most unusual parodos: how does the formal structure relate to the events of the story? The rather long prologue falls into two scenes, the second taking place before the school and culminating in Strepsiades' meeting with the school's director. In the parodos the actual entry of the chorus into the theatre is preceded by prayers invoking their presence and by songs which they sing off-stage and followed by a lyric dialogue with Strepsiades which leads to his self-dedication (263-475). Only the brief 'interview' of the prospective student separates the parodos-complex from the parabasis, which is performed while Strepsiades is supposedly beginning his education. His expulsion from the school occurs after two different approaches to teaching him have been tried (627-804). Strepsiades' expulsion, the second downturn in the story, ends the sequence which began with his decision to go to school himself. But now there is a new beginning: Pheidippides, after some pressure from his father, agrees to enter the school. What, then, was the dramatic purpose of his initial refusal? Why did Strepsiades attempt to undergo training? To these questions we shall return.

The prologue of the second action, though comparatively short, also falls into two sections and ends in front of the school. Not only, however, does it offer a revised and abridged version of the original prologue; it also shows what Strepsiades had learned, or rather it shows him imparting to his son some of the new ideas and information he has acquired. The new action, which of course has no parodos, proceeds straight to the agon, an argument between two personifications making their sole appearance, at the end of which Pheidippides enters the school as the pupil of the victorious speaker (1112). Once the rudimentary second parabasis, during which his education is presumed to begin, is over, there is an unexpected development: we do not at first see the pupil, but his father, a Strepsiades who is apprehensive about the imminent day of reckoning but hopeful that his son has learned to speak well. The father's joy on perceiving his son's accomplishments is expressed in an encomium before they go in to celebrate (1213). It seems now that nothing remains but to show the creditors worsted by Pheidippides and driven off, so that the feast may run its course. Instead, although two creditors do appear in turn, it is Strepsiades who dismisses them, using scraps of learning combined with violence, and re-enters his house (1214-302).[4] After only a few lines from the chorus to indicate that rejoicing is premature, Strepsiades once more emerges, calling for help. The final downturn has begun, and the conflict between father and son is embodied in the comedy's second agon, which results, like the first, in victory for the younger generation. When it ends, Strepsiades' hopes have been finally disappointed.

In the plays of New Comedy and their successors the happiness of the young man who has discomfited and defeated his seniors, often in gaining the bride he desires, tends to be the result which satisfies the expectations and pleases the sympathies of the audience. In *Clouds* the transfer of power works differently, it seems, largely because Pheidippides is distanced in dramatic terms and because he lacks the kind of support given in later comedies by companions of similar age and tastes and above all by the quick-witted, resourceful and unprincipled slave who manipulates people and events. Pheidippides' success does not give *Clouds* an unexpected, but still happy, ending: it is the means of producing a disconcerting and problematic turn. If Strepsiades were really in a tragic situation a tragic exodos would be in order, its sorrowful content appropriate to the circumstances of the story. In real life, on the other hand, or in a realistic narrative, emphasis would fall on the likely continuity and duration of debt and conflict, and not on an ending, happy or otherwise. It is natural for Strepsiades to be angry as well as despondent and it is his anger which enables the dramatist to bring off an ending which is striking and neat, if not altogether logical. Strepsiades sets fire to the school in order to punish the teacher whom he had charged with the task of educating Pheidippides. In so doing he recreates a moment from the prologue of the play. There the teacher had been shown above the roof; here the failed pupil, the victim of the successful pupil, briefly occupies a similarly elevated position.

Clouds is conspicuous among Aristophanes' plays for the amount of material it contains, both thematic, as we shall shortly see, and narrative. By contrast with *Acharnians*, whose action is complete when Dicaeopolis sets up his free market, several hundred lines before the end of the play, in *Clouds* the story continues to develop until the very last moment, and, whereas in *Knights* (which does not complete its narrative early) the prolongation of one single confrontation provides a large part of the dramatic substance, in *Clouds* the story itself, quite apart from its treatment, takes a varied and unpredictable course.

The vital issue in this story is that of parental authority. While he continues as head of the *oikos*, Strepsiades ought to be able to control his son. But having completely failed to limit his spending he next fails to persuade him to study rhetoric, at least until after his own attempt. And no sooner has Pheidippides mastered the art of argument than he uses it gratuitously and for trivial reasons against his own father; worse, he ends by 'proving' that it is right to beat one's parents (1410-50). The implication is that Pheidippides wishes to gain and keep the ascendancy over his father, although the time is clearly not yet ripe for him to become head of the *oikos*. His desire to dominate has not been provoked by any harshness on his father's part: indeed there are passages recalling the father's care for his infant son and showing the persuasive tones he adopts when speaking to the adolescent (1830 ff, 79 ff). It is as though Pheidippides were only his mother's son and looked down upon his father. It is worth repeating that the point of view throughout is that of the father: unlike a modern dramatist, particularly a younger dramatist, Aristophanes sides with the father. A few years earlier Athenian audiences had seen another father and son engaged in bitter debate. In Euripides' tragedy Hippolytus and Theseus each felt he had right on his side and Theseus' parental authority was reinforced by the curse of Poseidon. By contrast the superiority of Pheidippides, perhaps based on that of Hippolytus, seems all the more repugnant.[5] *Clouds* shows us a situation where both father and son are at fault and where the father's loving generosity is responsible for some of his son's selfish behaviour. Strepsiades was wrong to think that Pheidippides would use his skill in oratory only on those occasions chosen for him: Pheidippides has seen that the power to win an argument is a means to exerting power over people. What is the nature of the training that has done so much for him?

Rhetoric

A man who has incurred debts he cannot pay is unlikely to enrol for a course in public speaking as a means to financial solvency, although he may well cast himself on his creditors' mercy, using all the powers of persuasion he commands. If actually taken to court, pleas for pity having failed, whereas in our own times he will probably rely on the services of a member of the legal profession, in classical Athens he might obtain help from an experienced speech-writer (a consultant, in Dover's termino-logy), rather than depend on his own untrained powers.[6] In comedy, however, the author avoids the predictable, everyday solution: when Dicaeopolis had need of eloquent speech he borrowed what he wanted from Euripides; Strepsiades, who has already demonstrated an enviable ability to set out his circum-stances in a speech that might soften any creditor who heard it, embarks on a lengthier scheme.

Why does he want to go to school? Or more accurately, why does he want to send his son to school (apart from thinking it right that the cause of his troubles should do something to cure them)? At one level an answer to these questions is given in the course of the prologue: the institution to which Strepsiades plans to send his son contains people who 'teach you, if you pay them, how to carry the day in argument, whether your cause is just or unjust' (98 f, trs. Sommerstein). After a few lines in which Pheidippides speaks contemptuously about men who do not share a wealthy youngster's ideas about enjoyable activities, he asks what he is to study: 'It's said that they have in their house both the Arguments, the Better, whatever that may be, and the Worse; and that one of this pair of Arguments, the Worse, can plead an unjust cause and prevail' (112-15, trs. Sommerstein). Two points are important here, one moral, the other dramatic: Strepsiades goes on to tell his son that it is the Wrongful Argument he must learn; in effect he admits that defrauding creditors is wrong. As a pointer to what will occur later in the play, the lines are intriguing: one thinks at first hearing that the pupil will learn arguments as he might learn subtraction or spelling, but then one discovers that the Logoi actually have the power of speech.[7] The Logos then is endowed with a voice and can argue: the two Arguments may therefore be among the characters of the drama.

As we have seen eventually Pheidippides does go to school to learn the art of wrongful argument, remarking to his father as he goes, 'one day you'll regret what you're doing' (865). On arrival he makes such a poor impression that the Principal doubts whether he will be able to learn the 'arts of exculpation and summonsing and convincing flummery' (874 f), and absents himself from the proceedings: Pheidippides will learn from the two Arguments themselves (886 f). Two men come out, one old, the other young, and engage in the preliminaries to an agon, bandying insults and threats with great verve. It is noteworthy that neither of them mentions the school: it is just as though they were rival professional educators (like sophists), rather than fellow members of the staff of an institution. Their dialogue serves to introduce their attitudes, methods and personality in such a way as to illustrate and emphasise their mutual hostility.

At length the chorus leader calls them to order and instructs the Better Argument, the first speaker, 'who in former times garlanded men with virtues in plenty', to describe himself (959 f). The Better Argument immediately identifies himself as the upholder and inculcator of an educational system based on respect for justice and on prudent self-control. How well does he recommend himself as a practitioner and teacher of oratory? The critic could note the tripartite structure of his speech: in the first section he sets out the standards of behaviour prescribed and enforced in the good old days, giving abundant and detailed illustration of the points he is making. Most of the central part, addressed to the potential student, sketches the attitudes and conduct the young man will adopt as a result of his schooling (990-9). The peroration begins with a description of the pleasant surroundings in which Pheidippides will undergo his athletic training and ends by promising him excellence of physique. (One may observe in passing that much of what he says about discipline would be repugnant to Pheidippides and that all of it is irrelevant to his purpose in enrolling.) The speaker can paint a vivid picture and he deals surprisingly well with his opponent's sneers. In general his address probably resembles those made by physical trainers or doctors when advertising for pupils, except of course that there his contempt for modern youth would be out of place.

The Worse Argument, after cleverly referring to the riches to be gained by winning a case, states that he will show the weaknesses of his adversary's position by a series of questions. Having dealt with three minor points of difference between them in this way, he moves on to the last and most important, prudent self-control. In a continuous passage, addressed to Pheidippides, he asserts, in essence, that if the young man has oratorical ability he will have the power to enjoy all life's pleasures, licit or illicit, without fear of the consequences. So much for prudent self-control (1060-82). He clinches his victory by demonstrating that dissolute behaviour is the norm, among advocates, tragic poets and politicians and even among the audience.

Worse Argument has no educational programme to offer. He wins because he is quick-witted, confident, aggressive and audacious, and because, in advertiser's jargon, he knows how to supply a product which will appeal to the customer. His victory finally results not from eloquence or the adequacy of his case but from the way he exploits his opponent's answers for comic effect, rather in the manner of a cheer-leader. And when Better

Argument admits that self-control is the exception rather than the rule, we may recall that there was in his own speech more than a hint that he took a prurient delight in observing the young men whose chastity he praised.[8]

The dramatist chooses not to show the training which turned Pheidippides into an accomplished orator. When he argues with his father we can see that he behaves like Worse Argument, but we are unprepared for his mastery of all the arts of rhetoric. The new Pheidippides is competent in planning his material and in marshalling arguments; he is familiar with use of rhetorical signposts, of emotive words and clichés, of apt quotations, of appeals to higher authority. Already depicted as consciously superior to his father, he has further increased in confidence as a result of his training, so that he can even address him with condescension.[9]

Is it possible to estimate the impact of the two agones on the original audience? Might the older and more conservative among them be strengthened in their dislike of the new rhetoric by what they had heard and seen? Might the young be encouraged to model themselves on Worse Argument and Pheidippides (as the Aeschylus of *Frogs* would surely assert)?[10] What is certain is the brilliant sublety of the double contest. It is necessary for the plot that Pheidippides should win, and win by means of oratory as well as personality: his victory might have been a boring copy of that achieved by Worse Argument; instead, there is enough similarity (in attitude and in structure) to underline the affinities of the two representatives of youth and enough difference to avoid monotony. To give just one example, although each of them intends to shock, Worse Argument's dismissal of virtue is explicitly amoral and is accomplished almost playfully, as he gleefully outsmarts the old fuddy-duddy who has praised self-control. Pheidippides, on the other hand, argues coolly and politely that beating one's father is proper and beneficial. Where Worse Argument proceeds from verbal trickery through abuse to the bludgeoning of his opponent into admitting that the majority are dissolute, Pheidippides actually persuades his father to agree that his proposition is right and should be put into effect (1437-9).

Pheidippides' command of argument combined with a disregard of accepted values reduces his father to despair and anger, anger which should by rights be directed against the son. But

Strepsiades looks for someone else to blame. One possible target (there is another, as we shall see) is Pheidippides' teacher. Who is the teacher? Is it Worse Argument, as suggested by the first agon? Or is it the Principal of the school? Certainly it was to the Principal (if the manuscript attribution of these lines is accepted) that Strepsiades had entrusted his son with the instruction to 'sharpen him well . . . for minor cases and for greater issues' (1108-10) and it was to him that he had given a 'token of his appreciation' (1146 f) on his son's successful completion of the course.[11] At all events it is the Principal who has to bear the responsibility (for how could one punish an Argument?). However Strepsiades, clear that he wants to harm the people who had misled him, is still uncertain what to do. He turns to consult Hermes, whose statue stands nearby, and receives (as he makes out) the advice to set fire to the school (1484). So the play ends with Strepsiades sending down fire from above on the Principal of the school, the man who himself had first been seen looking down from above on gods and men (225).

The Chorus

Before choosing to punish his son's teacher, Strepsiades had charged the chorus with the blame for his sufferings. They, however, had immediately cast the guilt back at him: 'No, it is you who are responsible for your sufferings. You turned in the direction of wickedness' (1454 f). They go on to say that, when they had seen that he was 'in love with wickedness', they had deliberately encouraged him up to the time when they brought him to ruin, so that he would learn to fear the gods (1459-61). If we read this passage in isolation, knowing nothing of its context, what might we infer about the speakers and the play? We should surely suppose that the speakers were divine and we should also recognise as tragic the idea that gods urge on the sinner to his downfall. Verbal parallels for the Clouds' remarks are not wanting, but reminiscence extends beyond words.[12]

Deities who punish. Let us turn back to the second parabasis, where we can discover more about the nature of this unusual chorus. Here the goddesses are explicit about their powers to reward or punish: if the judges in the theatre 'help this chorus as is right and proper', their crops will be protected, if not, they will be damaged and destroyed (1115-30). These deities have the power to send or withhold rain and hail at their pleasure (and it is on the possibilities of harming and spoiling that they dwell at greater length). A chorus of avenging female deities who threaten to blight the land: the description would fit not only our chorus but also the Furies of the *Oresteia*:

> I am bereft of honor, unhappy one! And with grievous wrath
> against this land, alack,
> venom, venom in requital for my grief from
>   my heart shall I discharge,
> a distillation for the land
> intolerable; and after that
> a canker, blasting leaves and children.
>
>   (*Eumenides* 780-5, trs. H. Lloyd-Jones)

In the first parabasis the goddesses had emphasised that their habit of warning the people against wrongdoing and folly was a benefit, for which they did not receive due credit (576-83): in the *Oresteia* the Eumenides are presented as terrible beings who assert that fear promotes morality; their role is altered and expanded by Athene's persistent efforts to persuade them to give blessings in return for receiving new honour. In *Eumenides* Peitho (Persuasion) is appeasement effected by words honestly spoken: *Clouds* shows a use of argument so dishonest and debased that finally Strepsiades turns in disgust from words to action. Aeschylus' implacable and terrifying goddesses end as the Kindly Ones, 'doing good, receiving good, held in good honour' (*Eum.* 868). In this comedy, with its own 'tragic reversal', we see a transformation of goddesses equal and opposite to that portrayed in the trilogy. The goddesses are not, of course, anonymous avengers; they are Clouds, weather deities who can cause storms of rain and hail. In a more conventional account they could be depicted as agents of Zeus; here their independence and ability to do as they please are paramount. That weather deities should be formidable is readily understandable, even in the twentieth century; the two parabases illustrate the extent to which ordinary people and their activities could be harmed by sudden changes of weather. Yet the sinister nature of the Clouds does not depend on their meteorological powers alone, although it is associated with the phenomena of weather. The dweller in the mountainous land knows what it feels like to be walking through damp mist when clouds are low on the hills:

he is familiar with the way clouds descend and obscure the mountain tops, removing landmarks and making journeys risky. He has seen travellers vanish as the mist received them and so he can easily associate clouds with oblivion or deception or death. The sinister associations of clouds, which can be illustrated from literary sources, help to expand the chorus's potential.

Pindar, narrating the origin of the island of Rhodes, meditates on the gods' unwillingness to forgive men's failures when 'a dark cloud of oblivion' diverts someone from his proper course (*O.* 7. 45). In this case, although the worshippers forgot to take fire for their sacrifice, god sent a rain of gold upon them from a yellow cloud. Positive and negative, bright and dark clouds, a deity who overlooks deficiencies in men. In the myth of the punishment of Ixion, a warning to men of the dangers of ingratitude for divine blessings, Pindar tells how, when Ixion conceived a passion for the goddess Hera, wife of Zeus, 'it was a cloud he lay with, and he in his delusion was given the false loveliness' (*P.* 2. 36 f). Not a cloud of forgetfulness this time, but of delusion, preventing accurate perception of the person of the goddess, and contrived so as to deceive.

In one more example from a Pindaric ode the meteorological power of the clouds is expressed in military terms: Pindar likens this ode to a treasury at Delphi, standing firm in all weathers, even against the rain which comes relentlessly on, an army issuing forth from the rumbling cloud (*P.* 6. 10-12).

The Cloud goddesses are remarkable for their independence of movement: unlike other heavenly bodies, and unlike the Horae, they are not cyclical; the clouds do not dance to the music of time. As a cloud may suddenly appear in a clear sky and portend storm, as it may suddenly change its shape and colour, so the goddesses change. They introduce themselves as coming to rest on the 'wooded peaks of high mountains' where they shake themselves free of the damp mist surrounding them (279, 288 f). The goddesses' divine forms are obscured by moist vapour, which for their stage appearance they shed like a woman removing her cloak and throwing back her hood.

In attempting to understand the nature of the Clouds we have moved backwards through the play, from their self-justification, through their admonitions in parabases: it remains to show that their songs earlier in *Clouds* are much more conventional. In the odes of the parabasis they invoke deities: Zeus, Poseidon, Aether and Sun in the ode, Apollo, Artemis, Athene and Dionysus in the antode (563-74, 595-606); the form and style of their song is conventional, although the inclusion of Aether and Sun results from their own particular identity. Their opening song is hymn-like too, in that the goddesses exhort one another to float towards Attica, to gaze down at Athens famous for its temples and religious ceremonies, where at this very moment the spring festival of Dionysus is being celebrated with contests for choral groups (275-90, 298-313).

The School

I have so far presented a play, a tragi-comedy, in which the downfall of a father was brought about by the son's success in learning to use the Worse Argument. What I have not yet looked at, and have not needed to examine, is the whole section between Pheidippides' defiance of his father (125) and his reluctant consent to undergo training (866). A cavalier dismissal of roughly one-third of the play, of the scenes which for most people *are* the play? In order to estimate their importance, it is now time to go back to that moment in the prologue at which Strepsiades, faced with his son's refusal to attend school, decided to enrol himself, although he is, as he admits, 'elderly, forgetful and slow' (129).

When observed by someone from the twentieth century, the Reflectory which Strepsiades will enter and the elements of which it is composed seem only moderately strange, chiefly in that they are antiquated by our standards; it takes a considerable effort for us to realise exactly what constituted the school's undoubted oddity for the first audience. For centuries we have been accustomed to the idea of residential colleges, of education prolonged beyond schooldays, even available to the elderly. We associate religious communities with schooling. We are familiar with various fashions and techniques of learning, such as research, projects, lateral thinking, and even with 'progressive' schools which set out to show the benefits of some idiosyncratic educational philosophy. Just as Strepsiades managed to 'think away' his cloak (857), so we need, when approaching the Reflectory, to 'think away', as far as we can, everything that dims our appreciation of the novelty and uniqueness of Aristophanes' creation.

Before the teacher appears, the activities and nature of what I shall for convenience usually refer to as the school are described and presented. The 'small house' (92), clearly a residential establishment and equally clearly not an ordinary *oikos*, is inhabited, Strepsiades tells his son, by men who try to promulgate a new picture of the world and who also teach, for a fee, the ability to win arguments by fair means or foul (95-9). These men, who seem respectable to Strepsiades, are despised by his son as a bunch of pallid, barefoot impostors (102 f). With this description fresh in our minds, let us follow Strepsiades as he encounters the student whose cogitations his arrival has disturbed. The dramatist has chosen to present the school partly by report and partly by visual means in a scene of dialogue between the applicant for admission and the Student (whom we may think of as Head Boy or Senior Prefect). By the use of this method the humble credulous inquisitiveness of Strepsiades elicits from the Student anecdotes about the school's activities which are as amazing as they are ludicrous (144-80). Next there are revealed, at work in the courtyard of the school, other students engaged in researches into cosmology whose nature puzzles Strepsiades. Secondly he is shown apparatus used in astronomy, geometry and geography, the Student providing rather condescending explanations throughout (184-216). Third and lastly, he sees The Man, the Principal of the school, suspended on high (218).

The scene, admirable as a preparation for the epiphany which marks the conclusion of the prologue, also cleverly contrasts two sorts of credulity, the unquestioning acceptance by the Student of the activities of the school and Strepsiades' uncomprehending amazement which is increasingly punctuated by down-to-earth comments. In all this, there is no sign that in this establishment devoted to cosmological study there is any teaching of rhetoric: the subject is only mentioned when Strepsiades remarks that any expert on gnat's insides could easily get off when taken to law (167 f).

Thus far the school has been presented as an impoverished residential institution for cosmological investigations whose members should eschew long periods out of doors (175, 195-9). The school's Principal is also first seen engaged in cosmology, but soon there are indications that the institution is not one-sided and that its doctrines are more various than had first appeared. A casual oath uttered by Strepsiades to reinforce his promise to pay the required fee in return for training in the art of non-payment of debts is the pivot which turns the conversation, and the action, towards religion (244-6). The Principal, after stating his community's disregard of conventional deities, offers instruction in their religion and a 'meeting with our divinities, the Clouds' (252-3). At once the teacher is submerged in the priest and the pupil becomes a fearful candidate for initiation. In retrospect the Student's reluctance to admit an outsider to knowledge of the 'mysteries' of the school (140-3) may be seen as preparing for this development in which the 'little house' ceases to be an establishment for research and training and becomes a sacred building of the kind we chiefly associate with Eleusis. And we may perhaps recall the three stages of revelation of these 'mysteries', the last being the quasi-divine apparition of the Principal. Although Strepsiades is nervous, recalling the blessings reserved for initiates he reasonably enquires how he will benefit (259). He is promised excellence in argument, that is, he is told what he wants to hear and what will calm his fears. Nevertheless, the association of mystery – religion and eloquence has been made and made in advance of the arrival of the Clouds.

The school has one more aspect which requires comment and which is introduced by the Clouds themselves as part of their conditions for helping Strepsiades to achieve his aims. Having already praised their priest for his endurance of hardships (363), they now require a degree of asceticism on the part of Strepsiades, something which the frugal peasant is happy to undertake (414-22). His reward will be 'victory in action and deliberation and in verbal warfare'. The military language, in connection with a programme of self-denial, rigorous training and the acceptance of discomfort, carried out during a period of residence away from home, will have reminded the audience of Sparta's methods of producing a military élite.

A school for cosmology, an institution for training soldier-politicians, a religious body presided over by Cloud goddesses: are we to admire the rich abundance of this presentation or condemn its confusion of interests and the irrelevance of much of it to the needs of the play? At all events, there is only minimal connection between the material provided so far and the actual education of Strepsiades (the little we see of it). And, it may be added, there is no attempt to show that the first of his two periods of study has any connection with actual, or imaginable rhetorical training.[13]

Teacher and Pupil

Strepsiades' memory, or rather his forgetfulness, is a constant motif in these varied scenes,[14] or, to put it another way, much of his training consists in the presentation of separate items of information to be memorised, information to do with metre, the gender of nouns and similar linguistic topics (482-8, 636-93). Reasonably enough, Strepsiades considers all of this to be irrelevant to his needs: in modern jargon he is not 'well-motivated'. It is this forgetfulness which gives his teacher the prime reason for his expulsion. If we had formed a view of the school as a place where pupils carried out their own investigations, that view is countered by the form of teaching just described in which the teacher imparts 'facts' and the pupil is supposed to 'snap them up, like a dog' (491). Eventually, however, Strepsiades is told to think up a solution of his own to his problems (695), encouraged by the Clouds, and after some mental blankness he produces one or two ploys (747-73) rather like the trick the Student had earlier outlined as a means of obtaining money (175-9). Of course, in this temporary success Strepsiades owes nothing to the lessons he has just received; the ideas on which his teacher congratulates him call for ingenuity, lack of scruple, and a touch of witchcraft.

Learning through memorisation and inventing stratagems are at least intellectual exercises of a kind: Strepsiades' education has also a social dimension. The second reason given for his expulsion is that he is superlatively *skaios*; this adjective suggests both stupidity and bad behaviour, stupidity unredeemed by any attempt to improve. Elsewhere Strepsiades is called *amathes*, *barbaros* and *agroikos*, in contexts which suggest such renderings as 'uncultivated', 'uncivilised' and 'peasant-like' (*skaios* 627, 655, 790; *amathes* 135, 492, cf. 646; *barbaros* 492; *agroikos* 627, 646). The implication that he does not know the proper way to behave in polite society can be supported by his own words in the prologue (43-55) as well as by the Teacher's promise that instruction in metre will enable him to act the man of accomplishment on social occasions (649-51). In addition to failings attributable to his countryfied origins, there is no doubt that Strepsiades plays dumb and plays cheeky in response to the Teacher's authority. This 'naughtiness' which fits in well enough with other aspects of his characterisation is a familiar ingredient in comic school scenes, however unlikely it might seem in the case of a man driven to learn oratory by his debts.[15] Similarly, the Teacher is occasionally presented as formidable (195, 296), irritable (646, 726) and ready to punish a cheeky pupil (493), although for the most part willing to try to provide what Strepsiades wants and to adapt his teaching to suit his literal-minded, difficult pupil (494, 776 f).

The Clouds

We frequently talk of clouds coming from dews; and we actually see the heavy fogs become clouds. We see them go up to the tops of hills, and taking a swim round, actually come, and drop down upon us, and wet us through. But, I am now going to speak of clouds, coming out of the sides of hills in exactly the same manner that you see smoke coming out of a tobacco pipe, and rising up, with a wider and wider head, like the smoke from a tobacco-pipe, go to the top of the hill or over the hill, or very much above it, and then come over the valleys in rain . . .
    As we proceeded on our way from the bottom of Butser-hill to Petersfield, we saw thousands upon thousands of clouds, continually coming puffing out from different parts of these hills and towering up to the top of them.

(William Cobbett)

How large a part does the chorus take in the educational scenes and what is their function and significance? Earlier in this chapter the Clouds were seen as punishing and warning men, deriving their authority in part from their meteorological powers. Such is not the way we picture the Clouds in their earlier scenes.
    Strepsiades goes to the school to obtain help: the Principal of the school is the Helper, the counterpart of Euripides in *Acharnians* or of Heracles in *Frogs*, but a Helper whose part is extended, like that of Hermes in *Peace*. The *Clouds* enter the dramatic action as adjuncts of the Helper, divine patrons of the Reflectory.[16] It is not unusual for a chorus to enter in response to a request for aid, like the Knights in the previous year's comedy; what is extraordinary, even startling, is the appearance on stage of divinities when summoned by a mortal (even though this

mortal fulfils the role of priest and has already shown some pretensions to superhuman activities). Rather surprisingly the subject of the Clouds is brought into the conversation between Teacher and pupil as if by accident and it is only when the Teacher-priest delivers his elaborate invocation that their dramatic importance begins to be established. By addressing them as 'awesome goddesses' he enhances their dignity, and by adding the epithet 'thunder-fulminating' (Sommerstein's neat rendering) he points to their meteorological function, so important later. In the remainder of the invocation, also, he follows procedures conventional in hymns of this kind, referring to places at which the Clouds he summons might now be gathered. So far the supposedly new religion sounds remarkably like the old, an easy extension rather than a radical revision of old beliefs and an imitation of standard forms of worship.[17] The eyes of the spectators are raised skyward as Aether and Air are addressed and Clouds invited to be present. Was it at a clear sky that they gazed and were their reactions like those of Strepsiades regretting his lack of protection against rain, 'To think that I came out without my rain-hat' (267 f)? The priest's words suggest that the Clouds will be seen: the Clouds' words, immediately heard, speak of seeing, of looking down from a distance on the hills, well-watered land, rivers and seas of the earth. It is noteworthy that, unlike Aphrodite in Sappho's famous poem, the Clouds make no mention of the fact that their presence has been invoked.[18] In the second of their two stanzas (298-313) the 'rain-bearing maidens' sing their praises of Athens, their present destination, chiefly for its distinction as the site of the Mysteries and of temples and as the place where religious processions, feasts and festivals are held in due season. If some of the spectators had felt that invoking the presence of goddesses in a comedy was risky or actually impious, what could be more pleasant or reassuring than to hear such an encomium of 'Pallas' radiant land' (299)?

After this opening song the Clouds are silent until they address the old man and the priest (358 f). The interval, which is the time allowed for them to make their way into the spectators' sight and then into the orchestra, is largely occupied with further explanation of their nature. So far we have been led to think of them as supreme goddesses of a new religion which has replaced traditional deities, but at the same time to observe that they display characteristics easily associated with real clouds, such as resting on snow-topped mountains (270).[19] Now Strepsiades learns that they are 'mighty goddesses for men who are inactive' and that they provide thought and intelligence along with various oratorical accomplishments (316-8). Although nothing in the Clouds' song had the flavour of rhetoric, Strepsiades immediately replies, 'When I heard their voice my heart began to quiver and now it wants to spin arguments and natter about the niceties of smoke, to give back opinion for opinion and answer discourse with discourse' (319-22). Some lines later, the Clouds now visible, we discover more about the help they give their protégés, nourishing all those, to borrow a phrase, 'whose business is words', who do no manual labour, including those poets who specialise in writing dithyrambs about 'cloudy' subjects (331-4). For people of this kind the Clouds are Muses;[20] unlike traditional Muses these goddesses help seers and scientists and the only poets they favour are the dithyrambists, 'melodycurvers of the circular choruses' who, like dramatists, compete at the Dionysia. Just as the Muses were honoured by poets to whom they gave their gifts, so clouds are mentioned by the dithyrambists whom they nurture; their moist, dewy nature permeates the poetry. Like other 'idlers' the dithyrambists are rewarded, as Strepsiades observes, by the enjoyment of delicacies at the victory feast (338-9). (In these few lines Aristophanes can make fun of poetic rivals, largely by well-chosen quotation, and imply that only dithyrambists, not writers of comedy, can be charged with 'idling'.)

There is one more topic to discuss before the Clouds themselves are in a position to engage in the action, their capacity to change their appearance at will (348). When Strepsiades asks 'Why do the Clouds look like mortal women?' we may interpose with one answer: 'Because it is difficult to devise a convincing costume for representing a cloud.' (And the goddesses had already 'shaken off the rainy cloud' which disguised their shape (288).) However their present resemblance to women is explained in the text as a characteristic piece of behaviour. Everyone has seen a cloud shaped like a centaur or a wolf and so on; in fact the Clouds deliberately adopt the appearance of the person whose peculiarity they desire to mock, becoming deer when they see the cowardly Cleonymus, for exmaple (353 f). So, in answer to the original question, they are now women because they've caught sight of Cleisthenes! Not only does this passage contain an ingenious new approach to familiar targets (in a play lacking much jesting of this kind), but it suggests light-heartedly (what will be significant with hindsight) that the Clouds observe human failings.

The Clouds, now in the orchestra, after a brief greeting keep silent all the while their meteorological activities are set forth. (Did they withdraw and remain inconspicuous, impassive and unconcerned during the lesson?) This section (364-411), still in the long anapaestic lines well suited to weighty and pleonastic expression, might in fact be labelled 'theological': just as the Clouds were first mentioned after Strepsiades' reference to oaths 'by the gods' (246), so now the opening line is the statement 'They are the only goddesses; all the rest are rubbish' (365). All the meteorological lore about the causation of rain, thunder and lightning emerges in answer to questions about the effects of the removal of traditional gods, questions asked by a Strepsiades who knows that one god can succeed another, as Zeus had succeeded Cronos, and now easily takes on board the notion that Zeus has been displaced by Vortex, a splendid example of his capacity for misunderstanding (380 f). The lack of mental contact between the two participants in this scene, the 'scientist' and the literal-minded peasant, for whom weather has always been of practical importance, provides some of the humour; in addition the use of homely analogies, much favoured by instructors when explaining abstract or theoretical matters, juxtaposes the heavenly, the culinary and the intestinal to great effect (386 f, 408-11).

It is in their responsibility for changes in the weather that old- and new-style Cloud goddesses coalesce. By tracing their dramatic role from the end of the play back through the parabases, we have obtained a view of them as moral beings who reward or punish; and now on their first entry we have met cosmological divinities who were introduced by the priest of a new religion as exemplars of the workings of a scientific weather system in which the old gods have no place.

So much is said about the Clouds both before and after their appearance and entry that it is hard to realise how little they actually say on their own behalf, how much is put in the mouth of a witness by no means reliable or disinterested. In the scenes which precede the parabasis, apart from their opening song, the Clouds speak only in greeting (358-63) and in their dialogue with

Strepsiades (412-75), now to be discussed. After so many words which have nothing to do with Strepsiades' purpose in seeking to become a student in the Reflectory, we come back at last to the decisive moment of entry. The Clouds of course, unless by divine omniscience, should know nothing of Strepsiades' situation, though in fact they address him as 'hunter of muse-favoured speech' (358). (Perhaps they suppose any member of the school to require persuasive discourse for promulgating the New Learning.) The next time they speak it is to set out the rigorous discipline required of Strepsiades if he is to be victorious in action and counsel and the warfare of the tongue (419) and to promise that he, 'desiring great expertise', will be accounted 'fortunate in Athens and Greece' (412 f). Strangely, all this precedes their enquiry about the precise nature of his actual desires (427 f) and his reply: 'It's only this trifle I ask of you – to be best of all Greeks at speaking' (429 f). Strepsiades goes on to specify his wish to evade his creditors and the Clouds promise its fulfilment, instructing him to entrust himself to their ministers (436). His 'extravagant self-surrender', as Dover calls it, is followed by compliments and further promises of fame, happiness and wealth (437-75).

It is interesting to observe that the Clouds themselves do not promise to give Strepsiades directly the intellectual qualities and rhetorical ability he needs, or even to 'nourish' him (cf. 316-28, 331); he is to acquire his skill, if he observes the correct attitudes and practises self-discipline, from the Teacher who is their minister.

At this point we may take a final look at the structure of the comedy, a structure made lopsided by the length of the section devoted to Strepsiades' attempts at learning, or rather to the description of the school, its activities and doctrines. Why did the dramatist send Strepsiades to school? The first advantage of this surprising development was that it underlined the importance of Pheidippides' refusal to obey his father. Secondly, the scenes in the school required a different kind of pupil from the conceited Pheidippides who would not have given a moment's attention or credence to the Student's tales or the Teacher's theories. Moreover, how much better and more amusing that the pupil should be of an age with his instructor (or a bit older). Of course no sensible person could believe what was taught in the school or regard its investigations as worthwhile: a Strepsiades might react with a mixture of amazement, willingness to be impressed and occasional shrewd scepticism and these reactions are crucial to the viability of a dialogue concerned with matters remote from the knowledge of many of the spectators.

In T.S. Eliot's *The Family Reunion*, a play whose revisions were more extensive but better documented than those of *Clouds*, Agatha, with Olympian vision, speaks of men

> Reflecting a pocket-torch of observation
> Upon each other's opacity
> Neglecting all the admonitions
> From the world around the corner . . .

In studying *Clouds* it has been harmful to neglect admonitions from the world of Aristophanic comedy and take up a position Athenians of the 420s could not have envisaged in order to focus the beam from the pocket-torch of observation on one figure in one portion of the drama: 'Who studies this, travels in clouds.' 'Better not to sit by Socrates babbling; better not to ignore all that concerns the Muses.'[21]

Notes

1. See above, p. 6 ff. The articles which have most influenced this chapter are:
A.W.H. Adkins, *BICS* 15 (1968), 146 f.
A.W.H. Adkins, *Antichthon* 4 (1970), 13-24.
P. Green, *GRBS* 20 (1979), 15-26.
M.W. Haslam, *HSCP* 80 (1976), 45 f.
C.J. Herington, *TAPA* 94 (1963), 113 ff.
A. Koehnken, *Hermes* 108 (1980), 154-69.
E.C. Kopff, *GRBS* 18 (1977), 113-22 (and see F.D. Harvey, *GRBS* 22 (1981), 339-43).
M. Nussbaum, *YCS* 26, 43-97.
P. Pucci, *Maia* 12 (1960), 40 f.
C. Segal, *Arethusa* 2 (1969), 143-61.
L. Woodbury, *Phoenix* 34 (1980), 108-27.
2. The approach developed in this and subsequent paragraphs owes much to A.P. Burnett's *Catastrophe Survived* (Oxford, 1971).
Pheidippides' refusal does not spring from a desire to defy his father but from contempt for the members of the school and his fear of what his friends will think of him (102-4, 119 f).
3. See above, p. 50.
4. As in other scenes where unwanted visitors are driven off, verbal abuse, 'smart' talk and physical violence are combined.
5. *Knights* lacks devices for inducing sympathy for Sausage-seller or

Paphlagon; in *Wasps* the use of a third party, the slave, to set the scenes helps to keep the father in his comic place.

6. See further, Dover, *Lysias*.

7. The presence in the school of the Arguments not only gives them corporal substance but counters any idea that they are widely or generally available.

8. See Dover, *Clouds*, lxv, 216.

9. *Clouds* 1432.

10. *Frogs* 1053 f.

11. Both Dover and Sommerstein give 1105-6 and 1111 to Worse Argument; they do not mention 1146. A doubt must remain as to the dramatist's placing of responsibility for Pheidippides' training.

12. See Rau 174 f.

13. If there are doubts about the practicability of dramatising a training in rhetoric they should be dispelled by reading the opening scene of *Assembly-women*. One should note that the school appears to have no students of rhetoric and that Socrates has little of the orator about him.

14. e.g. 129, 481, 627, 785, 790.

15. See above, p. 75 f.

16. One may recall other patron deities like Hephaestus (metal-workers), Athene (weavers).

17. New divinities and new cults of old divinities continued to be introduced in Athens in the fifth century.

18. Sappho 1. Aphrodite's words indicate that the troubled lover has called upon her before the present occasion.

19. We are not sufficiently informed about the currency of legends in which the goddess Nephele ('Cloud') featured to say that the spectators would have her in mind, although in view of Strepsiades' allusion to Athamas in 257 it seems likely. See Dover and Sommerstein on the passage.

20. The success of 'seers', physicians, scientists and other experts depended on their ability to express their views persuasively; their subject-matter included theories and observations about the weather and its effects. For these people therefore the Clouds were Muses of a special kind.

21. *Frogs* 1491 f.

SELECT BIBLIOGRAPHY

Abbreviations are given in brackets following the entry. Other abbreviations used in the notes, apart from those of classical periodicals, as listed in the *Oxford Classical Dictionary*, refer to major Greek authors, e.g. A., S. and E. for the three tragedians, Ar. for Aristophanes.

Barrett, D. *The Frogs and Other Plays* (Penguin Classics, Harmondsworth, 1964).

—— and Sommerstein, A.H. *The Knights, Peace, The Birds, The Assemblywomen, Wealth* (Penguin Classics, Harmondsworth, 1978).

Buxton, R. *Persuasion in Greek Tragedy* (Cambridge, 1982).

Dale, A.M. *Collected Papers* (Cambridge, 1969).

Dearden, C.W. *The Stage of Aristophanes* (London, 1976).

Dover, K.J. *Lysias and the Corpus Lysiacum* (Berkeley and Los Angeles, 1968). (Dover, *Lysias*)

—— *Clouds* (Oxford, 1968).

—— *Aristophanic Comedy* (London, 1972).

Ehrenberg, V. *The People of Aristophanes*, 2nd rev. edn (Oxford, 1951).

Fraenkel, E. *Beobachtungen zu Aristophanes* (Rome, 1962).

Gelzer, T. *Der epirrhematische Agon bei Aristophanes* (Munich, 1960).

—— *Aristophanes der Komiker* (Stuttgart, 1971).

Henderson, J. *The Maculate Muse* (New Haven and London, 1975).

—— (ed.) *Yale Classical Studies* 26 (1980). (YCS 26)

Macdowell, D.M. *Wasps* (Oxford, 1971).

Moulton, C. *Aristophanic Poetry*, Hypomnemata 68 (Gottingen, 1981). (Moulton)

Newiger, H.-J. *Metapher und Allegorie* (Munich, 1957). (Newiger 1957)

—— (ed.) *Aristophanes und die alte Komödie* (Darmstadt, 1975).

Page, D.L. (ed.) *Poetae Melici Graeci* (Oxford, 1962) (PMG)

Pickard-Cambridge, A. *Dithyramb, Tragedy and Comedy*, 2nd edn, rev. T.B.L. Webster (Oxford, 1962). (Pickard-Cambridge 1962)

—— *The Dramatic Festivals of Athens*, 2nd edn, rev. J. Gould and D.M. Lewis (Oxford, 1968). (Pickard-Cambridge 1968)

Platnauer, M. *Peace* (Oxford, 1964).

Rau, P. *Paratragodia* (Munich, 1967). (Rau)

Rogers, B.B. *The Comedies of Aristophanes* (London, 1902-15).

Sandbach, F. *The Comic Theatre of Greece and Rome* (London, 1977).

Sifakis, G.M. *Parabasis and Animal Choruses* (London, 1971).

Sommerstein, A.H. *The Acharnians, The Clouds, Lysistrata* (Penguin Classics, Harmondsworth, 1973).

—— *The Comedies of Aristophanes*, vols. 1-4 (Warminster, 1980-3). (Sommerstein)

Stanford, W.B. *The Frogs* (London, 1963).

Taillardat, J. *Les Images d'Aristophane* (Paris, 1962). (Taillardat)

Taplin, O. *The Stagecraft of Aeschylus* (Oxford, 1977). (Taplin 1977)

—— *Greek Tragedy in Action* (London, 1978). (Taplin 1978)

Ussher, R.G. *Aristophanes* (Oxford, 1979).

Whitman, C.H. *Aristophanes and the Comic Hero* (Cambridge, Mass., 1964).

GENERAL INDEX

INDEX OF PASSAGES